The
Reconnected
Leader

'Only connect... Live in fragments no longer'
E M Forster

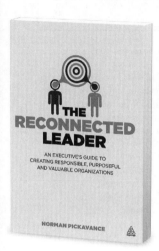

The Reconnected Leader

An executive's guide to creating responsible, purposeful and valuable organizations

Norman Pickavance

KoganPage

LONDON   PHILADELPHIA   NEW DELHI

First published in Great Britain and the United States in 2015 by Kogan Page Limited

2nd Floor, 45 Gee Street	1518 Walnut Street, Suite 1100	4737/23 Ansari Road
London EC1V 3RS	Philadelphia PA 19102	Daryaganj
United Kingdom	USA	New Delhi 110002
		India

www.koganpage.com

© Norman Pickavance, 2015

The right of Norman Pickavance to be identified as the author of this work has been asserted by him in accordance with the Copyright, Designs and Patents Act 1988.

ISBN   978 0 7494 7232 0
E-ISBN 978 0 7494 7233 7

British Library Cataloguing-in-Publication Data

A CIP record for this book is available from the British Library.

Library of Congress Cataloging-in-Publication Data

Pickavance, Norman.
  The reconnected leader : an executive's guide to creating responsible, purposeful and valuable organizations / Norman Pickavance. – 1st Edition.
      pages cm
    ISBN 978-0-7494-7232-0 (pbk.) – ISBN 978-0-7494-7233-7 (eISBN)   1. Leadership.
  2. Organizational change.   I. Title.
    HD57.7.P557 2014
    658.4'092–dc23
                                                                            2014039528

Typeset by Amnet
Print production managed by Jellyfish
Printed and bound by Ashford Colour Press Ltd

To Amanda
without whose patience and support
this book would not have happened,
to my parents
who taught me that you can achieve anything in life
if you apply yourself
and to the team at
Blueprint for Better Business
for their friendship and continued inspiration

CONTENTS

LIST OF FIGURES

LIST OF TABLES

Introduction

The tide has turned. Changes in our economic, technological and environmental ecosystems have unleashed unprecedented forces, dragging society by invisible rip tides into a great sea of uncertainty. Leaders of our largest institutions look increasingly cut off from what is going on around them. We are witnessing a change of era.

When eras change, the choreography of events no longer follows the narrative we are accustomed to. Everything seems disjointed as we are bombarded by conflicting signals.

At one level, life seems to be continuing the same as ever. At another, things no longer trend and new dynamics rapidly emerge, evaporate or explode, seemingly without cause or reason. Old approaches that used to work start to fail. This is what happens when eras change and it is at such times as this that effective leadership becomes more crucial than ever. Yet how should we lead if old certainties are getting washed away?

We first need to identify and understand the changing tides, before we can begin to formulate new solutions. Consider for a moment issues such as globalization and the rising power of the BRICS countries (Brazil, Russia, India, China and South Africa); the emergence of relational technology; increases in the world's population; the movement of billions out of poverty and mass migration of people from poor to wealthy zones; rapidly ageing populations in western democracies and ever-growing income disparity. How will all these forces combine, and how will they influence the way we see and operate in this world?

These are forces of upheaval, but they are matched by equally powerful outgoing rip tides. Here we see a collapse of trust in the corporate sector following the banking crash and scandals in every area of business, from rate rigging in our banks to bribery and mis-selling in pharmaceuticals, environmental catastrophe in the oil sector and phone-hacking in the media. Furthermore, global supply chains in major corporations have become so incredibly complex exposed to huge risks, as organizations have sought to make use of cheaper production opportunities in poorer countries, leaving their global brands exposed to uncertain practices around the world.

Meanwhile, the internet has given consumers and citizens a voice to expose malpractice and double standards and the power to organize protests faster than ever before.

A new narrative

Having identified what is happening we need to decipher what it means. This contests that these events are not, as some would have us believe, the consequence of a complete breakdown in the capitalist system. Rather, they have resulted from the way in which leaders have misjudged the change in era and, having misread the tides, are left increasingly high and dry, disconnected from our rapidly changing world and losing touch with new realities. At the moment, many are in a poor place to make the right choices about the future of their companies and their impact on the wider world.

The level of disconnection is illustrated most starkly in the degree to which leaders are apparently not learning lessons from major scandals. Lionel Barber, editor of the *Financial Times*, observed in a speech[1] that

FIGURE 0.1 A new landscape emerging for 21st-century leadership. Which path are you on?

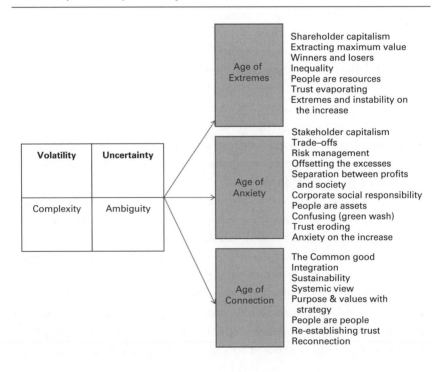

leaders in the banking sector have become 'detached from businesses, which had become too complex and risky ... beguiled by the prospect of easy returns ... detached from public opinion, still unable to understand the new post-crash world'.

We therefore need a new narrative, one which sees the interlocking nature of the forces we have outlined, which sees business as something that must contribute to the common good by becoming embedded in society. We will explore how this systemic understanding of our new environment can be brought together under unifying themes of interconnection and interdependence. In this new era, we need a new type of leadership delivered by different kinds of leaders rooted in the wider context of society and better able to connect with the world around them. These leaders will 'understand that their businesses are profoundly related to the communities in which they work [and will be] able to think differently and comprehensively about the larger environment in which they operate' (Gratton, 2014). Only by so doing can leaders start to rebuild trust, spark innovation, enhance the emotional vitality of their employees and increase the social wealth of their businesses and the communities they serve.

These, then, are the foundations for sustainable growth, but they are not easy or simple steps to take. To embark successfully on this journey will require leaders to undertake a shift in mindset about the nature of their organizations and their own roles; to rediscover the true purpose of their businesses and find more innovative solutions and to better integrate the challenge of long-term societal needs and short-term financial results. This book will argue that this is achievable if leaders get *reconnected*. That's the good news. The bad news is that time is running out.

The public are is rapidly losing confidence in business and trust is being lost. *Forbes* magazine recently indicated that business leadership is facing a major crisis – on a global basis less than one in five people globally trust that their leaders are telling them the truth (Llopis, 2013; Gratton, 2013). As leaders we have to wake up to the fact that 'No institution can operate without the consent of society' (Caulkin, 2013) and realize the extent to which that consent and the trust on which it is based are ebbing away. Trust is an intangible asset which is hard to monetize directly, perhaps precisely because it is *invaluable*. It is trust that makes customers commit to a retailer or to a brand and without it customers simply shop elsewhere to find a better deal. It is trust that creates environments in which people are willing to experiment and to share ideas and without it people hold back and innovation is lost. It is trust that encourages people to do more than their basic job, to make bigger commitments to their company and their colleagues, and without it people seek reward for each task performed. It is trust that creates these invisible and invaluable bonds.

But trust is on the wane just at the point at which we need it the most. We are entering a highly volatile period and a multi-polar world that promises to be a lot less predictable. Capitalizing on opportunities in this changing landscape calls for leaders who can understand issues in the broadest possible context; who see the interconnected nature of the world in which we live; who understand that their business can only succeed in a credible and sustainable way by recognizing the way that they and their organizations are connected to the people, communities and environments around them. As Unilever's CEO Paul Polman recently observed, 'Capitalism needs to evolve, and that requires different types of leaders from what we've had before. Not better leaders, because every period has its own challenges, but leaders who are able to cope with today's challenges' (Polman, 2014). These leaders will understand that business is here to serve society and that we need to find a way to do so in a sustainable and more equitable way, not only with resources but also with business models that are sustainable and generate reasonable returns. Our understanding of leadership will therefore have to evolve. 'Leaders will need the ability to focus on the long term, to be purpose driven, to think systemically, and to work much more transparently and effectively in partnerships' (Polman, 2014).

The thread that pulls these diverse themes together is the need for business leaders to reconnect with the world around them, with their colleagues and communities alike. These are enormous challenges and, unfortunately, many business leaders today are still seemingly unaware of the degree to which they have become cut off and isolated from people and events outside their current circles. This disconnection presents a huge risk for all our futures, because the leaders of our largest business institutions are the architects of the world in which we live. It is a risk that has become progressively evident over the past decade, with major business failings coming to light across all sectors of the economy.

In this book we will explore the nature of this breakdown – from the fraying links between business and its true purpose in society to the role of boards and the breakdown in the connection between leaders and workforces; the distancing that has occurred between organizations and their customers and the need to re-imagine innovation by strengthening the connectivity of the organization beyond its boundaries.

These risks appear all the greater when we consider that the modern corporation has been an engine for growth for over 150 years, transforming the lives of billions of people, improving living standards in the West and opening up the possibilities of progress from poverty for billions of others in the developing world. Life expectancy has risen globally and education levels have improved significantly in the West and in emerging economies, in part because of the contribution industry has made towards investing in the skills of its people. This period has been one of the fastest rates of advancement in our entire evolution. Extraordinary technology, which 40 years ago was only available in government space programmes, has now put computing power at the fingertips of our children, while the very strands of life are now being turned to our will as DNA is modified to cure previously incurable diseases and change lives. For some people, the life they lead and the luxury this affords would have been unimaginable years ago. Much of this has only been made possible by the rise of the corporation and the establishment of a stable society. Business has been to a large extent the vehicle through which this progress has been delivered.

At the same time, we are coming to recognize that this 'progress' has come at a cost and has not been as balanced as it needs to be, resulting in massive and growing income inequality across the world. Billions of people live in extreme poverty, surviving on less than $2 a day, while others have unimaginable wealth. In the West, the access to cheap, mass-produced food and drink is contributing to an epidemic in obesity and diabetes. Education standards remain poor in many areas and women and children are still being exploited in many parts of the world. We have also belatedly woken up to the fact that our natural resources are finite and the 200-year boom in the carbon deposit extraction is not sustainable, changing our climate in highly unpredictable ways and leaving a trail of pollution in its wake.

I will argue throughout this book that the problem lies not in capitalism per se, but in the way our major organizations are being led. Many, according to Porter and Kramer (2011):

> remain trapped in an outdated approach to value creation… They operate too narrowly, cut off from the rest of society, optimizing short-term financial performance in a bubble, while missing the most important customer needs and ignoring the broader influences that determine their longer-term success. How else could companies overlook the well-being of their customers, the depletion of natural resources vital to their businesses, the viability of key suppliers, or the economic distress of the communities in which they produce and sell? How else could leaders think that simply shifting activities to locations with ever-lower wages was a sustainable 'solution' to competitive challenges?

There is a growing disconnect between the way large corporations would like to see the world and what is happening in reality. Not for the first time are the needs of communities and the focus of major corporations diverging. We cannot, as Paul Polman, CEO of Unilever observed in an interview in the *Guardian* (London) 21 November 2011, 'have successful business in a broken society'. Furthermore, business appears to be increasingly unstable, prone to excess and calamity almost at one and the same time. It seems that we have entered an era where these giant business machines are as likely to be risk makers as they are to be problem solvers. Yet the reasons these risks are reoccurring are only slowly becoming appreciated. Today, it seems, a narrow conception of what capitalism is really about is preventing business from harnessing its full potential to meet society's broader challenges.

Evidence of a deeper problem emerges from a variety of sources. There will be many in the business community who accept that there are indeed wider problems in society and the environment, but feel strongly that it is not their role as business leaders to get too involved, because quite simply, their remit only extends as far as satisfying shareholder needs. Yet even in purely economic terms, there are seriously worrying signs that the current model by which leaders are running their organizations and the influence this is having on the performance of the economy as a whole, is no longer producing the results that we would expect or indeed require.

Following the 2008 crash, which shook western capitalism to its core with a near-fatal collapse in the banking system, we have seen the start of a re-evaluation of the strengths and failings of our economy. Recognizing that the economy has been perilously slow in its ability to recover, Harvard Professor Clay Christensen (2013) warns:

> There have been nine recessions since the Second World War. The 1982 recovery took economies the normal six months to reach prerecession peaks of performance. Getting back to the prior peak in the 1990 recession took 15 months. Our economic machine has now been grinding for 65 months trying to hit prerecession levels... there is something seriously awry.

A 2010 report from Deloitte Consulting showed that US companies' return on assets had dropped 75 per cent from their 1965 level, despite rising labour productivity. In fact, performance continues to decline, whether measured through return on assets, return on invested capital or return on equity. While this has been explained away as the result of macro-trends – the rise in outsourcing, the growth in intangible assets or the transition to a service economy – there are many academics and researchers who believe that these worrying signs are deep-set and cannot be ignored.

The Japanese economy has been stagnating for 20 years and offers a worrying vision of the future of the developed world. From the 1960s to the

1980s Japan led the field in so many areas but, since the 1990s, the stream of highly innovative ideas emerging there has reduced to a drip. There are several views on why Japan is in this situation, ranging from its ageing population to its inability to compete with lower-cost manufacturers in the rest of Asia.

The worry for other western economies is that they are on a similar trajectory. Innovation in the United over the past 30 years is now at one third of the level achieved in the 1950s, 1960s and 1970s. The UK's Parliamentary Select Committee for Science and Technology described innovation in the United Kingdom as being in a 'valley of death', blocking lab-based scientific innovations from becoming commercially successful businesses. In his book *The Innovator's Dilemma* (1997), Professor Christensen suggests that we have shifted our emphasis, placing greater reliance on efficiency-based innovation and improving productivity but not creating new markets or building new jobs. Professor Christensen has shown that good firms are usually aware of the innovations but their business environment does not allow them to pursue them, because they are insufficiently profitable at the start and their development can divert resources from maintaining short-term profitability. Ultimately such leadership choices are damaging our future competitiveness because sustainable success is closely linked to the characteristics of innovative organizations and innovation depends increasingly on how connected an organization is to a thriving innovation ecosystem.

Daniel Pinto is CEO and co-founder of Stanhope Capital, which with $8.5 billion of assets under management is one of the largest private investment offices in Europe. Pinto has become a vocal critic of the way western organizations are being run. He encapsulates the seriousness of the problems in his recent book *Capital Wars* (Pinto, 2014), cautioning:

> Western companies are now run by 'professional CEOs' who operate like unadventurous 'Administrators in Chief'... these executives are able to amass vast fortunes when successful but have little to personally lose when they fail. Disinclined to make the heavy investments required to ensure the leadership of their companies in the long term, they have learned to manage their careers more skillfully than the futures of their business.

This book argues that it is leadership that is falling short, lacking either the audacity of vision or failing to find an authentic voice as it strives to answer a range of difficult and demanding questions. The public know this and are disquieted by it. They can see that leaders have become leaden footed and unbalanced in the face of a shifting and increasingly unstable world. Business will continue to be under siege, seen as part of the social, environmental, and economic problems we face, as long as companies are perceived to be prospering at the expense of the broader community. As long as people question the wisdom of their leaders they will withhold the trust that they might have once placed in them and the legitimacy of business will continue to fall. The challenge we face is that without trust in both our leaders and the institutions they represent, society will struggle to address the bigger, more difficult and more important questions that lie ahead. Groundbreaking innovation will be deferred because it will require risks to be taken and taking risks only works when trust is shared. Clearly, there is a need to fundamentally re-imagine our approach to leadership.

Re-imagining leadership: A recurring phenomenon

In re-imagining leadership, we should take heart, as this is not a new phenomenon. It has occurred on several occasions throughout history and on each occasion has been driven by a seismic shift in the way our economic environments operate. Each time, business has survived but leadership has had to radically adapt. It is this ability to adapt that is perhaps the greatest strength of capitalism. We are at one of those inflection points today.

The work of Russian economist Nikolai Kondratieff (1892–1938) captures these shifts in the landscape of events and provides us with a fuller historical context. His analysis (Kondratiev, 1984) was based on a 1,000-year assessment of economic cycles across the globe. He predicted, for example, that there would be a great crash in the early decades of the 20th century and that this was the result of a long cycle of growth coming to an end, rather than an inevitable Marxist rise of the proletariat (Kondratiev was shot by Stalin for holding such 'anti-communist' views). Today's investment banks around the world still model with interest Kondratiev or 'K waves' to identify their influence on long-term expansions and contractions and the associated booms and busts in markets.

This notion of the mega trends was built on by several other economists, including Daniel Smihula (2011) who argued that each wave was marked by the rise of a specific technology which dominated world production, driving demand, growth and living standards and then fading. Smihula went on to suggest that each wave is now lasting for shorter periods, with greater economic turbulence as a result. With the ending of each major cycle of growth and technology, a different type of capitalism has emerged and with it, a new style of leadership.

FIGURE 0.2 Kondratiev wave diagram

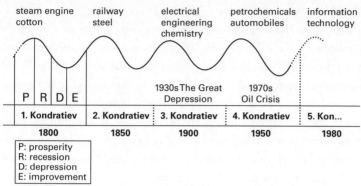

Note: Economist Daniel Smihula's observation: wave cycles are compressing and are therefore more frequent

When we look at how leadership has historically mapped these mega-trends, we can see how the perception of business has evolved. In the Middle Ages, commerce was looked down upon in many western cities and the money handlers were marginalized in cities like London. In 15th- and 16th-century London, business leaders were physically locked in an area known as the Steel Yard, because they could not be trusted. (The Old Steel Yard is now the site of Cannon Street station, coincidentally also home to the UK's Confederation of British Industry or CBI). This image of business leaders gradually changed and according to Oxford Historian David Priestland (2012), by the 17th century they were beginning to be seen as 'Moral Merchants', whose arrival presaged the beginning of the industrial revolution. The zeitgeist at that time repositioned merchants as 'exploring heroes', as seen in Daniel Defoe's *Robinson Crusoe*. By the beginning of the 20th century, the first wave of mass industrialization had resulted in power becoming concentrated in the hands of relatively few industrial titans like Rockefeller, Carnegie and J P Morgan. It took almost 30 years and two presidents to challenge and dissipate those powers through Theodore Roosevelt's anti-trust legislation and Franklin D Roosevelt's New Deal. This new era ushered in a fresh expectation of leaders of large corporations – that they should become stewards, not only of their industrial enterprises but also respected figures with a prominent place in society, expected to discharge a wider responsibility. This new model of leadership transformed what had gone before and reflected the beginning of a long era of 'professional management', led by Alfred P Sloan who had taken over the running of General Motors in the 1930s and transformed it through cutting-edge management techniques. It was an approach that was widely copied and, by the 1950s and 1960s, came to epitomize the way people thought organizations should be run.

The last time such a great shift in era occurred was at the start of the 1980s. Following the oil crash, 50 years of planned capitalism was replaced by a very different model of deregulated free-market thinking. Failures in leadership were repackaged as an inability to control misaligned and intransigent blue-collar unions. The upheaval which followed was marked by industrial action on both sides of the Atlantic, with ill-equipped managers struggling to negotiate changes in working practices, while production was transferred to developing countries as manufactured goods were imported into the West from Japan, Korea and China.

What also emerged in the 1980s was a new kind of leadership, caricatured in the 1987 Oliver Stone film *Wall Street*, in which a ruthless Gordon Gekko saw only the value of 'the deal' and not the human, ethical or other consequences. A rational and sanitized version of Gekko-like leadership has emerged as the dominant force in business since the 1980s. It is an outlook on business and life which has pushed us into extremes of rational individuality, in which people find themselves working in increasingly atomized units and ever deeper silos increasingly detached from the society. It has shaped an hourglass economy, where some benefit hugely from a global and technology-enabled environment and where the rest find their skills and circumstances trailing so far behind that they can never hope to catch up or participate fully.

The conventional theories we have relied on for the last 30 years have now passed their sell-by date. Behavioural economists have, according to Eric Beinhocker and Nick Hanauer (*McKinsey Quarterly*, September 2014),

> economists have accumulated a mountain of evidence showing that real humans don't behave as a rational *homo economicus* would... Andy Haldane, the chief economist of the Bank of England, notes that the conventional theory views the economy as a rocking horse that, when perturbed by an outside force, sways for a while before predictably settling back down to a static equilibrium. But, as Haldane has pointed out, what we saw during the crisis was more like a herd of wild horses – something spooks one of them, it kicks another horse, and pretty soon the whole herd is running wildly in a pattern of complex, dynamic behaviour... The economy – a complex, dynamic, open and nonlinear system – has more in common with an ecosystem than with the mechanistic systems the neoclassicists modelled their theory on... It suggests that markets are evolutionary systems that each day carry out millions of simultaneous experiments on ways to make our lives better.

For these myriad connections to work, learn and evolve they require on essential ingredient – trust.

However, the trust that once oiled the wheels of commerce – the trust that is key for risks to be taken – is being drained out of the system, like oil from a gearbox. Gears that once moved smoothly now grind and grate upon each other. When trust has gone, business runs on a less efficient basis; customers never become loyal; employees never fully commit; organizations continue to function but the creativity, passion and joy of working together with people in a joint endeavour disappear.

The critical importance of having institutions we can trust was set out in the masterly *Why Nations Fail* (Acemoglu and Robinson, 2012). They argued that institutions are the critical infrastructure needed to run a good and successful society. If we cannot rely on people in business to do what is right, then how can we run a society which has come to rely to such a large extent on business? The philosopher Alasdair McIntyre has identified that society has adopted a kind of compartmentalization between what is fair and trustworthy in our personal life and what is seen as fair game in business circles. McIntyre (2000) explains, 'By compartmentalization I mean that division of contemporary life into distinct spheres, each with its own highly specific standards of success and failure.'

Diminishing circles of trust

Building on McIntyre's ideas, I would propose we can view these spheres as concentric circles. In the centre is a small group of immediate colleagues, family and friends; the next sphere has our wider business dealings and is an area that has become increasingly grey; and finally there is the sphere, which marks the boundary of the law. The inner or central circle has become progressively narrower over the past 30 years. According to Margaret Heffernan in her thoughtful book *Wilful Blindness* (2011), these central groupings contain people we trust more because they are more 'like us'. This desire to feel comfortable with people we share an affinity with can influence all of our significant life choices, from whom we marry, to where we choose to live, to whom we form friendships with. Because we feel most comfortable in these settings and because we now have more freedom to move and locate ourselves wherever we chose, we can pick environments in which we like to live. In the United States, Bill Bishop (2008) has studied this phenomenon extensively and observes that most Americans have been increasingly 'clustering in communities of like-mindedness'. So, as people marry the same types and send their children to similar types of schools, the less likely we are to meet individuals from other groups or with different views. This retreat into ever-smaller circles is reinforcing existing social groupings and paralysing social mobility, which has consequently been in reverse over the past decade. This trend is as prevalent in China as it is in the United Kingdom and even Sweden is now following in the steps of the United States.

People operating within these narrow circles become far less comfortable with individuals who have different outlooks on life, beyond their immediate environments. Clearly this has huge consequences for society and politics but in business, this tendency to withdraw into a tightly defined inner circle filled only with like-minded individuals, disconnected from the wider world, can have dramatic and damaging effects on the future success of an organization and the people in it.

Organizations are only just starting to understand the full implications of their executive population becoming increasingly disconnected from their people, their customers and society at large. Boardrooms filled with identikit individuals, from similar backgrounds and with familiar views, are inevitably reducing the range of perspectives the board can bring to any given market challenge.

Beyond the inner circle of trusted people is the increasingly grey world of business operations, where some leaders have, perhaps unconsciously, adopted different standards of behaviour. They have treated others, be they employees, customers or suppliers, differently to the way they would perhaps treat close colleagues, friends or family. To illustrate how such different standards can occur we will take a step back and consider a different era.

Authors Rodolphe Durand and Jean-Philippe Vergne, in their thought-provoking book *The Pirate Organization* (2012), compare the development to the captains of pirate ships cruising off the Americas at the end of the 17th and 18th centuries. The piracy in the Caribbean occurred because vast wealth was at stake; the rules of the high seas were unclear in these unchartered waters and the respective governments of Britain and Spain did not have the resources to adequately police what was going on. The authors suggest that we see similar conduct amongst today's top leaders of internet, coffee are pharmaceutical companies, who scour the world in search of the optimal tax domiciles. They argue that this kind of piratical thinking has always been present in business and has been instrumental in creating today's business culture. Over the past 30 years, such attitudes have migrated from the outer limits of the business practice towards the mainstream.

The outermost ring of the circles of trust is defined by law. Patrolled by the State, this boundary has been on the retreat – because of the prevailing

FIGURE 0.3 The rise of the grey area

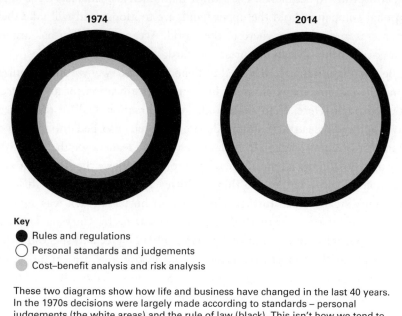

Key
- ● Rules and regulations
- ○ Personal standards and judgements
- ⬤ Cost–benefit analysis and risk analysis

These two diagrams show how life and business have changed in the last 40 years. In the 1970s decisions were largely made according to standards – personal judgements (the white areas) and the rule of law (black). This isn't how we tend to operate now. There are fewer and fewer people we feel we can trust completely – and so business 'rationale' replaces judgement.

There has always been a grey area around the way business has been conducted which concentrates on the financial assessment of risk and benefit. As free market thinking has brought about deregulation over the last forty years this grey area has expanded to encroach on the black area in the diagrams. Market logic has taken over much of what was previously governed by the norms of behaviour and good judgement. As a result, what we think about business and how much we trust it has deteriorated markedly. People – employees and customers – now have relationships with business which have been reduced to the purely transactional, where the dominant partner in the transaction is always the business and the business case is what justifies the decision.

Individuals in the 1970s still trusted a wide circle of people and extended that trust to business and institutions. People were in it together and not just out for themselves (however innocent that now sounds). Now the commercial outlook has influenced the way we look at things and more of life has moved from being *relational* (doing the right thing, being fair, open and honest) to *transactional* (what do I get and how much will it cost?). This harder, coarser approach results in everything being defined by endless, catch-all contracts. In the worst case, no one can be sure any longer of the right thing to do, leaving only two questions for the business leader: Is it legal? And does it make me money? Sandler has called this the shift from a market economy to a market society.

logic that business needs light-touch legislation, the difficulty in controlling footloose global businesses and an increasing desire by business itself to lobby government to alter the legislature. This is what Professor Rebecca

Hammond at Harvard Business School calls 'the active corruption of the regulatory system'. Hammond (2013) observes that all governments are under pressure to acquiesce. They know that much is at stake as large international companies hold the upper hand, are footloose and will take their businesses and jobs anywhere in the world. Accepted wisdom has argued that governments should not press too hard.

Beliefs about markets, the need to financialize the way we run organizations, the extreme focus on individualism, the justification for all our decisions through reference to shareholder value creation – all of these ideas have captured the entire economic debate and been absorbed into the bloodstream of business leaders. It explains why many leaders see the world the way they do. On the whole, leaders have come to believe that this approach is the only logical way to run things. However, the absorption of this way of seeing extends much further. The extent of business reach was summarized in an interview with *Rolling Stone* Magazine by Chrystia Freeland (2012), journalist and author of *Plutocrats* (2012). Freeland suggested that the people at the top of organizations and institutions are capturing the political system – what Citigroup's chief economist Willem Buiter (2008) calls 'cognitive capture'. Freeland explained:

> His argument was that part of the reason the financial crisis happened, is the entire intellectual establishment, not just people inside investment banks, but regulators, academic economists, financial journalists, had all been captured by the financial sector's vision of how the economy should work. And in particular, light touch regulation ... And I think what you see increasingly is, elites like to think of themselves as acting in the collective interest, even as they act in their personal vested interest.

Expecting State legislation to fill the gaps left by 30 years of deregulation may take a long while and, in the meantime, allows business leaders to ignore the fact that much of the greyness about 'the right thing to do' has always been within our own sphere of influence.

Why aren't we learning the right lessons?

Since the crash of 2008, there has been a growing acknowledgement that business has fallen short of the expectations of wider society in several important respects, along with a dawning realization – in some quarters at least – that no institution can operate without the consent of society as a whole. Why then has business found it so hard to learn the right lessons or conduct a re-examination of its methods? This appears particularly baffling when the consequences of failure are exposing business and society to such significant risks.

The answer to this paradox may lie in the German idea of *Weltanschauung*, a word first used by the philosopher Immanuel Kant in the 18th century to mean 'world outlook'. Kant (1790) was articulating the sense that we all have a frame of reference, or framework of beliefs, through which we interact with and interpret the world. *Weltanschauung* serves as a way of thinking about how the world works and, at its deepest level, articulates a fundamental orientation of the human heart. If our world view stays the same, it becomes almost impossible to learn new and challenging lessons without causing some kind of dissonance or mental stress. When dissonance does occur leaders, like all people, try to reduce it by avoiding situations and information which could increase the feeling of discomfort. According to Professor Leon Festinger (1962), this occurs because of our basic human drive for internal consistency, without which individuals can become psychologically distressed. In other words, people prefer to ignore difficult realities, rather than have to change their world view.

Given these basic human traits, we need to acknowledge that the process of changing such fundamental perceptions as to how business works, requires a very different approach to all that we do. We need to introduce far greater interaction and connection with a different range and type of people than those we see on a daily basis within our increasingly isolated corporate bubbles. We need to engage with 'people who have had different experiences and can convey a different reality' according to Professor Ib Bondebjerg (2013), from the University of Copenhagen. My point is that a reconnected leader has to bring this different range of experiences closer to their everyday lives, to exert a bigger influence, better equipping themselves and their organizations to understand the changing global reality in which we all live.

This book argues that the business community has been slow to learn from its mistakes because the *Weltanschauung* of those in leadership positions has become increasingly insular, narrow and constricted, cut off from so many important stimuli, so that leaders are no longer capable of seeing the new picture that is emerging.

This process of disconnection has pervaded business since the 1980s and has been reinforced by the practices leaders have been encouraged to adopt. This has created organizations that have diverged from serving the interests of the customers, employees and the rest of society. It has also led to a growing sense for many individuals that they are leading a divided life, where it is no longer possible to behave the same way at home and at work.

Is it possible to change this world view? I will argue that we can. I will show how leaders can change the way business operates, by making reconnections at every level of activity, enabling greater inclusion, innovation and improvement for the benefit of the many, and not just the few.

A framework for 'reconnected leadership'

Throughout this book we will explore a new framework for leadership, constructed around those areas that make, shape and influence connections and relationships. This approach will examine, at different levels, how leaders can embrace, contribute to and ensure that both business and society reap sustainable benefits from our interlocking and shared interests.

The framework is constructed around three pillars of leadership focus:

- purpose;
- leadership practices;
- personal leadership.

The section on leadership practices is expanded to cover specific practice areas, and together these form the eight steps to becoming a reconnected leader. Each of these steps is set out in outline below and form the basis for Part Two of the book.

FIGURE 0.4   Reconnected leadership model: The three pillars

The 3 pillars of the reconnected leadership model are explored in detail throughout the book. This chart provides a high-level overview. Leadership practices are expanded in the next slide. Together they form 8 steps to becoming a reconnected leader. The model is designed to help leaders think about how they make, shape and influence those connections and relationships which matter the most, when building a sustainable business. The approach will enable leaders to embrace the interlocking nature of business and society, improving the direction that they provide to their organization over the long term.

Step 1: Purpose

This first element addresses how leaders can work with their organizations to explore, develop and connect their people through a set of principles designed to help build a strong sense of purpose. This represents a focal point stone to help leaders to reconnect their organization with employees, customers, suppliers and communities through an exploration and development of the organization's core purpose. It is designed to ensure that their business is focused on serving the common good, treating people with dignity and respect both inside and beyond the organization and ensuring a fair return for responsible investors. The purpose will be one that will last, that will inspire people within an organization, help people to innovate and perform better and in so doing forge a connection between the activities of the organization and broader society.

Steps 2–7: Leadership practices

These practices offer ways that a leader can foster connections through six key themes:

- building a reconnected board;
- creating reconnected work environments;
- nurturing a spirit of shared enterprise;
- connecting with communities;
- fostering customer connections;
- inspiring connected innovators.

Step 2: Building a reconnected board

This considers how boards need to adapt, ensuring they not only connect with what is happening on the frontline of their own businesses but also address their crucial responsibility to make their organizations more transparent, more inclusive, more open to scrutiny and more accountable to society as a whole – not just a limited section of it.

Step 3: Creating reconnected work environments

This considers how leaders can reconnect with the people in and across their organizations, creating environments in which people can thrive and flourish. This element addresses how leaders can help their organizations to treat everyone with dignity, enabling open and constructive dialogue and nurturing all who work for them, both directly and indirectly, to learn and contribute.

Step 4: Nurturing a spirit of shared enterprise

This looks at how leaders can use connections to forge a spirit of shared enterprise, where a true sense of common ownership and accountability are combined to inspire and foster innovation and lasting commitment.

Step 5: Connecting with communities

This relates to how leaders can reconnect with the world around them, by personally becoming more closely involved in communities and environments and by understanding how their supply chains work in practice and how their products and services actually serve society. In so doing, leaders will start to see people affected by their decisions as members of their own community.

Step 6: Fostering customer connections

This considers how business leaders can build lasting relationships with customers, dealing more honestly and openly in sharing knowledge and helping customers and suppliers to make more informed choices.

Step 7: Inspiring connected innovators

This looks at how business can become a guardian for future generations by fostering collaborative innovation both within and beyond the organization – investing in developing skills, knowledge and understanding in wider society to encourage informed citizenship.

Step 8: Personal leadership

This addresses the implications of reconnection in terms of a leader's personal actions and responsibilities. This explores how leaders can better relate to the wider community and reorient their role to offer dynamic solutions in turbulent times. Finally, we consider how leaders must reflect on their personal behaviour, how they act as role models for others and how their reconnected leadership approach can shape new kinds of relationships and expectations

In the following chapters we will explore each of the elements of the *Reconnected Leader* framework in greater detail. We will argue that we can develop a different kind of leadership that is capable of making different

FIGURE 0.5 Reconnected leadership model: Practices

kinds of choices; however, such a transformation will require leaders to reconnect in a profoundly different way to the world around them, and to what matters most to the common good. Such reconnected leaders can again be trusted as catalysts for growth and positive change, bringing a humanizing quality to both business and the rest of society.

Trust between society and business is today at an all-time low. However, the steps set out in the Part Two of this book can help to open a fresh dialogue between business and society, unlocking new energies and potential. This dialogue is essential because business leaders cannot gain a full insight of the issues faced without establishing better connections with wider society.

However, to frame these leadership solutions, we first need to understand the true nature of the problems that organizations currently face. We must first consider what has happened over the past 30 years – how the great disconnection between society and business has occurred and the role that business leaders have played in this. Armed with these insights, we will be in a better place to shape a new route map for reconnected leadership.

---

1   Can banking clean up its act? *Financial Times,* 1 May 2014

PART ONE
The great disconnection

The great disconnection

> *We don't see things as they are, we see them as we are.*
> **(ANAÏS NIN)**

Are we learning the right lessons?

In order to understand the role that leaders could play in bringing business back into step with the wider needs of society and a changing world, we need to first produce a better diagnosis of both what has been happening inside our major organizations and why these organizations are seemingly causing as much harm as good. Without this, calls for an alternative route forward for business will always flounder.

This section therefore looks first at a number of the major business 'failures' that have occurred over recent years. In considering these examples, we will excavate a number of underlying causes or themes. These case studies and themes will form the backdrop to the book and will serve to frame our alternative model of *Reconnected Leadership*.

In our discussion of recent crises, we will draw on case studies across a wide cross-section of the economy:

- oil;
- pharmaceuticals;
- banking;
- food;
- retail.

In our analysis of the root causes of these crises and the implications for leadership, the following themes will be addressed:

- ethical policies;
- mindsets and belief systems;
- careerism;

- the disconnected board;
- the disposable workforce;
- big data and the age of the smart machine;
- engineering out human connections;
- the forgotten many;
- fragmented performance;
- the executive club;
- losing touch with customers;
- stifling innovation;
- the unintended consequences of good governance;
- the downsides of a digitally enhanced corporation.

We will begin our analysis by considering recent crisis in various sectors of the economy, starting with oil.

Big oil

At 9.45 pm on 20 April 2010, a geyser of seawater erupted 250 feet up into the night air in the Gulf of Mexico, bringing brown sludge spurting to the surface and then a rush of methane gas. The men around the wellhead knew they only had seconds to shut it down but despite their frenzied efforts, attempts to activate the blowout preventer failed. Minutes later the methane ignited and a massive fireball exploded into the sky. The explosion could be seen on the shore 35 miles away, and was so large that it was picked up in space by US satellites. It killed 11 crewmen instantly.

The spill quickly turned into an environmental tragedy, killing marine life and impacting hundreds of miles of coast. By 2013, BP had budgeted $37.2 billion for spill-related expenses. To really understand why this human and environmental disaster happened and to develop some insight as to how an event on such a calamitous scale could have occurred, we have to look further back in BP's history.

BP started life as the Anglo-Persian Oil Company and grew organically until 1978, when it acquired Standard Oil; in 1998 it merged with Amoco to form one of the world's biggest companies. It promised its shareholders that the Amoco deal would deliver 'significant cost efficiencies', by bringing the two organizations together (Harding and Rovit, 2004). These synergistic benefits were at the core of the deal and the new CEO of the combined company, John Browne, set about delivering his commitments by ordering a

25 per cent reduction in costs across the business, to be achieved over three years. Every site in the enlarged BP was to honour this cost reduction commitment, irrespective of the state of their operation.

The managers at one facility in particular knew how difficult this would be. At the Texas City refinery they had already spent several years stripping costs back to the bone. Yet they, like everyone else in the organization, were exposed to the same pressures so they further reduced manning levels and maintenance schedules – not because they were specifically told to undertake those particular actions, but because they knew they had to hit the 25 per cent target somehow. The writer Margaret Heffernan (2011) observes: 'when employees were surveyed on corporate priorities, they cited as number one "making money" and number two as "costs and budgets"'. While explicitly BP had a very strong safety culture, implicitly managers knew they were operating in an even stronger one – to drive out costs. As the pressure mounted in the vast corporate cost-reduction programme, BP managers were invited to meetings to discuss their progress and to explain themselves if they weren't on track. Everyone knew what counted, what you needed to do to get promoted, what you needed to deliver if you wanted to avoid the excruciating spotlight. 'Cost out' was the mantra which everyone throughout the hierarchy lived by and if you were failing to contribute you would be asked quite publicly: Which part of '25 per cent' didn't you understand? Things could not have been clearer but the potential consequences of these decisions were never discussed.

Then, on 23 March 2005, a hydrocarbon vapour cloud explosion occurred at a BP isomerization process unit, killing 15 workers instantly and injuring more than 170 others at its Texas City refinery. So significant was the disaster that BP commissioned an independent review by former US Secretary of State James Baker III (2007). Four days before the report was published, Lord Browne announced he would be standing down in June of that year, 18 months ahead of schedule. The report, according to the press, had 'savaged BP', which was charged with criminal violations of federal environmental laws, and resulted in record fines.

That the Texas City disaster occurred in the first place is a tragedy, that only five years later the organization could have been responsible for the world's biggest oil spill should be cause of concern to all. It indicates that one of the world's largest organizations, filled with some of the smartest people in business, has failed to grasp what really caused the failure. It had failed to learn the right lessons, but why?

It is easy to examine these incidents in isolation, but that would be to miss a far larger point. For at the same time as the oil industry was trying to clean up its act, the drugs industry was suffering its own litany of failings.

'Big Pharma'

The giant pharmaceutical sector shares many similarities with big oil. The modern drugs industry is dominated by a small number of big companies, grown to super-size so that they can manage the vast investments and huge downside risks associated with long-term business cycles and uncertain outcomes. We will see that in Big Pharma these enormous pressures for success have caused some leaders to become disconnected from the very principles laid out in their own ethical codes.

In 2013 in the US, \$5.5 billion of fines were handed out for mis-selling and malpractice. The Department of Justice issued record fines to a string of Big Pharma names, including previously trusted household companies. Eli Lilly, had trained its sales force to disregard the law by selling Zyprexa, an anti-psychotic drug, to treat elderly patients with dementia. AstraZeneca had been promoting its anti-psychotic, Seroquel, to treat sleeplessness, when it had only been cleared to treat schizophrenia. Abbott Laboratories had been fined \$1.5 billion for training its sales professionals to target Depakote®, an anti-psychotic, at nursing homes to treat dementia.

GlaxoSmithKline (GSK) is another drug major, regarded as one of the most professional and respected organizations in the sector. Its mission states: 'Our commitment is to be a responsible, values-based business [this] underpins everything we do, including our sales and marketing practices, our relationships with suppliers and how we conduct and report our research' (GlaxoSmithKline, 2014).

It goes on to say that 'All business decisions are guided by our core values. We expect all employees to commit to transparency, show respect for people, demonstrate the highest integrity, and be patient-focused.' Despite this, GSK was fined \$3 billion for promoting and misbranding the drug Paxil to treat patients under 18 years of age for depression, when the drug had never been approved for use with that age group. The actual complaint details how GSK manipulated the findings of one of its test studies to reach the false conclusion that Paxil was effective against depression in adolescents (Whaleen *et al*, 2012). A GSK employee recommended revising a section of the study relating to side effects, removing the finding that serious side effects like worsening depression and hostility were related to the treatment, and replacing it with a statement that headaches were the only side effect considered to be treatment-related. This study was subsequently used by GSK to promote Paxil for children and teens to the medical profession. The US Deputy Attorney General, James M Cole (2012), said of the judgement that it 'underscores the Administration's firm commitment to protecting the

American people and holding accountable those who commit health care fraud,' going on to observe that: 'At every level, we are determined to stop practices [that] violate the public trust – and this historic action is a clear warning to any company that chooses to break the law.'

The $3 billion fine against GSK occurred in 2012, at which point GSK promised to clean up its act. However, as Philip Ball further observed in an article for the *Guardian*:

> While these fines sound like staggering amounts of money to most people, a fundamental problem is blatantly and painfully apparent, fines don't work. They simply do not curtail behaviour when applied to corporations. They've become little more than an expected annoyance, a risk to be mitigated, a cost that is calculated into the price of doing business.[1]

A year later, this observation seemed to be borne out when GSK's Chinese operations were accused of unethical activity in the bribery of officials. GSK's HQ in London initially claimed to be unaware of this, yet 10 months later police at the Ministry of Public Security in China said that 46 suspects at GSK's Chinese subsidiary had been identified as part of a 'bribery chain', funnelling money to hospitals and doctors. It was alleged that the bribes were paid for by inflating the price of drugs up to seven times their normal sale price. As these allegations landed on the desk of CEO Andrew Witty, the public relations response[2] explained that, any such actions in China were not sanctioned and were outside the clear code of ethical conduct that the Group had in place. However, as a former global partner in one of the world's top accountancy firms explained to me,[3] ethical codes such as that at GSK have been implemented by many global organizations, primarily as a preparatory legal defence. This was meant to ensure that the board could always distance themselves from the actions of errant individuals. While there is no suggestion that this is what GSK has done, what is clear is that the attempts to clean up the way the business works following the Paxil scandal are not getting the cut-through they need. Once again it seems that Big Pharma, like 'big oil', has failed to learn the right lessons from these major failures and massive fines.

Concerns about business behaviour are not isolated to a small handful of western companies. In the pharmaceuticals sector it is a phenomenon that is growing globally. As BBC Business Editor Robert Peston observed: 'Maintaining ethical and legal standards in a sprawling global business appears to be a "challenge" for a striking number of multinationals'.[4] As a case in point, the online newspaper *The Hindu*[5] explained why Dinesh Thakur had become a whistleblower at drugs company Ranbaxy. He had identified the discrepancies between Ranbaxy's records and the data filed with regulatory agencies in 2004, showing how widespread and systematic questionable behaviour had become, stating it was 'penetrat[ing] the very DNA of the organization'.

The unethical practices of the drugs industry has also become endemic across the banking sector.

Big banks

In the wake of the financial markets crash of 2008, several large banks have set about upgrading their compliance teams, the internal compliance leaders who are there to ensure that staff within those institutions obey the rules. Indeed every banker in the western world has now received extensive compliance training. The question for the boards of these institutions is whether any of these measures will actually prevent future malpractice and their own future 'Deepwater Horizon'. So far the signs are not promising.

In the banking sector, after various reports into what banks needed to do differently post-2008 crash, there were still cases of malpractice emerging up to 2013, from Libor to Foreign Exchange fixing to mis-selling policies.

A case in point is the UK Lloyds banking group, which was fined £28 million by the Financial Conduct Authority for breaching guidelines, applying pressure to staff through its bonus scheme to mis-sell financial products. Lloyds staff reported that, 'The only thing that matters is hitting sales numbers, not the needs of the customer.'[6] It was reported that a climate of fear pervaded their regional offices, as people worried about being demoted for failing to hit sales targets. Lloyds may now have to set aside £100 million to cover compensation costs to customers. As one individual impacted by the scandal observed, customers have a right to expect better from our leading financial institutions. The environment at Lloyds sounds very similar to that at BP. No one said, 'Go out and break these rules.' However, people in the frontline felt that they had no alternative but to act in line with what was implicitly expected of them.

Barclays also found themselves at the eye of the storm of public outrage over mis-selling and rate rigging. It is worth pausing on the scandal around Libor (London interbank offered rate) rigging. Despite the claims of some who would have us believe that it was only a technical matter that affected a small circle of banks, early estimates showed that the rate manipulation scandal cost US states, counties, and local governments at least $6 billion in fraudulent interest payments, and a further $4 billion that government had to spend to unwind their positions exposed to rate manipulation.

In the United Kingdom the unfolding scandal about who knew what resulted in the resignation of the chairman and chief executive of Barclays Bank. The crisis was felt to cut so deep inside the bank that incoming Chairman Sir David Walker appointed Anthony Salz, a respected city lawyer-turned-investment banker, to conduct an independent review of what had been going on after the bank was fined a total of £290 million by UK and US regulators for attempting to rig the key Libor interest rate between 2005 and 2009. Salz's view (2013) was that these events were shaped predominantly by Barclays' culture, which rested on 'uncertain foundations': 'There was no sense of common purpose in a group that had grown and diversified significantly in less than two decades.' The result, the report said, was a 'strong drive to win', which led to an 'over-emphasis' on short-term financial performance, reinforced by a bonus and pay culture that rewarded money-making over serving the interests of customers and clients. The report also said there was a sense that senior management did not want to hear bad news and that employees should instead solve problems on their own.

The situation is no better in the United States where, in June 2013, The Bank of America was found to have systematically lied to homeowners, fraudulently denied loan modifications and paid their staff bonuses for deliberately pushing people into foreclosure. This long-suspected practice was revealed in sworn statements by six former employees acting as whistle-blowers in the federal court. 'Bank of America's practice is to string home-owners along with no apparent intention of providing the permanent loan modifications it promises' said Erika Brown, one of the former employees.[7]

A recent BBC Radio interview illustrated that confidence in the banking business is fast being replaced by cynicism. Following further announce-ments of corporate malpractice, the BBC's Business Editor and author Robert Peston had been brought into the Radio 4 studio early one morning in December 2013 to comment on recent events. He observed drily that the banks were now so commercially driven that individual bankers had become wired to think in a purely entrepreneurial way, 'getting round' any obstacles – including 'the rules' – that may have been in the way of mak-ing money. Peston suggested that it would now be almost impossible to expect them to behave any differently. Bankers, he argued, were leaving themselves open to the fate of all commercial people, prone to act in an unscrupulous way.[8]

We have to recognize that sentiment towards business has seriously shifted. This is a difficult and unaccustomed position for business lead-ers and many are still struggling to accept that this is what is going on.

Meanwhile, other sectors of the economy have not remained immune from this malaise, as we shall see when we consider an example from the food industry.

Food

In China, fast food chain KFC (formerly Kentucky Fried Chicken), owned by parent company Yum! Brands, has been subject to much criticism when a KFC 'half-price chicken' promotion went viral online after consumers found they were only receiving half the amount of chicken that they would normally get in a 'family bucket meal'. The promotion wasn't a promotion at all and people were left feeling cheated. This may sound like a small faux pas but for KFC this disaster came hot on the heels of earlier bad press that they had been working with suppliers who were injecting excessive levels of antibiotics into their chicken to help fatten them more quickly. China currently accounts for 40 per cent of KFC's total sales. This case shows just how rapidly trust in a big brand can be impacted when customers feel that they have been cheated or mis-sold. The scale of the negative reaction on China had a major negative impact on Yum! Brands's share price.

Big retail

The retail sector is increasingly morphing to reflect sectors where 'big' can be applied. This is particularly true in the general food and merchandise sectors where Walmart, Tesco, and Carrefour dominate globally alongside the leading domestic grocer. Concern about the integrity of the food we are provided with is therefore very much a global issue. Following in the wake of a European scandal into the substitution of cheap horsemeat for other processed meats in British supermarkets, a wholesale investigation into the food industry was undertaken. While the horse meat substitution did not directly represent a health and safety threat, it showed that the food chain of many companies had been seriously compromised, with leaders not knowing what subcontracted partners across a range of European countries were adding as ingredients on their behalf. Customer confidence was significantly shaken and sales of processed meat products tumbled. It served to illustrate just how stretched boards can be when it comes to providing the necessary scrutiny, particularly in the way global food supply chains are managed. Paul Hopkin (2013), a Director at the risk-management specialist Airmic, observes: 'The relentless pressure to cut prices has led to the creation of supply chains of mind-boggling complexity and business models that no one properly understands. When you consider the speed with which information travels, boards should not be surprised when public relations disasters such as the horse meat scandal take place.'

These challenges come to light when leaders simply assert that a business is behaving to a particular set of standards, set out in the company's ethical policy. However, in practice, such guarantees are getting more difficult to assure, particularly where leaders believe that standards are followed by relying on a command model of responsibility, where leaders agree standards of performance and cascade these responsibilities through the hierarchy. The risk of complexity on leadership standards was illustrated by the Business Continuity Institute (BCI), who carried out a comprehensive review of supply chains for 532 organizations across 68 countries. It identified the risks for supply chains that now routinely outsource and offshore production, making it increasingly difficult for leaders to monitor supply chains adequately.

We can see this playing out in the way some organizations are unaware of who their suppliers are subcontracting work out to. The risks here mount when cost pressures lead to smaller suppliers further down the food chain compromising on quality, ethical and labour practices. How leaders shape standards of behaviour across their extended organizations is a pressing challenge, one that is not yet being considered by many organizations today.

Unfortunately these 'oversights' seem to be happening with increasing regularity, and not only in the food sector, as was illustrated by the collapse of the Rana Plaza textile factory, in April 2013, which killed 1,100 people in Bangladesh. Here the boards of several global garment companies had not shown sufficient curiosity into the working practices or safety of facilities in their Bangladeshi manufacturing partners, before outsourcing low-cost production to them. Leaders are simply not connected enough to the reality of what is happening in their operations on the ground. The Rana Plaza disaster happened despite evidence from the Tazreen factory fire only a year before, killing at least 110 garment workers. Corporate decision-making seemed to be wholly focused on the cost benefit of moving production to Bangladesh where the minimum wage is $37 a month. While these industries can help to raise people out of poverty, it is, in the words of John Gapper of the *Financial Times*, 'unacceptable for hundreds of workers to die in preventable industrial tragedies'.[9]

What do these multi-sector failures teach us? First, that many business leaders are – perhaps understandably – struggling to grasp that these issues are of their own making. This point is central. In our analysis, we need a coherent logic that explains why business has become as dysfunctional as the case studies above would indicate.

Leaders have unconsciously architected business systems that have caused these problems. This was perhaps not deliberate, much in the same way that a town planner architects congestion on our roads if they fail to ensure sufficient provision for public transport. Rather, leaders have done so unintentionally and unthinkingly because they are insufficiently in sync with the way the world around them works.

Ethical policies

The leaders in all those businesses we have reviewed thus far would no doubt see themselves as decent, hardworking individuals doing tough jobs for demanding shareholders. It is true that most had policies in place that set out high standards of behaviour. As the Baker report into BP found (2007), in the main, there haven't been any 'deliberate or conscious' efforts on the part of leadership to short-circuit safety. Yet it is here perhaps that the real insight lies. Leaders are, unconsciously in many cases, shaping cultures that implicitly undercut their own stated ethical standards, by implementing practices that lead to fragmentation, both in the workplace and in the way their organization interacts with the world around them.

In this regard, we can see three important factors emerging from our examination of corporate failure:

- First, there is the *implicit culture*, which defined what the real priorities were in the business, along with any stated priorities and over and above any ethical code. In BP's case, those 'real' priorities were all about costs.

- Second, there were a set of *systemic practices*, which characterized how leaders went about making things happen. At BP, people saw the performance focus being applied to cost-cutting objectives and the associated career sanctions and threat of personal humiliation associated with not hitting these targets. In the final analysis, these practices overrode any policies about safety either in oil exploration or in drug development.

- Finally, there were the underlying *belief systems*, which leaders used to justify certain decisions, while neglecting to consider fully the implications of these choices. This last characteristic has been described as the 'corporate moral personality'.

When viewed as living systems in this way, it is perhaps clear why good people do the wrong things when working in these large organizations. As quality guru William Edwards Deming observed (2000): 'If you put a good person in a bad system, the bad system always wins.'

Indeed, research on the use of ethical codes in business indicates that on their own, such approaches have little impact on the people's behavior. The 2005 US National Business Ethics Survey (ERC, 2005) compared the impact of organizational culture and formal ethics programmes on behaviour. It found that even though the number of formal programmes – ie written standards of conduct, ethics training, the ability to report complaints anonymously, etc – had risen over the previous five years, positive outcomes of those programmes had not. The study found that, although applied ethics policies did have some impact, organizational culture was far more influential in determining the outcomes of those policies. Furthermore the overriding focus on achieving (short-term) results and other organizational pressures were likely to create a culture in which employees are afraid to raise ethical concerns, even though formal measures such as speak-up phone lines may be in place. The Institute of Business Ethics' 2004 survey (Webley and Dryden, 2005) found that about one in three respondents who said that they had observed unethical behaviour in their organization had not reported it, stating that they felt speaking up would either jeopardize their job or alienate themselves from their colleagues. These observations support one of the central analyses of this book – that leaders have created the conditions in which ethical issues are more likely to occur. The critical question, therefore, is who sets the cultural tone of an organization and the answer is that leaders do.

A 2005 American Management Association survey[10] found that the factor most likely to compromise an organization's standards, mentioned by nearly 70 per cent of the respondents, was 'pressure to meet unrealistic business objectives and deadlines'. Commenting on this survey, a report in the *Business Ethics European Review*[11] observes that when reward systems are disproportionately dependent on the achievement of goals, the temptation to cut corners can be difficult to resist – a point we will examine later in the book.

Why competitive pressure crowds out ethical policies

Machiavelli observed: 'How we live is so far removed from how we ought to live, that he who abandons what is done for what ought to be done will rather bring about his own ruin than his preservation.'[12]

With the increasing pace of business, leaders are expected to operate pragmatically, not to hang on too tightly to projects they believe in: business moves on at such a pace that what was right yesterday can often look wrong today. The abilities to adapt and be agile are today's essential qualities. This quick-fire pragmatism, compartmentalizing our decisions and disconnecting our personal feelings from their work actions, has become an essential part of the business survival toolkit. 'It's not personal, it's only business' has become our de facto modern mantra.

In the view of John Darley, eminent Princeton psychologist, malpractice occurs because under pressure, people overlook the moral and ethical dimensions of the task: 'In very competitive environments, where you are under a lot of stress, a lot of cognitive load, you won't see that there is a moral consideration at all' (O'Brien, 2011). In the case of BP, the risk of harm to the men on the rig or the environment simply did not weigh heavily enough on people's minds because of the commercial business pressures. In the case of the drugs industry, the risk of harm to patients simply did not weigh heavily enough on the minds of the people involved in the mis-selling of drugs and one can imagine the similar circumstances arising inside a major bank when the pressures to do a deal or hit a number serves to equally crowd out virtue. Darley continues: 'Most issues start with an intuitive act not a deliberate one.' For example, 'when a sales person in a bank is selling a mortgage product to people who may not be able to afford them, they are in a highly competitive environment, under a lot of pressure to perform'. These are environments where people are thinking fast so they don't monitor the morality of their actions. As Margaret Heffernan (2011) noted: 'If you look at how it all plays out, you see conditions of high stress, competitive environments, compensation structures, company politics – the high stress tends to distance moral reflection.'

The effect of power and authority on people within an organization was perhaps most powerfully illustrated in the work of psychologist and social scientist Stanley Milgram. Influenced by the effects of the Holocaust, Milgram ran his now-famous experiments, which showed that people would obey authority figures even when asked to do things that were morally repugnant. The experiments began in 1961, three months after the start of the trial of Adolf Eichmann. Milgram devised his study to answer the question 'Could it be that Eichmann was just following orders?' By getting people to administer electric shocks to others, Milgram (1974) proved that even when the destructive effects of their work become patently clear and they are asked to carry out actions incompatible with fundamental standards of morality, relatively few people have the resources needed to resist authority. So people are capable of doing things because they think the work or the organization demands it, even when these actions are completely at odds from anything they would do outside the organization.

So the risk then is not that corporations, in the words of James Baker (2007), 'consciously or deliberately' look to break or ignore the rules; rather that the very *environments* which corporations create for people to work in are conducive to those rules being broken. People are only human and respond to the very real pressures to conform to the expectations that the organization has of them. As a result, we find individual leaders not really thinking about people as people outside their own immediate circle of trust. From that point onwards the dice is then very heavily loaded so that people don't just ignore the moral consequences of their actions; they hardly think about them at all.

In today's business environments, with the high turnover of CEOs and each new one arriving with a different vision and fresh demands, individual leaders and managers are left with little to personally hang on to. Inevitably this leaves many operating at the level of the lowest common denominator: 'the things that everyone can agree and act on, as opposed to the highest standards which everyone can aspire to' (McIntyre, 1984). This is at odds with how people would like to be and the disconnection that leaders feel, between their desire to do those things that have meaning and are meaningful and the reality of the latest set of changes, can cause real tension. When the pressures to go along with things are weighted so heavily, how can we shift the balance back for individual leaders and decision makers, such that they do bring to front of their minds the moral consequences of their actions at the point when the important and everyday decisions are taken? In subsequent chapters, this book will argue that we need to help leaders to reconnect with their people and environments, to reduce the moral distance between their decisions and the people they are likely to impact.

For leaders to stand their ground and do what is right, rather than what is just most commercial or most convenient, they need to feel like they are standing on a firmer structure than the one they see around them today, where the narrow and pragmatic pursuit of short-term results can either overpower them or leave them in a moral vacuum.

Leaders shape the culture of their organizations based on their own underlying belief systems. What then, is shaping these beliefs?

Mindsets and belief systems – 'a distant signal'

One of the people who has most profoundly influenced leadership beliefs over the past 30 years has been Chicago economist Milton Friedman who said in an article in the *New York Times*: 'There is one and only one social responsibility of business – to use its resources and engage in activities designed to increase its profits, so long as it stays within the rules of the game.'[13] 'Corporations do not have responsibilities,' Friedman said; 'only executives do, and their responsibility as agents of their owners is to maximize shareholder returns.' This notion of *agency theory* gradually gained a hold and by the late 1980s had a tight grip on the thinking of almost everyone in business, a position that has remained unchallenged until very recently.

Its impact was magnified by another idea, which had been embraced by the political and intellectual community – that of the need to liberate the individual. It's an idea that stretches back to the 17th-century Enlightenment. This philosophy gave birth to the modern notion of the self-defining individual standing clear of any entanglements with others, except in so far as they can do him or her some advantage. This idea of the self as an unencumbered individual became the dominant idea of modern secular liberal democracy. It is an individualism that is now taken for granted as normal, indeed normative. When such an individual engages in finance or trade or economics, then in the thinking of major policy makers, he or she becomes the autonomous rational creature, *homo economicus*. These ideas had been pushed to the fore by Ayn Rand, an American intellectual who came to prominence in the late 1950s and who articulated an extreme version of this logic. She published a collection of essays under the provocative title *The Virtue of Selfishness* (Rand, 1961), in which she rejected altruism and applauded egoism as an ethical ideal. The rational self-interest of *homo economicus* was not just how things were, but how they ought to be. Considerations of what was fair or just didn't come into it.

The degree to which these ideas were embraced by those shaping economic policy was widespread on both sides of the Atlantic, with Alan Greenspan, the Chairman of the US Federal Reserve between 1987 and 2006, an avowed follower of these free-market ideas, perhaps the most high profile. Accordingly it is perhaps understandable why a variety of research shows that many business leaders may have been seen to be less than fulsome in the support of principles set out in their company's own code of ethics because they were unconsciously operating from a different set of unspoken beliefs about the way the world should work. This disconnect between beliefs and actions impacted at the personal level. When leaders are driven by self-interest, they will inevitably struggle to set a more inclusive personal example on a day-to-day basis. People read these unspoken signals from their leaders. They notice how they *are* more than what they do, and they remember what leaders do far more than whatever they may say. It should then not come as a complete surprise to find that because of the way more junior managers regarded acts of apparent self-interest by senior leaders within their organizations, that high standards of personal conduct are not regarded as a priority by managers within their organization or their teams.

How could business leaders fail to see a bigger picture emerging? I will argue that if leaders have had to fully commit to the juggernaut of business, they will become consumed by business life, cut off in many ways from more everyday troubles of the public, far more in touch only via a preoccupation with the performance of their organizations' short-term returns and the immediate group of people around them. Consequently, any influences wider society may have to offer inevitably recede, and become at best a half-heard and distant signal.

Careerism

Becoming consumed by the demands of business life has been part of the deal business leaders have signed up to, in their struggle to reach the top of their organizations. In return for giving their all to this way of living and working, people who follow this path can expect to achieve what society has defined as a 'good life'.

Of course an interest in one's career has generally been thought of as a good thing. However, since the 1980s careerism has taken on a different order of magnitude becoming something of an invisible movement within sections of society, a means of achieving satisfaction and meaning in life through progression at work. It has gone hand-in-hand with a 'total work' mentality, where the job has simply become the most important thing requiring complete and total attention. The advent of mobile technology has accentuated this invasion of work-life into personal space, such that individuals are always connected to their jobs, at the behest of the latest summons or 'emergency'. This isn't simply about the growing capability or pervasiveness of the technology; it is primarily about the greater significance that society has attached to work.

Careerism has grown because to many, it has become the only means by which they can demonstrate their worth. Its importance has left people transfixed by personal achievement, at the expense of community participation. Careerism has become the route to accruing value in a society obsessed by material gain; the distance progressed up the corporate ladder a yardstick for a person's value.

But careerism has also been about survival, in a society where collective support from family or community has got thinner and where the sense of being on your own has grown stronger. Career has been the only constant companion as people have scaled the corporate hierarchy, moving locations and companies many times over to get wherever they have wanted to go. Careerism articulated to people, in an accessible and palatable form, a level of individual freedom and what it could provide, ushered in by the prevailing economic forces of the 1980s. As the sacrifices individuals have had to make have continued to mount, the price they have exacted has also gone up in a kind of Faustian pact. People have felt justified in expecting ever-bigger pay cheques and bonuses, which also provide them with a rationale for all the hours spent in the office. Senior managers fixated on career success have, by dint of the amount of time and energy expended on managing their career, had little time for anything else. And so the sense of disconnection from the rest of life has mounted.

If leaders expected this of themselves, then surely they could expect the same outlook and sacrifice by the people who worked for them. As Schor (1992) points out in *The Overworked American*, it was those people with a total work mentality that set the pace inside organizations and put particular pressure on the rest of their business to do the same. As a consequence, the total work mindset has spread through the organization. The business side of life has come to dominate everything else, crowding out other activities, whether that be missing the children's school concert or the visit to the theatre or simply spending time with friends and family on a Sunday rather than preparing for another week in the office. In spite of the calls for greater work-life balance, the reality for most is that the balance continues to tilt the way of business. As a consequence it has lessened the broader perspective and civilizing influences that life and society can provide. 'The careerist becomes fixated on the particular limited ends, whether their own or their organizations to such an extent that larger ends like human dignity or the common good become thwarted' (Naughton, 1996).

The career then has become an aspirational – some would say essential – element of modern business life. For careerists it provides a rationale for the personal sacrifices they have made, while for many it is associated with the sense of obtaining higher positions and the power and wealth that go with them. Thirty years ago, a career was primarily undertaken within a single organization. In many ways it therefore reflected the journey that an individual took, the contribution made and the friendships formed along the way within an organization; these multi-faceted relationships gave a career a context and consequently greater meaning, because it was about a *contribution* to something that was greater than, yet still connected to, the individual. Now the career experience is far more of a solo voyage. A career has become an intensely personal and insular thing. It is *my* career, a thing I am encouraged to own and can take pride in. It has also become a way of looking to the future on what may lie ahead for me or reflecting back on personal achievements in the course of a good career. Few others can plot the respective highs and lows, let alone understand the significance of the contribution or sacrifices made, because there has been no one else there who has seen the voyage from start to finish. In this sense, the career as a vehicle for gaining real personal satisfaction is starting to develop a hollow ring. For many, all that is left is the sense that they are working professionally to the best of their abilities and that they are being well rewarded for their efforts; yet all of this somehow feels empty. As people move between companies so much, their sense of career achievements can – at best – be savoured alone.

It explains to some degree why, when the rate of a person's career progress slows, people are often so quick to feel let down, to feel angry, demotivated and to seek alternative options externally, because the other rewards which used to come with careers, like friendship and seeing a company that you have contributed to develop and grow, are now much rarer; the only currency to measure the worth of a career that is left is financial. 'How can we know who we are when we are scattered like dust motes in the wind? How can we reconnect with ourselves? Where do we begin to look to find our "all-together" self?' asked Michael J Naughton (1996).

Careerism as we have seen has been an important motor behind the rise of individualism in business. However, have we been so focused on our self-interests that we are finding it harder to establish important bonds with others? I will argue that this has been an inevitable consequence of the way many leaders have had to adapt to fit in with our prevailing business culture. In the next section we will see that it has been almost inevitable that as we focused more time on our personal interests, we have had less time for others.

The disconnected board

Boards are now heavily made up of independent non-executive directors. These individuals have become a powerful group, determining the direction and investment priorities of a business, while ensuring commitments to shareholders are met and governance standards are maintained. These individuals now form a hardly visible elite, often sitting in multiple boardrooms and relying on their network of contacts for influence and leverage. Meeting collectively at global network gatherings, they exchange insights and develop an increasingly collective perspective on what is and is not accepted wisdom. At the top of this group, a kind of super league has emerged, people who have access to prime ministers and presidents around the world to lobby discreetly for policies that support their organizations. They exchange insights with journalists in return for favours. The world, it might seem, is in their hands and while we don't really know who these people are, we are encouraged to believe that these organizations are run professionally and in the best interests of all. Unfortunately this group has become unintentionally insular, living in a boardroom bubble, insulated from all but the narrowest of financial stimuli, needing to radically reconnect if they are to regain trust and rebuild legitimacy.

This growing isolation is starting to impact directly on the performance of business itself. Cass, one of the UK's top-ranking business schools, conducted an analysis of 18 corporate scandals around the world over the past 20 years.[14] To understand whether these failures were random acts or had elements in common, it studied a wide range of corporate crises, including those suffered by AIG, Arthur Andersen, BP, Cadbury Schweppes, Coca-Cola, EADS Airbus, Enron, Firestone, Independent Insurance, Northern Rock, Railtrack, Shell and Société Générale.

The Cass report makes it clear that there is indeed a pattern to the apparently random circumstances causing companies in completely different sectors to fail. The Cass study identified six key questions highlighting underlying board weaknesses. All the factors related in some way to the degree to which board members were in touch or connected with what was really going on at the heart of their own business. The six key factors or questions were:

1 Are the people held responsible for running these organizations sufficiently connected to what is really going on in their business?

2 Are they getting all the information that they need to accurately evaluate performance?

3 Do they have the necessary experience and expertise to test the judgement of operational directors, such that operational misfortune could have been avoided?

4 Are they taking a broad enough view of the responsibilities of the organization they are responsible for?

5 Are they upholding the long-term purpose of the organization, ensuring the business continues to operate in the best of interest of customers, suppliers, employees and communities?

6 Are they being held to account for the decisions they are making?

What is equally worrying are the instances where non-executives fail to exhibit a strong and personal connection to the values and purpose of the organization they are governing, evidenced in their unwillingness to address any improprieties they may witness. Once again many non-executives will rail against this observation. However, Ernst & Young (EY) the global accounting and professional services firm, produce an annual fraud survey, which polls directors in 36 countries across Europe, the Middle East, Africa and India. The 2013 survey revealed that nearly half of all board members and senior managers are aware of irregularities in their own financial reports as companies struggle to maintain healthy balance sheets. The EY review identified that 42 per cent of directors had seen irregular financial reporting in their own companies and one in five had personally witnessed financial manipulation from overstating revenues or mis-selling products to customers. In a *Financial Times* article David Stulb, EY's Global Head of Fraud Investigation, reported they had found that an alarming number of companies seem to be comfortable with unethical conduct, including reporting revenue early or under-reporting costs or encouraging customers to buy 'unnecessary stock'.[15] How is this possible given that one of the primary roles of non-executives is to ensure good governance? One conclusion may simply be that with so many businesses engaged in such activities they have become almost accepted as standard practice and not seen as worthy of ruffling too many feathers.

All of this might suggest that the codes of corporate governance introduced over the past 20 years are not providing the necessary spur or spine for non-executive directors to take business to task. Another alternative is that they simply do not set too much store by these codes of practice and consequently haven't fully implemented these codes themselves. In 2012, the accountancy firm Grant Thornton conducted an analysis of the effectiveness of the voluntary code of conduct.[16] It found that only 51 per cent of the UK's top 350 businesses were complying with the

UK Code of Governance; that companies were providing far more information about their operations but the quality of the reports were no better; that many companies were providing no clear pointers on their strategic vision; and that only one in five were linking their strategy to risks and KPIs. Indeed, on risk management many companies simply repeated, in copy-paste fashion, what they had written the year before with only 40 per cent of companies implementing a committee to monitor the major risks facing the business. Furthermore, the Grant Thornton report indicated that the people who are supposed to be providing independent scrutiny of boards and their operations, the auditors, were still involved in very close relations with large companies where average tenure was reaching 33 years, which if nothing else suggests that there are serious risks of familiarity not breeding the right level of inquisitiveness.

The apparent failure of some boards to connect with issues inside their organizations has led to an increasing number of employees going beyond their internal board governance structures, turning to whistle-blowing. According to the UK Financial Ombudsman Service, the number of complaints against businesses has doubled since the beginning of the financial crisis.[17] If boards are losing connection with some of the issues facing their organizations, what about the broader connections, between leaders and the wider workforce?

The disposable workforce

There are structural shifts occurring in the way our workforces are structured and viewed. We are witnessing a global workforce on the move, which bankers euphemistically refer to as the 'great re-balancing', with a levelling of pay in every country down to the lowest common denominator. Every country seems to be involved in some way, acting as donors or recipients of labour. Countries like the Philippines pride themselves on being mass exporters of labour, with an estimated 3,000 workers leaving the country's shores every day, while Qatar is a mass importer of labour – as are many countries across the Middle East. Qatar is using this global labour source to construct stadia for the 2018 World Cup. The workers come from everywhere but largely from the Indian sub-continent.

Meanwhile in Canada, according to senior Canadian economist Armine Yalnzyan (2012): 'There is recognition of a two-tier society developing, one made up of citizens with full rights and another comprising an underclass of "rent-a-workers" brought in from overseas.' In the United States,

Bloomberg's online magazine highlights the life of single mother Tammy Smith, a call centre worker: 'She is paid by the minute, 25 cents per minute in fact, but only for the minutes that she is actually on the phone with customers. Tammy is classified as an independent agent; she has no health insurance, no retirement benefits, no sick days, no vacation, no severance, and no access to unemployment insurance.'[18] In Taiwan, employees at Wintec, a subcontract manufacturer for brands like Apple and Nokia, work 70-hour weeks for 83 cents an hour, have no rights and endure shocking workplace conditions. While Apple has a code of employment practice, this seems to be ignored and the factory workers claim: 'Our bosses are blind and deaf.'[19]

There is a wider point here. Allowing people to be seen and used as a commodity is a slippery slope, which can result in the complete breakdown of human dignity and respect at work. A case in point is the UK farmers who are supplying millions of eggs to supermarkets via big brands like 'Happy Eggs'. This company uses agency labour to collect the eggs in a vast operation across the United Kingdom. One supplier had their licence to operate removed after a raid by the UK's Serious Organized Crime Agency (SOCA) liberated 30 trafficked Lithuanian workers who had been kept in debt bondage and forced to work 17-hour shifts. Many seeking work find themselves reduced to mere components in a vast global supply chain, part of a disposable workforce. At the extreme end of the disposable workforce is the re-emergence of human slavery. Modern slavery has crept from the margins of life to form a part of the long supply chains that serve our daily needs. The value of the slavery business is now put at $31 billion according to David Bastone in his book on global slave labour *Not for Sale* (2010). As respectable organizations are finding (if they choose to look), they have growing number of people potentially working indirectly within their global supply chains who are in some form of debt bondage or slave labour.

In striving for lower costs and greater flexibility, leaders have started to make a distinction between the people who matter – the top talent whom they value and want to connect with – and the people who work at the disposable end of the workforce, with whom connections are being lost. Again, this may be an unconscious act, but the reality is that if an organization has decided that roles can be contracted out to agency providers, or the individuals can be employed on some form of temporary arrangement, or to be self-employed, then there is an implicit statement that these people don't matter as much. Business leaders may object to this observation, but the reality is that for many in low pay and low skilled roles, their employment lacks security, stability or opportunity to progress. This lack of connectivity between those in leadership roles and large parts of the workforce shows up in many ways, not least of which are productivity, performance and engagement levels. US Gallup workforce engagement survey data charts the continued decline of engagement levels to their lowest levels ever, while in the United Kingdom the Macleod Employee Engagement Review found that declining workforce engagement levels were costing the UK £25 billion a year in lost productivity (MacLeod and Clark, 2009).

How can leaders, for whom the management of people has historically been a major part of the job, become so disconnected from their people? One factor that is playing an increasing part in the breakdown of ties is the way technology is increasingly being used.

Big data and the age of the smart machine

When management thinker Peter Drucker imagined a future where a CEO could act like a conductor of an orchestra, without hierarchy and dealing directly with frontline teams, he had seen this as the positive potential of technology. As ever, Drucker (1964) was prophetic in the image that he created. However, he would have been disappointed that the ubiquity of information systems has meant that in many of the most technologically well-equipped organizations, decisions are no longer taking place at the right level; instead they are sucked up the hierarchy to be overseen by higher levels of management through information technology embedded into every laptop and smartphone, allowing someone's every movement and action to be observed and second-guessed.

This was exactly what Jeremy Bentham had in mind when in the late 18th century he designed his first Panopticon prison (Semple, 1993). The word Panopticon derives from Greek mythology, where the many-eyed Panoptes kept watch over the entrance to the realm of the gods. The aim was to observe everyone inside the institution from a single vantage point. These ideas were developed further in the 20th century by the French philosopher Foucault (1977), who believed that the process of subjugating individuals to an all-seeing power would ultimately lead to a process of 'behaviour normalization', as people internalized the fact their every action was being observed.

The technology that enables the all-seeing gaze of the watchman is now present across business, watching staff in every call centre and increasingly down on the production line, but also through the application of interconnected 'big data' technology, which allows a single manager to know whether an individual is at their desk, to note how many times they have been on the internet and what calls they have or haven't made. It is a level of surveillance that not even Orwell could have fully imagined. Pulling information to the centre – this growing panoptical approach to management – keeps managers away from having to connect with real people and squeezes out the desire of those being observed to innovate and experiment, as people wait to be second-guessed by those in charge, rather than risking creativity and initiative. The resulting reduction in individual autonomy breeds stress and feelings of frustration, not only for those who are watched, but also for leaders (the watchers), as it acts to distance and ultimately disconnect them from developing a human relationship with their colleagues on the office or shop floor.

In her seminal work *The Age of the Smart Machine*, Soshana Zuboff (1988) observed that smart machines created the risk that people would lose their first-hand experience of the real world and be reduced to being observers of dials. This loss of connection and feel for situations can reduce their judgement and confidence in decision-making. It is a point that was echoed by Matthew B Crawford in a *New York Times* article in 2009: 'In the boardrooms of Wall Street those who sit on the swivel chairs tend to live remote from the consequences of the decisions they make.'[20] Both of these thinkers are, in very different ways, exploring the risks that result from leaders becoming disconnected from the people and core operations of their businesses.

Engineering out human connections

Yet despite the abundance of technology, which should have made life simpler with less need for management supervision, there are now more managers than ever before. A recent US survey indicated that there is now one manager for every 10 people.[21] Given all the technology we have discussed and the ability to monitor activities remotely, what are all these managers for? Renowned business strategist Gary Hamel proposes that management is now the least efficient activity in all of business and that this inefficiency stems from a top-heavy management model that is both cumbersome and costly. In a *Harvard Business Review* article, Hamel (2011) observed:

> The most powerful managers are the ones furthest from frontline realities. All too often, decisions made on an Olympian peak prove to be unworkable on the ground ... [A] multi-tiered management structure means more approval layers and slower responses. In their eagerness to exercise authority, managers often impede, rather than expedite, decision making.

Layers of management would perversely appear to be leading to those at the top becoming distanced and increasingly disconnected from those on the front line.

Few organizations even ask the question: How can we design this organization, to give individuals a greater opportunity to bring their whole selves to the work? In fact these days, beyond the rhetoric of employee engagement, such work and job design is rarely a practical consideration. This is seen in the 'Process' view of organizations developed by computer scientist Michael Hammer, which regards business as a series of logically related tasks, performed to achieve defined business outcomes. In effect, it is a descendent of a 'Taylorist' view of work, with each task broken down into its component parts. However, in removing 'unnecessary' process steps, leaders have also engineered out many human connections that went along with work (Hammer and Champy, 2003; Denning, 2010). The payroll clerk, who knew the personal circumstances of the staff, has gone. The sales administrator who built connections with the client organization has long since disappeared. An even bigger implication is that, with this fragmentation of person from person and of task from purpose, people no longer feel connected to what they do; they have lost the sense of being part of a shared endeavour, in which everyone has their part to play. The consequences of this can have a profound impact on employees' sense of ownership for the outcomes of what they do, as changes made by leaders seeking to squeeze out the last drops of efficiency lose instead whole buckets of meaning, and without meaning, as we will see later, work becomes drudgery.

There is another, perhaps even bigger, point at stake here: when people can no longer see the connection between what they do and the impact that it may ultimately have, they stop caring as much about what ultimately happens with the customer. As they lose sight of the purpose of what they do, they fail to value the consequences of things going wrong. This disconnection between actions and consequences is at the heart of so many cases of individually unthinking acts that cause damage. We encourage our children to mature by helping them to take on more responsibility for the consequences of their actions, yet it seems in much of the workplace we are doing the opposite. An extreme form of this trend is the outsourcing movement that has taken out whole organs from the corporate body, transplanting activity out to people who have no connection with the core purpose of the business. It can deliver significant short-term economies but in the process unseen nerves are severed, hidden connections are lost and much of the value created between people evaporates. A case in point is the way in which cleaning services have been outsourced in hospitals. No matter to what degree the cleaning crews feel a sense of responsibility for hitting specific cleanliness targets, they are never going to see the patients on the wards they clean as 'their' patients, with all the consequent ownership and sense of responsibility that a nurse feels.

In their treatment of organizations as purely process-based, leaders risk disconnecting employees from the meaning they derive from their work, breaking connections between colleagues and neglecting the benefits workers can bring by connecting what they are doing to a wider sense of the common good. It is a high price to pay and one rarely factored into the benefit analysis of many re-engineering and outsourcing discussions.

The forgotten many (our broken approach to talent management)

According to the PricewaterhouseCoopers (PwC) consulting group's annual global survey of CEO perspectives, a lack of talent is now seen as a top three issue for companies, inhibiting their ability to achieve future growth.[22] Mercer Consulting believes that this issue will be compounded by the demographics of western nations, where ageing populations will leave a huge 'skills' gaps on retirement (Hankin, 1997). The net result is that our organizations are becoming less resilient and less able to respond to the volatile demands of global markets.

Between 2000 and 2008 the recruitment industry in the United Kingdom grew by 167 per cent. In India today young technicians and programmers play 'corporate hopscotch', moving rapidly from one company to another in a bid to drive up their pay rates. There is little loyalty and a lot of movement, but why?

The McKinsey-inspired *War for Talent* (Hankin, 1997) has led leaders to focus on a smaller and smaller cadre of people at the top of an organization: the top one per cent of 'talent'. These individuals are subjected to rigorous reviews by boards and are likely to receive investment in management programmes and one-to-one coaching. The downside of this intense focus is that 99 per cent of the population feels like they have missed out. While a small section of people are managed as an elite group, the disconnection with the rest can have a highly damaging effect on confidence and performance. This observation was illustrated by psychologist Albert Bandura, who identified that the vast majority who know that they are not in the group earmarked for the future, are disinclined to commit fully and in turn become less connected with the long-term goals of the organization.

This observation ties in with another the trend that has emerged over the past decade in which a new CEO starts rebuilding the top teams as soon as he or she arrives. This process of top team development has moved from a long-term process of cultivating internal talent over years, to a short-term recruitment assembly process bringing talent together from many different organizations with no connection with the historical roots of the company they are joining. Talent development processes which used to take years, to inculcate and anchor people in the traditions and meaning of an organization, are now packaged into 'on-boarding' events which will always struggle to inculcate the 'feeling for the company', leaving the new crop of senior leaders permanently disconnected from the organizations and people for whom they are responsible. This may start slowly but ends up being a constant process of dilution, as each new leader hired wants to, in turn, hire their own 'hand-picked' teams. Consequently, a continual stream of new people coming into an organization breaks the connections with a company's culture and history, diluting it to such a degree that what started as a unique company ends up like any other 'me too' organization. This point was illustrated by Philippa Lally (Lally *et al*, 2009), who showed how the 'habitats' in which people operate form 'commitment devices', providing the basis for creating role models and a source of constant feedback on expected and unacceptable behaviours. Employees who form the core of the business sense that they are being managed by leaders who do not share the same love or passion for the organization that they have built up over years and has become part of their lives. This leads to a schism in the belief of the people in the business and the leaders who are running the organization and partly accounts for the low levels of trust we discussed earlier. Furthermore, as people recognize that moving from one company to another is often the best way to get on and move ahead, they develop an interest in their personal career to which they remain loyal, but loyalty to anything else or anything greater is lost. Sadly, few of the banks experiencing major scandals in recent years have made the link between the constant flows of talent in and out of their organizations and the cultures that no longer know what they stand for. This is something that no new-hire introduction course on corporate values is ever going to fix.

Fragmenting performance

The CEO

James Gorman, installed as CEO at Morgan Stanley after the 2008 crash, made the following observation on the culture of the banking industry: 'We need to change the perception that it's the individual that's the hero. I think that investment institutions need to wake up and see that well managed, high engagement and therefore healthier organizations perform so much better and so deserve their investments.'[23]

It isn't only leadership behaviour that fosters the cult of individualism. Most management processes now place such a heavy emphasis on the individual and the individual's contribution, that there is little space for the consideration of collective concerns. This division of performance into individual fragments forces a disconnection between people in organizations – a disconnection that team-building and communications events try to remedy, but they cannot address employees feeling that they are actually being told to paddle their own canoes very hard indeed. This underlying sense of individualism leads to talent reviews focused only on individual stars and reward structures in which there can only ever be winners and losers. Performance reviews rate each individual; 360-degree appraisals reinforce the sense that what counts is the perfecting of individual competencies; and development plans are designed around individual needs. This obsession with individualism can put a huge strain on relationships and often causes the bonds between people to fray. This emphasis on the individual at the expense of the 'connected whole' when combined with short-term financial performance targets, can lead to the creation of highly 'toxic cultures', as observed by Anthony Salz in his review of Barclays Bank (Salz, 2013).

Of course, every company would like their performance management systems to help to motivate staff to perform at their best, to learn and to grow. Unfortunately, our current approach to performance tends to do the opposite because of the way goals are set, feedback is given, and how people are measured (Rock *et al*, 2013a). Deci and Ryan (2002) have argued that performance and reward systems in many US organizations practice what they call 'coercive controls', using reward mechanisms which compare the performance of one group with another, to force particular performance outcomes to occur. This approach is adopted by over a third of US organizations[24] and in part explains why employees' focus narrows to deliver only what is expected and not necessarily what is required. Rather than connecting managers to the potential of their staff and bringing out the best in people, these traditional performance management approaches cause a large slice of the population to shrink and hold back.

Unfortunately many leaders now use performance reviews as a centrepiece activity in their relationship with employees. Perhaps this is a source of one of the greatest disconnections. In a survey of employees, Globalforce (2013) found that 75 per cent of respondents thought the annual performance appraisal process was one of the most demotivating activities of the year.[25] This chimes with other evidence indicating that people feel that their efforts to do a good job are not recognized, with almost a third of people saying that this factor has been central to their decision to look for an alternative role. In fact, according to a recent report from Rock *et al* (2013b), only 8 per cent of human resource executives thought that performance management made a significant contribution to business performance while a massive 86 per cent of companies are not happy with performance management as it stands. The current approach to performance management is perhaps at its worst when managers seek to complete a bell-curve analysis of the performance of their teams or divisions. In this approach there must be a normal performance distribution with 10 per cent of performers at the top and 10 per cent at the bottom, who are 'acting as a drag' on the organization. This detached and mechanistic approach often follows a macho logic once espoused by Jack Welch, former CEO at General Electric in the US, and is now common practice in many organizations, where the bottom 10 per cent of people identified in performance reviews are periodically culled from the organization because their performance falls short of the 'bar' that had been set and raised each year. The image of a cull of people is a powerful and disturbing one. Unsurprisingly it fills organizations with a certain apprehension, and causes many to focus on hitting their targets without paying heed to any of the wider consequences that this may have.

Yet many senior leaders will struggle to see how these performance practices cause significant disconnection between what they say and what they are really expecting their people to do. These are factors that were clearly evident in the cases of BP, GSK and Barclays. As McKinsey's Global Managing Director, Dominic Barton, observed: 'Top teams [are] working overtime to meet near-sighted targets – and they are blind to the impact of their actions on any broader measure of value.'[26] Individuals, he said, 'have lost sight of the broader goals of a free-market economy'. Many organizations would argue that their organization is based on collective team efforts and the best long-term interests of the whole organization. They will point to the countless meetings and away-days, motivational conferences and mission statements that their organizations have in place to reinforce company values and collective efforts. Yet so little of this activity seems to be having anything other than a transitory effect on staff morale and instead results in high levels of cynicism. This is because it doesn't line up with what people experience in reality every day at work.

The executive club

Pay for those at the top of organizations is now on average 110 times that of those at the bottom (rising to 250 times for the very highest paid). In the United Kingdom, CEO pay is currently rising at five times the rate of shop floor workers. According to Chrystia Freeland, author of *Plutocrats* (Freeland, 2012), the past 25 years has witnessed the arrival of a 'new managerial aristocracy', with superstar managers who are highly paid and equally highly mobile, in a 'new virtual nation of mammon', fuelled by new technology and the accelerating pace of globalization. These highly paid individuals are increasingly disconnected from the world around them, living in their own 'Executive Club' bubble, cut off from the realities of their operations, or its long-term purpose.

Tellingly, Citibank now divides the world from an investment perspective into two blocs: the super-rich and the rest. Citibank calls this the 'Hour Glass Economy' and are advising 'smart money' to invest in the stocks of either luxury goods producers or deep discounters (Leonard, 2012). Citibank now tracks the performance of stocks using their Hourglass Index, and points out that it beat the Dow Jones Industrial Average by 45 per cent between 2009 and 2011 (Freeland, 2012). Meanwhile, people at the top of the Hourglass seem to see themselves as the rightful meritocratic winners of a tough global competition.

According to Professor Mihir Desai at Harvard University, 'Rising income inequality can be traced back to the proliferation of high powered incentive contracts for managers and institutional investors' (Desai, 2012). The US and the UK now have the biggest income disparities, between the HNWIs (High net-worth individuals) and the rest, but this issue is not isolated to the Anglo-Saxon business world. Seemingly disparate protests on the streets from São Paulo to Turkey are, according to the *Financial Times*, united by common underlying tensions.[27] Increasingly, 'highly educated and growing youth populations, living in urban sprawl, suffering record unemployment and huge income inequalities are finding their voice and connecting through mobile technology' and are, according to the *Financial Times*, starting to exert pressure.

So the practice of rewarding a few people at the top disproportionately to the vast majority at the bottom is fuelling the sense of disconnection, not only in business but also with the wider world that people experience in day-to-day life. These levels of pay play a contributory role in locking people at the top of organizations into a lifestyle that is effectively cut off from the day-to-day lives of the majority of people. Given that most products and services are designed for mass market consumption, the very different life experiences that leaders have because of the way they are remunerated inevitably hampers an organization's ability to connect with its ordinary customers.

Losing touch with customers

Over the past 30 years, the giant corporations that dominate the world's business landscape have succeeded in bringing an unimaginable amount of choice to our doors. The overall quality of products is far superior to anything that was previously available and the price makes it accessible to nearly all in affluent western societies. The price of all this convenience has also come down as a percentage of our monthly expenditure, and until recently there has been more disposable income to spend on holidays and entertainment. Vast supply chains connect local retail stores with goods made in the four corners of the globe, putting luxury within the reach of ordinary people.

So customers should be feeling pampered and happy. However, it appears that the more that has been made available, the more expectations have risen, and the less happy we have become. It seems that we don't forgive processes which fail and hate it when a de-personalized and faceless company seems to be exploiting us; it leaves us feeling out of control and slightly paranoid. We start to worry and ask ourselves: if a bank or insurance company or supermarket can do this, what else are they capable of? Trust – that essential invisible quality which holds things together – quickly evaporates.

Stifling innovation

For all the talk about innovation being key to growth, many leaders seem to operate by a set of hidden principles designed to prevent innovations from surfacing or succeeding. At their heart, these principles seem designed to reduce connectivity both within their organization and between their business and the world outside.

Leaders do so by being suspicious of new ideas and require extensive reports on every piece of expenditure they have. They limit connectivity by keeping people very busy on the task in hand, leaving no time to experiment or to explore the ideas that others may have. At the same time, the ability to connect with others beyond the immediate group is hampered in the name of competitiveness, with internal groups encouraged to fight over resources so that rather than collaborating, individuals end up challenging the quality of each other's work. In this way, leaders become architects of the organizational bunkers and silos that create many losers and few winners.

Cutting off innovation is rarely done deliberately and consciously, rather it occurs through a number of disconnections, which leaders create through a series of seemingly unrelated actions. We can see in an example at Intel, how a strong performance culture can stop people making the connections with the future and stifle innovation.

CASE STUDY Intel Corporation

In 2008, as new fields in computing and social networks were opening up, Intel Corporation launched its New Business Initiative (NBI), designed to retain its world-leading position (Shih and Thurston, 2010). But the programme is now widely viewed as a failure, with every one of the 42 ideas that reached take-off point as new business concepts failing to get the backing they needed within the organization. A 2010 Harvard Business School paper by Thomas A Thurston examined why the programme had floundered. The programme had the remit to identify, fund and develop new businesses through the exploration of new technologies, new products, new markets, and new distribution channels. The programme had an investment horizon of 5 to 10 years. NBI operated as a largely autonomous unit. Unlike the relatively formal and structured annual planning and budgeting processes that drove sustained success in the microprocessor segment, NBI typically committed only seed capital to new business ventures, ramping up its commitment as strategic and financial milestones were reached. Intel took a rigorous approach to understanding competitors, technology, customers, market structure and a host of other variables when analysing opportunities for growth.

Unfortunately for Intel – and for everyone else who seeks to innovate – data about the future could only be limited and so many important but unanswered questions remained. Because of this inherent ambiguity, great ideas which were ready for take-off did not get backed by business unit leaders who felt that they could not justify the expenditure on an investment that only had a 'possible' future value, compared with the investments they knew about in markets they understood, delivering a known return and ensuring near term business targets were hit. Intel's own financial metrics thus prevented it from getting the benefit from the programme. The business unit leaders placed a greater priority on continuing to deliver the numbers and because of this relentless pressure to deliver, the managers made the only rational choice available to them given the dynamics within their organizations (we will return to the topic of measurement later).

The unintended consequences of good governance

In November 2011, Bob Diamond former Chief Executive Officer of Barclays Bank, one of the world's largest financial institutions, gave the inaugural BBC Business Lecture to a group of leading figures from the British establishment. His words have proved to be strangely prophetic:

> Soon after the financial crisis of 2008, I was at a meeting in Washington with a group of US senators. They had invited me to provide a point of view on new legislation aimed at ensuring we never have to go through the events of 2008 ever again. While I was there, a senior economic adviser at the White House put a question to me. 'Do you think banks can be good citizens?' he said. I wanted to answer yes, but before I could reply he said: 'If the answer is yes, think about the fact that no one will believe you.'[28]

Senior leaders of our largest organizations are bright people who understand the breadth of issues set before them, so how can the view of corporate leaders and wider society become so disconnected? One overlooked factor lies in the way business leaders evaluate the dilemmas they face and the way they, in turn, make decisions.

Leaders are today schooled to consider matters of profitability, share-price and reputation alongside challenges like carbon footprints, pollution levels, and worker exploitation. In large companies these factors are 'dealt with' quite logically and often at great length in risk committees, which score and evaluate each 'risk 'item and rank them on a matrix. In the process of these reviews the orientation to the matters at hand changes, key points are discussed, but the process itself reduces the considerations to purely 'intellectual problems', factors that can be dealt with by 'managing the necessary trade-offs'.

Unfortunately many of the challenges we face today do not lend themselves easily to such simple business-type calculations. After all, it's hard to do a profit-and-loss account on the impact of opening a mine up in the middle of a pristine piece of jungle, when the consequences for plants and animals are difficult to quantify, yet the 'benefits', taxes and profits to be realized are so significant.

Issues discussed at corporate risk committees are therefore no longer about right and wrong, but rather about risk and mitigation management. Many leaders would hold that this is the only way that these factors can be dealt with rationally, yet others would counter that this kind of trade-off mindset has in and of itself led business leaders to become increasingly amoral in their outlook. A viewpoint reinforced, as we will see later, through the tendency to fine an organization for transgressing the law, as opposed to sending people to jail. This is a form of sanction that can be weighed monetarily (but not morally) against the benefits to be gained by an organization. Whatever the case, these 'good governance' processes have come to dominate business practice everywhere and are serving to unintentionally and unconsciously distance leaders from the reality and consequences of their decisions. How do we enable leaders to connect with the world around them?

The downsides of a digitally enhanced corporation

We go through life mishearing, mis-seeing and misunderstanding so that the stories we tell ourselves will add up.

(Janet Malcolm)

It isn't only extreme rationality, risk management and the relentlessness of the daily schedule that is getting in the way of senior leaders hearing what they need to hear. They are also engaged in a 'communications war', to manage the reputation and associated share price of their organizations. However, while this confidence game seems essential in 'managing the image' and reducing risk, it also has a downside in that the very act of the managed communications environment can distort a leader's sense of the reality of what their organization is really doing convincing themselves as much as it convinces others, that the image is the reality.

This is a natural trait. Human beings, it seems, are wired to edit the world to the way they would prefer to see it. In a recent discussion in London, James Kilner (2014) spoke about 'The Curated Ego' based on his neuroscience research at University College London. Dr Kilner reflected on the phenomenon of the selfie (taking a picture of yourself on your mobile) which has been practised by prime ministers and presidents alike. He observed that for the first time in history we are able to take and retake as many pictures as we like of ourselves until we produce an image that comes closest to matching our perception of what we think we should look like. In his research, he found that we are systematically more likely to choose digitally enhanced versions of ourselves to the stark realities. It is natural to want to put the best possible image of ourselves out there; the problems come when we start believing that the image is in fact reality. Rather than having a mature dialogue based on a more 'balanced picture', as we shall see, it seems that corporations are intent on producing the commercial equivalent of 'selfies'.

Corporate leaders can create a 'digitally enhanced version' of themselves and their companies in three ways:

- First, by exerting their influence over governments, lobbying heavily for – and frequently getting – the laws they want. Corporations can do nothing other than 'look good', if they 'break no laws' by continuing to operate within the rules, and indeed many corporations may well argue that this is a perfectly legitimate activity in a 'free society'. However, if you were a successful tennis player and you could change the rules to allow only the richest players to buy bigger tennis rackets, then you would expect to win more games. This may be perfectly understandable leadership behaviour if all you want to do is 'win'. However, if you see the needs of a 'bigger game', then you might question how this approach was helping to encourage tennis talent at the grass roots, you might ask if it provided good entertainment for the fans, who may not continue to turn up to one-sided games and you might even question whether it was fair and effective in promoting a true spirit of competition. Such is the plight of so much professional sport. Nonetheless, according to the Centre for Responsive Politics in the United States, corporate expenditure on lobbying in Washington by the pharmaceutical industry alone was $2.7 billion between 2008 and 2013; the insurance sector spent $1.8 billion over the same period; the oil and gas sector spent $1.5 billion, as did the computing sector. Lobbying firms go as far as pay individuals to stand in line, so that 'their people' get to sit in on the public debates, and crowding out ordinary citizens from participating in the process of government. In turn, the process of government is becoming less open and less trusted. As with any investment, organizations wouldn't spend the money if they weren't getting a reasonable rate of return.

- The second area that corporate leaders seek to enhance their image, reputation and standing is perhaps best illustrated by the level of corporate expenditure on public relations, which was $7 billion in 2011, up 8 per cent in even in the depths of the recession. This public relations management of reality is increasingly subtle with large corporations paying considerable amounts to have purportedly independent comment on their business practices. Barclays Bank for example paid Ernst & Young to carry out an audit of its performance against its 'Citizenship Report' launched by Bob Diamond in 2012. There was nothing wrong or false in the report but did it convey a wholly truthful picture of Barclay's activities? The EY report was based only on the input and assessment of Barclay's own staff. Barclays paid handsomely for the report, because they knew that by having the EY names on a document about the progress the bank was making towards becoming a better company, would add credibility to its actions. The Ernst & Young report never even mentioned the Libor rigging scandal, or indeed the impact of mis-selling, in its evaluation.[29]

It took the escalation of the Libor crisis and the exit of the Chairman and CEO at Barclays, to allow the independent Salz Review to occur. Published in April 2013, it was the first time the internal culture of the bank had been identified as being at the root of the scandals the bank had been involved in. Waking up to these realities is incredibly difficult for any leader if they are immersed in a warm bath created by their own PR machines. It starts to explain in part why it is proving so difficult for leaders in our biggest corporations to learn the right lessons.

- The third and final way that corporations seek to enhance their image is through the management of corporate social responsibility. In the preface to their book *The End of Corporate Social Responsibility* Professors Peter Fleming and Marc T Jones (2013) identified that the most popular image used to communicate CSR on the internet was a fragile earth held by a giant pair of corporate hands. This was clearly designed to demonstrate the care that business has for the planet. However, the authors highlighted a potentially darker meaning, showing corporations with so much power that they do indeed hold the earth's future at their will. Yet we never see the face of the business leaders in the darkness that surrounds the image and the small earth seems somehow powerless to resist. Nonetheless, corporations are spending a colossal amount on CSR budgets. The top 10 most respected organizations in the United States, a list that includes, Microsoft, Google, Disney and BMW, spent in excess of $1 billion on the agenda in 2012. According to a report by the Reputation Institute in 2013, 73 per cent of customers want to see companies doing CSR work.[30] However, perhaps most tellingly,

FIGURE 1.1 From stakeholder management to reconnected leadership

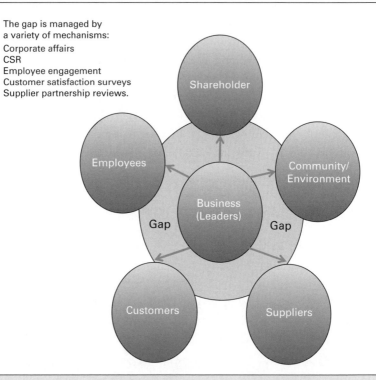

The gap is managed by a variety of mechanisms:
Corporate affairs
CSR
Employee engagement
Customer satisfaction surveys
Supplier partnership reviews.

Shareholder

Employees

Community/Environment

Business (Leaders)

Gap

Gap

Customers

Suppliers

Purpose: to maximize returns to shareholders, enhance reputation and minimize risks

The stakeholder management model, has become pervasive in modern leadership thinking. It assumes that the role of leadership is to *manage* the relationships between each of the parties, everyone, forging a balance which is in the best long-term interests of the company. It reflects a powerful mindset which sees the world of business as somehow apart from the rest, with a need to manage the relationships of people who have a notional stake in the business.

Key points to note:
Business is at the centre of the model.
There is a gap between business and each of the distinct interests of the stakeholders, which are presumed to have different and potentially competing interests and are managed in that way.
Various governance approaches seek to evaluate the distinct aspects of each strand of a company's relationships. The risk of disconnection is high. The challenge of seeing all these stakeholders in such a compartmentalized way is an increasingly onerous management burden.

only five out of the top 100 companies on the reputation report were seen to be delivering on their CSR commitments. These insights suggest that while business leaders are spending billions on enhancing their reputation and image, the public have discerned that there is a disconnect between the air-brushed version they see and what they have increasingly come to believe.

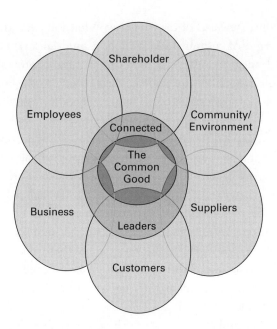

Purpose: to maximize returns to shareholders, enhance reputation and minimize risks

Rather than managing each stakeholder separately, here the leader finds connections and shared interests to form a distinctive, unified approach to deliver sustainable returns for everyone. The leader is helping to pull things together rather than keep things apart. This requires integrated, dynamic and agile orientation and a far deeper appreciation of the needs and opportunities presented by the model. The reconnected model assumes that business does not stand at the centre of things or apart from them. Instead it plays a vital role in serving the common good of society. The role of leadership is therefore to make connections between the interests of business and those of all other constituencies in order to enhance the good of all. By doing so the business leader is creating a sustainable model for their organization within society, enabling the business to continue to evolve to changing needs. Operating like this requires leaders who are far more connected. The governance outlook shifts from seeing sustainability as an add-on activity – managing various stakeholders and the corporation's reputation – to one which is integrated into the core activities of the business whose purpose is to thrive within a thriving society.

Conclusion

In the early part of the 20th century at the height of great technological advancement in coal and steel and rail, two American presidents realized that business leaders had assumed too much power and that this was no longer for the benefit of American society as a whole. The era of the Roaring 20s and *The Great Gatsby* also witnessed a concentration of wealth in the hands of few people during what became known as the Gilded Age. It was therefore against a backdrop of intense animosity and upheaval that a programme of reform was introduced which curtailed the monopolistic tendencies of some of the largest corporations and reframed the role of business leaders to become stewards of the economy. What followed after much turmoil was a period of sustained innovation, growth and renewal, led by a new cadre of leaders like Alfred P Sloan of General Motors. We are once again at one of those inflection points, when society as a whole recognizes that the old ways of working have to change, when the need for more inclusive growth and the end of almost oligarchic power is plain for all to see.

Up to now, few on the part of business have had opportunity to break from the pack, yet many recognize that there is a pressing need to change. To turn around a growing anti-business sentiment will take a breed of business leaders with the vision and courage to mark out what such a transformation could look like in its totality. Yes, pay structures need to be reformed; yes, we need greater employee engagement; and yes, technology will be a huge enabler of new ways of working. But how can all these ideas come together to form a compelling new direction, which business leaders and society as a whole believe will enable them, their organizations and the societies they serve to be more successful?

The thread that pulls together all of these ideas is set out in the second section of this book under the banner of *connectivity*. Without being connected to the issues that others see, it will be difficult for many in business to grasp fully the remedies that are needed for a different future. From the need for a leader to establish personal connections with the poorest and most disadvantaged members of their community to the new connections they must forge with customers to bring different and deeper relationships. This sense of connectedness beyond the normal confines of our business experience will define what the new era of leadership is all about.

Part Two of this book will mark eight steps required to start that journey.

---

1 Philip Ball, GlaxoSmithKline's bribes are evidence that Big Pharma isn't working, *The Guardian*, 4 July 2012

2 GSK: Living Our Values: Anti-bribery and corruption programme 2010, GSK Press release, 15 July 2013

3 Off-the-record observation

4 BBC Radio 4 *Today* Programme, 16 July 2013

5 Drugs, Ranbaxy and lies, *The Hindu*, 29 May 2013

6 BBC Radio 4 *Today* Programme, 18 December 2013

7 Keith Wagstaff, Former employees say Bank of America lied to a lot of homeowners, *The Week* Magazine, www.theweek.com, 18 June 2013

8 BBC Radio 4 *Today* Programme, December 2013

9 John Gapper, Business must take the lead on Bangladesh's working conditions, *Financial Times*, 1 May 2013

10 Pressure to meet unrealistic business objectives and deadlines is leading factor for unethical corporate behavior, American Management Association and Human Resource Institute survey, 16 January 2006

11 *Business Ethics European Review*, **17**, Oct 2008

12 Niccolò Machiavelli, *The Prince*, Oxford University Press, 2008

13 *New York Times*, 13 September 1970

14 *Roads to Ruin*, Cass Business School Report, July 2012

15 Franny Rabkin, Tolerance of fraud rises, *Financial Times*, 23 May 2012

16 Effectiveness of the Voluntary Code, Corporate Governance Review, Grant Thornton, 2012

17 Financial Ombudsman Service, May 2013

18 The disposable worker, *Bloomberg Business Week* Magazine, 7 January 2010

19 Workers' rights in the global electronics sector, *Good Electronics*, November 2012

20 *New York Times*, 28 May 2009

21 Jim Clifton, Gallup Chairman and CEO, *The Chairman's Blog*, June 2013

22 PwC 15th Annual Global CEO Survey, 2012

23 M J Moore, *Bloomberg News*, 8 November 2010

24 Jenna McGregor, *Bloomberg Business Week Magazine*, 8 January 2006

25 *Empowering employees to improve employee performance*, Globalforce survey, summer 2013

26 Dominic Barton, McKinsey's Global Managing Director, Blueprint for a Better Business Conference, October 2012

27 Philip Stephens, Prosperity fuels protest in the new age of unrest, *Financial Times*, 30 June 2013

28 Inaugural BBC Today Business Lecture, 3 November 2011

29 Jo Confino, Has Barclays brought corporate responsibility reporting into disrepute? *The Guardian*, 2 July 2012

30 CSR RepTrack 100 Study, Reputation Institute, 2013

PART TWO
Eight steps to becoming a reconnected leader

Introduction: The arrival of the connected era

02

Throughout history, waves of technology innovation have led to long periods of growth followed by major market collapse, driving fundamental shifts in the way organizations have been led. The last major shift of this kind occurred at the beginning of the 1980s, ushering in an era which saw the world move 'from a market economy to a market society' (Sandel, 2012). Once again, we are now seeing the end of one era and the beginning of another as part of capitalism's continuing process of renewal. The period that began with the crash of Lehman Brothers Bank in September 2008 has witnessed the unravelling of many previously accepted market practices through a variety of business scandals and associated loss of trust. As we saw in Part One, this has led to a disconnection between business leaders and the rest of society. There is now a growing recognition that old leadership models are out of balance and in need of overhaul. The challenge now is for leaders to appreciate what this change means for the way in which they run their organizations. Part Two of this book will consider how leaders can undertake this challenge.

The start of this new 'connected era' saw the first iPhone launched in 2007 and the first iPad in 2010. These new technological advances may still be in their infancy, yet they have already served to break down barriers, bring people together and redefine markets. This technological enablement has also given people around the world powerful tools to organize and voice their views in a way that had not been previously possible. We saw this only too clearly in the protests at Tahrir Square and across the Arab Spring more generally. However, despite the flurry of articles about the power of social media 'kicking off' everywhere, technology does not in itself provide sufficient insight or indeed the answers we are looking for in how best to lead in this new era. It is simply an enabler in much the same way that the railways and electrification changed the way work and life could be organized.

The pace of globalization also took a sharp turn upwards in parallel with the arrival of the new technology. The first conference of the five most advanced 'developing' nations, the BRICS (Brazil, Russia, India, China, South Africa), occurred in Yekaterinburg in Russia on June 2009. By 2015 they will have established a 'New Development Bank' to rival the role of the World Bank and the International Monetary Fund. Technological advance is acting as an amplifier for globalization and other emerging phenomena of our age, including population growth, demographic change, migration and climate change. These megatrends are converging and are starting to change the way people look at things. This shift is not simply about angry protests on the streets but is about something far deeper. For the first time in a generation, accepted ways of thinking and organizing are being questioned fundamentally. Together these factors are compressing the world around us, making what was once remote and distant increasingly part of our newly connected and increasingly shared existence.

An example from Africa illustrates just how interconnected we are becoming and the resultant challenges and opportunities that we face. In Ghana, the local and traditional clothing industry is being crowded out of business by the cheap imports of second-hand clothes donated to charity shops by fashion-hungry Brits spending £60 billion a year on new clothes. Bought in vast bales off the boats that land every week, these clothes (which the UK charity shops cannot sell) are sold on markets around Ghana as *obroni wawu* – 'the dress of the dead white man'. The trade has virtually killed off the traditional culture of local Kente cloth-making. The irony of course is that the British consumer can only afford to throw so many clothes away because they are bought relatively cheaply from the cheap labour factories of Bangladesh. This 'global cycle' is having the knock-on effect of closing all bar one of the 40 textile factories in Ghana.

However, the compression of these global factors doesn't end there. Youth unemployment across Northern Africa is resulting in ever increasing numbers of unemployed men going in search of opportunities, crossing the Sahara before embarking on dangerous voyages across the Mediterranean Sea to find work in Europe. This influx of illegal immigrants from North Africa increases the supply of cheap labour into the European labour market, effectively suppressing wage rates in Europe, and unintentionally contributing to low-income lifestyles and patterns of exclusion amongst young people.

This example not only illustrates how closely our economic lives are now tied up with each other, but also shows how culturally intertwined we have also become. African men with a Muslim background are moving to French cities and other parts of Europe in far larger numbers than ever before, radically changing the cultural dynamic. Meanwhile, in Ghana there has been an erosion of traditional cultural ways, with industries and traditions all but dying out to be supplanted by 'throwaway' western fashions. The example serves to illustrate how interconnected leadership thinking will need to be if it is to find sustainable answers to such complex issues in the new connected era.

The implications of this new era are about opportunity, conflicting demands and confusion in equal measure. It requires a different kind of leadership capable of thinking and acting in a far more systemic way, identifying lasting solutions to the real challenges we face rather than fixing problems which too easily resurface in another guise elsewhere. To paraphrase a quote from Andrew Grove, the former boss of technology firm Intel, in this new era 'only the reconnected will survive'.

In Part Two we will therefore set out an eight-step framework to help leaders to reconnect and to start to take a more systemic outlook, developing a fresh and different perspective on their organizations and their own personal leadership approach.

Step 1: Discovering the power of purpose

03

> *Profits are like happiness in that they are a by-product of other things.* **(RATAN TATA, PRESIDENT OF TATA GROUP)**

Introduction

As we saw in Chapter 1, many leading organizations focus primarily on delivering superior shareholder return as the principle purpose of their business. Yet this can have unforeseen and negative consequences. So in this chapter we will examine how leaders can build a stronger and more sustainable foundation for their organization, which reconnects employees, customers and the wider community within a business's core purpose. The approach is designed to help business leaders connect the contribution they and their businesses can make to the common good, while also delivering a fair return for responsible shareholders.

In Chapter 1 we also saw that businesses based on narrow conceptions of shareholder return have this narrow financial logic woven into every fibre of their organization and into every domain of activity. This starts with the way the board itself works and spreads out to determine how employees are managed through to the relationships with customers, suppliers and the wider community. Thus, the true purpose of a business ultimately takes on a pervasive form. As Lau Tzu observed in *Tao Te Ching*: 'Watch your thoughts: they become words. Watch your words: they become actions. Watch your actions: they become habit. Watch your habits: they become character. Watch your character: for it becomes your destiny.'

Developing a sense of purpose is therefore the essential first step in our eight steps towards reconnected leadership. In this chapter we will consider how leaders can develop a purpose that acts as a powerful focal point for all other activities within the organization. As we will see in subsequent

FIGURE 3.1 Reconnected leadership model: Purpose

chapters, the principles set out in the development of a strong purpose are in turn embedded in the development of new leadership practices, which inform the way an organization's purpose is brought to life.

Why develop a purpose?

Leaders who want to create the necessary conditions for sustainable results – and a life they can value – need to find a counterbalance to the relentless pressure to deliver. If left unchecked this can create increasingly myopic and imbalanced leadership prone to poor choices. The way leaders can find this counterbalance is to reconnect themselves and their people through a strong and powerful sense of purpose for their organizations, which can sustain and guide them even under intense pressure.

The importance of establishing a sense of purpose was set out by respected business adviser Gurnek Bains (2007), who encapsulated purpose as: 'An invigorating sense that goes beyond business success, and which makes people feel that are improving society as opposed to just servicing a tactical need.' Bains goes on to claim that having a purpose creates, 'a culture that allows people to be themselves and to feel they are personally making a difference, utilizing all their distinct talents'. Purpose then, offers the potential for us to bring our common and shared humanity back to the workplace.

People working for an organization with a strong sense of purpose also experience a direct business benefit. Deloitte Consulting's 'Core Beliefs & Culture Survey' (2013–14) found that a company with a strong purpose is probably more confident in its prospects, and as a result, invests more heavily in initiatives that lead to long-term growth.[1] The report found that 82 per cent of respondents working in an organization with a strong sense of purpose believed that their organization would grow over the next year. In comparison, only 48 per cent of respondents working for companies without a sense of purpose were optimistic about growth prospects. According to respondents, it is this sense of deeper and longer-term commitment that is the main driver of confidence in purpose-driven companies.

But if leaders believe the creation of purpose is really about delivering better short-term shareholder returns, they will create a level of 'instrumentality'

FIGURE 3.2   Development of corporate purpose forms part of a closed system

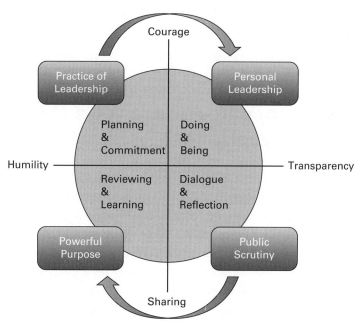

The development of corporate purpose is part of 'closed system'. Unlike other 'Box ticking" or external standards-based approaches to corporate ethics, the standards set are developed and owned by the leadership of an organization. The 'challenge' then comes from having to explain how you have actually performed to the public at large. This is a new level of accountability – for boards – and is currently only seen in Senate Committees or the Public Accounts Committee in the UK, through a curated dialogue with informed and interested sections of society. The curating of meaningful discussions with the public, such that informed scrutiny is possible, is something we will return to in Step 2 – Chapter 2, and is covered in the responsibilities of the reconnected board.

that colleagues, customers and community members will see through and feel they have been cynically manipulated. This is why so much of the corporate social responsibility (CSR) agenda is regarded with suspicion. The difficult step that a leader must therefore take is to embark on developing a purpose that is genuinely about making a contribution to the common good. Done in the right way, this will provide customers with products that are truly good and services that truly serve. Organizations that take this path will be better placed for long-term success.

However, while lifting business's sights in this way, leaders must also help to cultivate more rounded expectations of business activity by society. Having a purpose is not about achieving perfection as there are no perfect organizations, nor should we expect there to be. We must instead cultivate a greater sense of realism and humility about what business can achieve. What we can – and should – expect is that leaders will work to be true to their guiding purpose and in doing so will produce more sustainable organizational performance. Such honesty, while incredibly difficult, will over time produce a more trusting dialogue with society.

How a leader develops and connects with their purpose is therefore pivotal to the long-term success of any organization and we will now consider this in more detail.

The power of purpose: Are you a Mode 1 or a Mode 2 organization?

In this chapter we will look at an alternative approach to purpose from the kind of narrow financially orientated purpose that currently dominates organizations. The contrast was captured by Professor John Kay at a conference hosted by the 'Blueprint for Better Business' organization, where Kay considered the impact that having everyone connected through a true sense of purpose could have on the fortunes of an organization.[2] To clarify why purpose is so important, Kay set out the difference between what he called 'Mode 1 organizations' and 'Mode 2 organizations'. He illustrated his points through a case study on ICI, once one of Britain's largest, most successful and most admired global organizations. Kay observed that, in its 1987 annual report, ICI's stated purpose and mission was to be 'the world's leading chemical company serving customers internationally, through the innovative and responsible application of chemistry and related science'. The purpose statement goes on: 'Through the achievement of our aim we will enhance the wealth and well-being of our shareholders our employees our customers and the communities which we serve and in which we operate.' Kay described this as a *Mode 1 organization purpose*, and we can see that it brings to the fore the focus on those operational activities which were at the core of what the business was about and importantly helped to make it distinctive – 'the innovative and responsible application of chemistry and related sciences' – so that the 'wealth and well-being of shareholders, employees and communities which we serve' can be enhanced. However, following a takeover battle in the early 1990s, ICI had a fundamental review of its aims and by 1994 had split itself into a pharmaceuticals business called Zeneca (now part of AstraZeneca) and a core chemicals organization. ICI then re-crafted its purpose statement in that year's annual report to read: 'Our objective is to maximize value for our shareholders by focusing on businesses where we have market leadership, a technology edge, and world-competitive cost base.' This statement could have been written about almost any company and reflected what Kay called a *Mode 2 organization*. He then went on to examine the two statements in detail and identified three important differences. First, in Mode 1, operations are the primary focus, 'serving customers ... through the responsible application of chemistry and related science' whereas in Mode 2, the primary focus is financial where, 'our objective is to maximize shareholder value' has jumped to the top of the list. Second, in Mode 1, ICI had a strong stakeholder orientation, 'enhancing the well-being of shareholders, employees, customers and communities'; while in the Mode 2 statement, it talks exclusively about only one stakeholder, 'maximizing value for shareholders'. Finally, the Mode 1 statement focused on a core competence, which allowed it to move into new areas of business as those needs arose, through its 'application of chemistry and related science'. This led the organization to move from a focus on dyestuffs and explosives in the 1920s to the invention of several petrochemicals products such as perspex, polythene, crimplene, and beta-blocker drugs. It is also interesting to note that after it set up its pharmaceutical business in the 1950s, ICI did not make any money out of it for over 15 years until beta blockers came on stream, something that most, if not all organizations would struggle to do in today's short-termist investment markets.

But in its move to become a Mode 2 company in 1994, ICI narrowed its purpose to focus on existing businesses where it already had 'a market leadership' position. Interestingly, this move coincided with the appointment of ICI's first external CEO (a point to which I shall return later) and an acquisition spree, which resulted in ICI developing a debt-mountain of £4 billion.

TABLE 3.1 Example of ICI: Showing Mode 1 and Mode 2 approaches

Purpose Statement	Mode 1 approach	Mode 2 approach
	'The world's leading chemical company serving customers internationally, through the innovative and responsible application of chemistry and related science'. 'Through the achievement of our aim we will enhance the wealth and wellbeing of our shareholders our employees our customers and the communities which we serve and in which we operate'	'Our objective is to maximize value for our shareholders by focusing on businesses where we have market leadership, a technology edge, and world competitive cost base'
1) What is the focus of activity?	**Operational Focus:** 'application of chemistry and related sciences'	**Financial Focus:** 'To maximize value for our shareholders'
2) Is there a unique or generic mindset?	**Unique mindset:** 'the innovative and responsible application of chemistry and related sciences'	**Generic mindset:** "maximizing value for our shareholders" (statement could belong to any company)
3) What is valued? and Who is value being created for?	**Value:** 'Wealth and well-being for shareholders, employees and communities'	**Value:** Value for shareholders only
4) Inspiring Outlook (Narrow or Wide / short or long term?)	**Wide/Future focus:** The world's leading chemical company	**Narrow/Today focus:** 'Focusing on businesses where we have market leadership'
5) Serving or Competing?	**Serving** 'serving customers internationally . . . and the communities which we serve'	**Competing:** 'a technology edge, and world competitive cost base'

ICI's original Mode 1 statement contained a real sense of aspiration, to be the 'world's leading chemical company', which by 1994 had disappeared. While ICI's share price climbed to a high in 1997, it then deteriorated progressively over the following decade and by 2008 what was left of ICI was bought by AkzoNobel. Sadly, ICI no longer exists.

There are few organizations that have managed to craft and stay true to purpose over the long term, such that it forms the very the fibre of their organization. As we have seen in the ICI example, organizations and leaders can lose track of what they are about and where they are going. Organizations, like people, find it difficult to live up to the aspirations they set for themselves. However, a leader who has reconnected with the long-term purpose of a Mode 1 organization can use this as a source of courage, helping them to take tough decisions in the short term 'knowing' that they are doing the right thing over the longer run. In such a way a reconnected leader is better placed to cultivate shared connections across an organization developing a deeper sense of trust with employees, suppliers and customers alike, that while they may not always like the decisions that such a leader has to take but they understand the direction and trust the basis from which tough decisions are being made. Perhaps one of those with the greatest examples of working in this way is the Tata Group in India.

CASE STUDY Tata – India

Tata represents approximately 10 per cent of the value of all companies in India. It has a purpose which has guided the organization for over a century. Following a visit to Manchester in 1875, Jamsetji Tata, the company's founder, had been inspired to open a steel-making plant. In 1912 Tata began supplying steel for the new railways across India and has continued to innovate ever since – not just in markets, products and services but also in the way it has treated its people and its customers. In 1912, it was the first company to introduce an eight-hour day for its workers, at a time when Britain and the rest of the world were still demanding 12 hours. In the 1920s, it was one of the first companies to introduce paid leave. This leadership approach extends into environmental policy, the level of engagement with the local community and the way people are developed. Unlike so many other companies, Tata backs up its words through real commitment and true connections, with close to 30 per cent of group profits after tax being spent on supporting social causes.

At the Tata Group they had this to say about their purpose:

[W]e are committed to improving the quality of life of the communities we serve. We do this by striving for leadership and global competitiveness in the business sectors in which we operate. Our practice of returning to society what we earn evokes trust among consumers, employees, shareholders and the community. We are committed to protecting this heritage of leadership with trust through the manner in which we conduct our business.[3]

Tata has always been values-driven. There are five core values which underpin the way Tata do business, which are set out at every one of its sites. They are:

1   *Integrity*: We must conduct our business fairly, with honesty and transparency. Everything we do must stand the test of public scrutiny.

2   *Understanding*: We must be caring, show respect, compassion and humanity for our colleagues and customers around the world, and always work for the benefit of the communities we serve.

3   *Excellence*: We must constantly strive to achieve the highest possible standards in our day-to-day work and in the quality of the goods and services we provide.

4   *Unity*: We must work cohesively with our colleagues across the group and with our customers and partners around the world, building strong relationships based on tolerance, understanding and mutual cooperation.

5   *Responsibility*: We must continue to be responsible, sensitive to the countries, communities and environments in which we work, always ensuring that what comes from the people goes back to the people many times over.

The language used by Tata in its values statement are markedly different in tone from that used by many other organizations particularly in its desire to be transparent, 'capable of standing the test of public scrutiny'. It also highlights a strong sense of solidarity in its commitment to ensure 'what comes from the people goes back to the people'. Like all organizations Tata does have imperfections, but the sense of purpose which they have cultivated since the company was formed with its commitment to improve the quality of life of the communities they serve, has helped successive generations of leaders at Tata to ensure they stay connected with all their people across what is now a vast and increasingly diverse global business.

CASE STUDY CVS – USA

For any purpose statement to form part of the lifeblood of an organization, it must become integral to continuing decision-making and shape the policy and practice of an organization. Another organization that has chosen to reconnect with its core purpose is CVS in the United States. CVS is a huge retail presence in the United States with a near-$80 billion market capitalization. In early 2013, the pharmacy chain captured headlines for shaking up the business model of the chain's 7,600 stores, for their decision to no longer sell tobacco products. The decision will cost the business about $2 billion dollars per year in lost sales. However, for CEO Larry Merlo, the decision to stop selling cigarettes was as much about the purpose of the organization as the economics. 'Everyone has a personal story, a friend or loved one who was killed by smoking,' said Merlo. Indeed, smoking continues to be the leading cause of premature death in the United States. The CVS move sets the company apart from its peers by choosing to forego short-term profits for a long-term vision of the company as a healthcare provider. 'Tobacco was always a sticking point when it came to building relationships with hospitals and physicians' practices,' said Merlo. 'They asked if we were really committed to this vision as we sold tobacco products. It had become a complete contradiction to the health outcomes we were trying to achieve', he added.[4]

CVS is looking to meet a growing demand for health services as tens of millions of Americans gain insurance through President Barack Obama's signature healthcare reform and as the country's elderly population balloons. As more people need medical care, the United States is facing a shortage of doctors. That is where CVS sees an opportunity. By 2017, the company plans to open 1,500 in-store clinics offering basic services such as immunizations and preventive care. The new vision for CVS will see the organization become an extension of a physician's office. The move demonstrates how a focus on purpose can produce a benefit for society and for shareholders at the same time, rather than doing the right thing as an add-on activity. President Barack Obama, a big supporter of this move, observed:

> As one of the largest retailers and pharmacies in America, CVS Caremark sets a powerful example, and will help advance my administration's efforts to reduce tobacco-related deaths, cancer, and heart disease, as well as bring down health care costs—ultimately saving lives and protecting untold numbers of families from pain and heartbreak for years to come'.[5]

The CVS example is powerful because it demonstrates how, by reconnecting with its true purpose, an organization can integrate its profit and growth ambitions with a positive impact on society to achieve a real point of difference in a highly competitive environment.

CASE STUDY Pixar – USA

Another example from a different sector is the animation company Pixar. Making great films is what attracts people to Pixar: it makes them feel proud and energizes them, and it's why they stay. However, Pixar realized that it had lost its sense of balance as an organization when its focus on delivering results started to have a hugely negative impact on its people.

In the making of the film *Toy Story*, highly dedicated staff had given everything to the cause of making the film a great success, but at a high personal cost. People were working seven days a week over a gruelling nine-month period in order to complete the film. By the end of the nine months, a third of the staff had repetitive strain injuries. It forced the leadership team to ask: 'What have we become?'[6]

Pixar recognized that it had drifted into dangerous territory by moving away from its overall purpose and putting the film ahead of the well-being of its people. The experience made the company reconnect with its core belief that people must always come first. It recognized that if its purpose was to make great films, then as a creative organization, great ideas could only come from great people. Pixar realized that people needed to be the priority. Its leaders arrived at a clear understanding that focusing on profit first would lead to compromising its purpose by sucking the passion and energy out of the people in the organization. The leadership team agreed that as 'ideas come from people, people need to be the priority'.[7]

These are laudable goals but what did they mean in practice? What is clear from understanding the Pixar culture is that they have not compromised on the standards of excellence they expect from each film that they make, and this pressure as Ed Catmull, then CEO observes, is self-imposed. No one at the studio wants to produce some films, which are 'just OK'. What they have done however, is completely redesign the nature of work. Creative talent is given complete control over every stage of the development of their ideas, and a peer culture has been created to encourage everyone in the company to help each other to produce their best work. One practical technique they have used is to have the teams share unfinished work on a daily basis. 'By doing so people get used to opening up about things which are not perfect and it gives others the permission to comment on each others' work' (Catmull, 2008). They have also created a far greater level of subsidiarity in the workplace through which there is little reliance on formal 'management structures' and everyone is expected to do whatever they need to do, and talk to whomever they need to talk to, to fix issues quickly. In other words they have created a completely different kind of organization, a true community where real virtue is built around creating long-lasting relationships.

CASE STUDY   Handelsbanken – Sweden

A joint venture, between the Management Lab at London Business School and the Department of Strategic Management and Globalization at Copenhagen Business School, has created a five-year programme to understand how companies put in place innovative ways of managing apparently conflicting strategic imperatives. (The research undertaken was later published as Birkinshaw *et al*, 2014.)

One of the companies featured in the case studies from this research was a Stockholm-based bank, Svenska Handelsbanken, which stands out as an extraordinarily resilient and successful operation. Unlike a number of its competitors, Handelsbanken steered a course through the Swedish financial crisis in the early 1990s and it has subsequently sailed through recent banking turbulence with uninterrupted growth and top ratings for customer satisfaction.

How has Handelsbanken been so consistently successful? According to Birkinshaw *et al* (2014): 'Its purpose seems unoriginal: simply, to be customer-focused.' However, rather than just talking about customer focus, Handelsbanken has built a management model that supports its goals. First, the bank's structure is highly decentralized. Managers of individual branches have much more discretion regarding loans and employee salaries than is customary in the industry. This reduces the cost of information transfer and supports rapid responsiveness to changing market conditions. The company was also a pioneer of the 'beyond-budgeting' movement; it has moved away from setting budgets on a top-down basis and instead expects branch managers to set their own targets.

At Handelsbanken, there is no emphasis on maximizing shareholder returns; the goals are simply to track a moving target by always having higher customer satisfaction and profitability than a weighted average of the competition. These goals are then linked to a combined profit-sharing and employee stock ownership scheme called Oktogonen. Profits are shared equally across the organization (rather than on an individual basis) and when the bank's after-tax return on equity is higher than the industry average, shares are issued to all employees. This model has been employed since the 1970s, so that today employees own more than 40 per cent of the total equity and many long-term employees have become millionaires. This equal profit-sharing scheme is an excellent example of how financial rewards can strengthen a purpose-driven goal rather than displace it.

CASE STUDY   HCL Technologies – India

Another case study included in the research programme was HCL Technologies. Headquartered in Noida, India, it was a second-tier player in the highly competitive Global IT services sector when Vineet Nayar became President in 2005. Nayar decided to differentiate HCL through the quality of its leadership and by having a radically different purpose for the organization – putting his employees first and enabling them to create value in their relationships with customers.

In his book *Employees First, Customers Second*, Nayar (2010) explains that he first got everyone to accept that the company was underperforming and needed to change and then put in place a series of specific initiatives that were designed to help employees service their clients better. Nayer then led all his managers and leaders to place the results of their 360-degree appraisals online to make them more accountable to their employees. He also created a 'service ticket' scheme, so that if an employee wasn't happy about something he could open a ticket to get the attention of the relevant manager. Nayar tracked the number of tickets opened, and the speed with which they were closed, as an indicator of employee well-being. As these initiatives began to take hold, Nayar captured his philosophy with the slogan 'employees first, customers second'. Further initiatives were added, such as the 'Employee Passion Indicator Count' (EPIC) survey, which was used to identify the key passions of employees and to steer them towards jobs where these could be put to use.

By 2012, HCL had recorded an industry-leading compound annual growth rate of 24 per cent. The research showed that many employees had bought into

Nayar's 'employees first' model and saw the company as a highly attractive employer. Turnover rates were lower than in competitor companies, and the highest ratings on the EPIC survey were on collaboration and client service. We will explore the way in which HCL leaders connected with their employees in more detail later in the book.

How do I discover and shape the purpose of my organization?

'To *live differently we need to think differently*'

(Matthew Taylor, CEO Royal Society of Arts[8])

As we saw in Chapter 1, there have been many organizations which have developed purpose or ethical statements but then rapidly reverted to their own insular journey, delivering against a narrow set of targets for the corporation alone and not the delivery of the wider good. In such environments how can leaders break out of this 'locked in' thought process and behaviours? A second challenge facing leaders is that the development of corporate purpose is that it can quickly appear to be purely instrumental or self-serving. In other words, it positions what the business is doing is all about delivering a benefit for the wider community, but everyone, both inside and outside the company, knows that leaders are only 'positioning things' in this way in order to win more business or improve the bottom line.

How then do business leaders arrive at a sense of purpose which is truly connected to the wider needs of customers, employees, society and the environment, yet is relevant to the core activity of their organization?

This can present real dilemmas for any leader, because constructing new purpose using the same old building blocks as every other business may well end up generating broadly similar results to everyone else. So if we truly wish to think differently about our organizations, we need to start back with first principles to find a different source code for thinking about how business operates.

In order to address this challenge, in 2013 a small group of leaders from a diverse range of backgrounds came together. The group included an eclectic and inspiring mix of experienced individuals from Asset Manager Old Mutual, Guardian Media Group, Unilever, Accenture, Harvard Business School, former Partners from KPMG consulting, leaders in sustainability, international leaders from J P Morgan, former director generals from the British government, leaders from the not-for-profit sector, journalists, business commentators. The group had joined forces following a surprising series of meetings which had taken place between bankers and industry leaders, including Unilever's CEO Paul Polman and Vodafone's Vittorio Colao, and Cardinal Nichols, the Roman Catholic Archbishop of Westminster. The meetings had occurred because of a deep sense that business was failing and the bond of trust between society and business was being lost.

The group was set a challenge to create an alternative 'blueprint for a better business', which synthesized the best insights available from multiple sources into a coherent framework. The purpose was to enable a fundamental re-examination of modern business leadership, looking at industry and commerce with fresh eyes, at both the personal and organization level. Explorations into science, faith and philosophy unearthed a rich vein of thinking which, surprisingly perhaps, spoke with a common voice about the nature of our shared humanity and purpose. These 'deep roots' demonstrated to the group that a framework could be based on both timeless provenance and the latest scientific insights. At the crux of discussions was the notion that redefining the purpose of business in society and re-connecting business and society are interdependent goals. We recognized that we couldn't just be another group of business leaders trying to rework stale ideas. The aim of the blueprint was to shift the focus from an insular one, in which business leaders think purely about what is good for their own organizations, to an outward one which connected individual leaders and the purpose of their business to the context of the world around them in pursuit of the 'common good'. In so doing the Blueprint for Better Business set out a framework that would help to unite corporate purpose and personal values to serve society. The aim of the initiative is to encourage businesses to define and operate to a purpose that serves society and respects the dignity of people, and to nourish a culture through which behaviours needed to deliver that culture can flourish.

To explain how simple yet radical a departure this is from current thinking, I have set out some of the insights from the research The Blueprint for Better Business conducted, from the fields of philosophy, faith and science.

Insights from philosophy

The foundations of Western thinking can be traced back to Greek philosophers and to Aristotle in particular. He asserted that we are all teleological creatures, by which he meant that our underlying purpose in life is to realize the talents we all have to best effect for the benefit of others. He argued that the purpose of a good society is to help us nurture those talents through the formation of habits. He went on to describe how excellence and virtue resulted from repeated practice, made possible by the environments in which we live. He believed that central to the role of all institutions is the creation of conditions in which virtue can flourish. Some two thousand years later, Edmund Burke arrived at a similar conclusion about the role of institutions and society. In his biography of Burke, Jesse Norman (2013) synthesized Burke's thinking as follows:

> The social order does not merely rest upon the virtue of those in positions of power; more fundamentally, it rests upon the habits and behaviour or 'manners' of those in all walks of life. Man is a social animal; people naturally imitate each other; they co-operate and compete; and they establish practices, habits, rules and codes of behaviour which make this cooperation and competition possible. Individually, good habits become internalized into virtues; collectively, they create institutions, and the result is what we would now call social capital or trust.

Burke went on to argue that it was a mistake to see people as a mere individual atoms. 'In effect', he said:

> it is a denial of their collective identities as participants in a social contract or between the generations: a denial of the covenantal nature of society itself. It seeks to assert the primacy of the individual will, and sees all social constraint as fetters to be thrown off. Liberty becomes license: the absence of impediments to the will. The danger then is that liberal individualism makes people profoundly selfish; that they slip from an enlightened to an unenlightened self-interest.

This logic developed by philosophical thinkers over two millennia chimes with what is today emerging from modern scientific research into the way the brain works.

Insights from science

The Royal Society of Arts (RSA) has been running a programme since 2009 called the 'Social Brain'. Based on recent discoveries in neuroscience, its aim is to better understand our brain functions and to identify to what extent we are making the most of our talents. Its most recent findings have highlighted the different thinking patterns of our left and right brains: one side deeply analytical, compartmentalizing and individualistic; the other side engaged in finding connections, an integrative and creative processor which sees the deeper meaning in things. Since the enlightenment the analytical and individualistic side of our natures has been more highly valued. However, the research indicates that this has been at the expense of the development of all our natures. Given these insights, Jonathan Rowson (2011) observed: 'Social context can no longer be seen as an afterthought, a variable to be controlled, but is instead a defining feature of how we think, learn and behave'.

Further research into the wiring of the brain highlights a fascinating link back to the thinking of Aristotle. MRI scans reveal that our brain's wiring is like the muscles in our body. The more we use certain connections, the more connections and synapses are formed; the more we fire signals down the nerves, the wider they become, like our own internal broadband. It's why for London cab drivers the part of the brain that's responsible for navigation has been found to be 20 per cent bigger than that of non-cab drivers. This is not because they were born like that but simply because, with repeated use, a lot more wiring and blood supply now goes to this part of their brain. Equally, if we fail to use parts of our brain they will atrophy. So the stimuli which we are exposed to literally shapes the way we are wired. The more we are exposed, the better the connections work and, intriguingly, the more we are able to read complex patterns, make connections and see how things are really developing. These connections start the moment we are born and UK research on human development shows that the size of our brains can be directly correlated to the degree and nature of human contact we receive in the first years of our lives. However, it is our continuing connections which shape the way our brains operate. All the research indicates that the brain has a high level of plasticity and is far more like constantly upgrading software code rather than being hard-wired, as previously thought. We can conclude that if leaders become cut off from the stimuli of new sources beyond their organization, then to use a sporting metaphor, they are far less likely to be able to read the new game that is developing and simply won't recognize the 'plays'.

New scientific developments have also shown that our genes are much less set and far more adaptive to our environments than we ever previously understood. Indeed, those elements of genes that have until very recently been thought to be 'junk DNA' turn out to be control panels which turn our genetic code on or off. This new area of research, called 'epigenetics', points to a level of genetic adaptiveness we had previously thought impossible, demonstrating just how responsive we are to our environments before changes get encoded in our DNA. We are, it would seem, designed at our most fundamental level to operate as social animals.

These developments in neuroscience and genetics are echoed in recent findings in psychology, particularly research by Edward Deci and Richard

Ryan at the University of Rochester and Martin E P Seligman, the Director of the Penn Positive Psychology Centre in the United States. Deci and Ryan's work (1985) shows that that our natural developmental tendencies do not operate independently, but instead require constant social interaction. They have demonstrated that, if we are to feel motivated to engage and commit to activities over the long term, we need to experience a blend of mastery (in the tasks we are responsible for), autonomy (in decision-making about those tasks) effective relationships (with those we interact with in completing the tasks) and purpose (a sense of meaning in what we do). Their work demonstrates that these factors foster the most high-quality forms of motivation, including enhanced performance, persistence and creativity. These are precisely the forms of behaviour that are required to succeed in our globalized and increasingly interdependent world. Seligman's work has also focused on those conditions that enable human beings to flourish. Along with fellow psychologist Christopher Peterson, Seligman (2004) has developed a handbook of *Character Strengths and Virtues*. This lists wisdom, courage, humanity, justice, temperance and transcendence as the critical qualities that lead to human fulfilment. What is again fascinating about Seligman's work is the degree to which there is a recognition that the development of these virtues are both essential for human flourishing and contingent on the relationships around the person. This need for relationships as an essential component in shaping our character is something to which we will return later. The degree to which a leader is connected with a breadth of influences can therefore be seen to have a profound effect on the 'roundedness' and 'rootedness' of the views they are capable of holding.

The field of economics has also recognized that we are far from being purely isolated rational creatures – that we are not, after all, simply *homo economicus*. It turns out that the connections we make with the world around us are far more important than was previously thought, in determining the choices we make about where and how we spend our money and the investments we make. In 1995, a then-unknown economist, Rachel Kranton, wrote a letter to Nobel Prize-winning economist George Akerlof, insisting that there was an alternative interpretation of the way people behaved when making economic choices. She argued that identity, formed through social interaction, was the missing element that would help to explain why people facing the same economic circumstances would make different choices. This was the beginning of a 14-year collaboration, leading to the publication of the book *Identity Economics* in 2010. This work illustrates how our conception of who we are is heavily informed by our social context and may well be the biggest single factor in influencing the choices we make in life.

Their research showed that the social preferences of the groups we associate with play a far bigger role in influencing our decisions and how we feel about the decisions we make, than we would perhaps like to admit to. As we discussed earlier, if we only interact with groups that are 'just like us' in outlook, our ability to take on other influences and the nature of our decisions are going to become seriously limited. We understand these risks when we consider those from poor and excluded backgrounds; we are far less likely to see the risks for those in power of leading lives that are equally isolated.

The outlook developed by Kranton and Akerlof reflect the need to consider the human dimension of economics in a very different way – people are not commodities. If we extend this logic further we arrive back with economist Karl Polanyi (2001) who would have argued that 'it is simply wrong to treat human beings as objects whose price will be determined entirely by the market. Such a concept violates the principles that have governed societies for centuries.' 'Life', he observed, 'has almost always been recognized as having a sacred dimension.' Polanyi's outlook was that people should never be seen as here to serve the market, rather that the market should be viewed as a social mechanism designed to serve human life. It is a challenging alternative to much of contemporary business thinking.

The plethora of findings and insights from a variety of scientific sources leads us to conclude that people are wired differently, not isolated beings but social animals, designed to continue to adapt to those environments to which we are exposed the most.

As the world becomes more interconnected this will have an increasing influence on how people see, think and feel about their worlds. If leaders are themselves not connected with all dimensions of society, then as we witnessed in Chapter?1, the risk of leadership appearing to be out of touch and imbalanced can only increase.

Insights from faith traditions

The great faith traditions, despite the conflict and tensions that we see around us, do have one thing in common: they have all developed a deep understanding of the human condition. What is fascinating is not just the commonality of these ideas but the fact that they have been based over thousands of years on observations and reflections on the way human beings actually are. This then, was the third area of influence that Blueprint for Better Business took into consideration. Recognizing that in corporate life, questions of faith have almost disappeared. Retreating from the public square, they are seen as just one of our many personal choices, with no part to play in our public lives. Some leaders may believe that any reference to faith should remain in the background, anachronistic to our pluralist society. Yet to do so would be to ignore not only a rich heritage of thought but also the linkages that exist between these insights and the thinking of modern psychologists like Daniel Kahneman in his *Thinking Fast and Slow* (2011), which demonstrates that we all operate on two levels, that which thinks purely in terms of self-interest and that part of us which thinks about the common good. These modern insights are completely in line with a huge archive of thinking and insight from the world's great traditions, whether Christian, Jewish, Muslim, Sikh or Buddhist. These traditions share many outlooks about the needs of individuals to pursue the common good and to treat our fellow humans with dignity and respect. 'Catholic social teaching' in particular has developed a repository of thought on the interconnection between the life we lead and the values we hold. It argues that we have within each of us a 'natural disposition' to seek out 'justice, courage, truth friendship and generosity'. According to modern theologian Herbert McCabe these dispositions 'project a certain ideal of life which can then provide a sense of direction or purpose and help to form and influence our moral judgements' (Pinckaers, 1995).

The concept of a common good emerged strongly in the late 1890s to address the crisis of the conditions of workers suffering as a result of the industrial revolution. Advocating a different path from either laissez-faire capitalism or communism, Catholic social teaching (Mich, 1998) stressed for example the need for a living wage for all workers. Later writings in this tradition describe the common good as 'the sum total of social conditions which allow people either as groups or as individuals, to reach their fulfilment more fully and more easily'. The common good is therefore a goal of all human life representing the good of all people and the whole person. In this sense, the goal of life in society is in fact the attainment of the common good.

One of the most interesting things about the common good is its emergent quality, something that individuals cannot create or do on their own. By its very nature it can only be created through people coming together to achieve something through mutuality of interest. The common good occurs out of an interaction between people, who recognize that a greater good is possible, that pursuing everyone's interests including their own can create new and better outcomes that did not and could not have existed before. It also presents the opportunity to create highly complex outcomes through relatively simple and natural individual interactions. Emergence can be found in many natural phenomena from the way bees swarm, birds flock or schools of fish suddenly change direction. It is how unified patterns form, seemingly from out of nothing, without direction or planned structure. We can also see emergent properties in human behaviour as the internet links millions of people together. Peter Miller, in *The Smart Swarm* (2010) observed: 'Whenever you have a multitude of individuals interacting with one another, there often comes a moment when disorder gives way to order and something new emerges, a pattern, a decision, a structure, a change in direction.'

Becoming purpose-driven

From these sources leaders can start to change the conversation. Using this definition of the common good we can perhaps start to see the possibilities of capitalism. Rather than a mechanism for financial gain, 'the genius of capitalism is that it both creates incentives for solving human problems and makes those solutions widely available' (Eric Beinhocker and Nick Hanauer (*McKinsey Quarterly*, September 2014). It these 'solutions to human problems that define prosperity, not money'. Beinhocker and Hanauer go on to assert that that growth should not be a financial measure; rather it should track the rate at which new solutions to human problems become available and accessible. Viewed in this light, developing a purpose for a business which is focused on solving human problems, business that is making life better for the greatest number of people, is a business that is stating to think about its role as serving the common good. Using a different language to shape alternative foundations for their business thinking, confident both in the provenance of those ideas and confident that the thinking is connected to the world beyond their organization. The first obstacle for many leaders who are contemplating this journey is where to start and how to engage colleagues in a discussion that appears sufficiently grounded in the realities of business life while also raising aspirations about what is possible. To ensure that this is a robust process, a leader will need to ask a series of challenging questions. What would it mean to become *truly* purpose-driven? What are the benefits of embarking on this journey for the organization?

It is one thing to understand intellectually the need for an organization to become purpose-driven. However, many business leaders may already feel that their own business already has a strong purpose. Therefore to help leaders critically appraise the degree to which their organization is truly purpose-driven, the Blueprint for Better Business developed an independent platform, a framework of five guiding principles which are central for allowing leaders to convene an intelligent debate, not only within their own organization, but also with wider society. The aim is to create an environment, in which through dialogue and relationship greater connectedness between business and society can be forged. This dialogue needs to be couched in a language which is relevant to all parties and not – as we find so much today – couched in the obtuse 'business-speak'. This is important because a strong purpose can form the basis of a business creating a new narrative through which leaders can make sense of what their organization does.

To facilitate the start of a new dialogue, each of these principles set out below have been framed as questions, to help individual leaders reflect on important dimensions of their business's activity and to facilitate dialogue with both colleagues and communities alike.

Ultimately, leaders and the people within their organizations must own their own purpose. By doing so leaders can determine the outcomes they want to see and start to engender greater trust. The principles that have been defined are therefore a way in which leaders can ask themselves the difficult questions to produce a level of clarity and honesty about the role of their organization. It is a path that is now being embarked on by several major global corporations including Unilever and Vodafone.

The five principles of a purpose-driven business

The five principles are:

1 *Does your business have a purpose that delivers long-term sustainable performance?* Is your business operating true to a purpose that serves society, respecting the dignity of people and so generating a fair return for responsible investors? Is it doing so in such a way that you welcome public scrutiny of the alignment between your stated purpose and your actions?

2 *Is your business fair and honest with customers and suppliers?* Are you dealing honestly and transparently with all who buy from or sell to you, seeking to build lasting relationships? Are you striving to ensure your suppliers also make a fair return, paying promptly what you owe? Do you expect your suppliers to do the same? Are you openly sharing your knowledge to enable customers and suppliers to make better informed choices?

3 *Are you a responsible and responsive employer?* Are you treating all your people with dignity and respect? Do you have fair pay and conditions for all, while expecting all your suppliers and subcontracting agents to do the same? Does your business respect and promote diversity, giving a fair chance to people from all

backgrounds, including the underprivileged? Does your business nurture all, and promote constructive dialogue about its behaviour and whether it is keeping true to purpose? Does your business foster innovation, leadership and personal accountability? Is your business creating, nurturing and protecting a thriving environment?

4 *Are you a good citizen?* Does your business consider each person affected by its decisions as if they were a member of your own community? Does your business make a full and fair contribution to society by structuring its business operations to promptly pay all taxes that are properly due? Do you provide opportunities for less privileged people? Does your business work to the highest standards even in markets where there is little regulation requiring this?

5 *Are you a guardian for future generations?* Does your business honour its duty to protect the natural world and conserve scarce resources? Does it contribute knowledge and experience to promote better regulation, to the benefit of society as a whole, rather than protecting self-interest? Is your business investing in developing skills, knowledge and understanding in wider society to encourage informed citizenship?

A purpose doesn't have to be elaborate or novel. For Handelsbanken, it was all about serving the customer; for Tata, it is about the communities in which the company operates; and for HCL, the purpose is employee well-being. The key point is that a purpose is about making a connection which stretches beyond benefiting just the companies, shareholders or individuals within the business. Indeed the evidence suggests the successful companies are the ones that were able to translate often pedestrian-sounding purpose into consistent and committed practice.

To start the process, leaders need to be willing to go back to first principles, to ask questions of themselves and of their teams about why they came into that business in the first place. Kami Lamakan, who runs a specialist business which helps organisations all over the world to bring purpose to life, observes

> People are in essence social beings, and it is people working together who create the great leaps that progress our societies. A business is one of the places where people work together, to create wealth and prosperity… advanc[ing] society in ways that go beyond the returns that they generate for investors and the value they can add for stakeholders. This is their purpose. For example, the businesses involved in building the Brooklyn Bridge weren't just creating a great feat of engineering. They were enabling the growth of a thriving city and the prosperity of a nation.

To tap into these insights, Kami and his team ask leaders to explore the history of their organization and their deeper hopes and dreams about the future. To some leaders still locked in to 2th-century ways of looking at things these perspectives can at first feel strained in a business context. Perhaps hope lies in the next generation of leaders who have a markedly different outlook from the current leaders.

A report by Cranfield University in the UK noted in October 2014 that 80 per cent of emerging business leaders believe that societal and environmental impact will be the most important indicator of future business success, with only 35 per cent holding profitability up in the same regard. This compared with 94 per cent of current CEOs who believe profitability will continue to be the key indicator of success and 88 per cent of current leaders saying the same for shareholder value, compared with only 27 percent of future leaders.

The report surveyed 50 CEOs and almost 150 MBA and MSc students and recent graduates across Europe. In addition to a marked shift towards societal impact as a measure of worth, it found nearly half of future leaders believe companies that focus solely on economic value will not have a competitive advantage in the future, compared with only 16 per cent of current leaders who said the same. 86 per cent of CEOs surveyed believed that businesses already have a clear social purpose compared to only 19 per cent of future leaders.

The two groups also had different opinions about the barriers facing businesses that seek to combine social purpose with profit. According to the report, 66 per cent of current CEOs view external factors such as Government and regulations as the main barrier, while the majority of future leaders cite internal factors, such as current management attitudes (55 per cent).

'While it's not surprising to learn that social purpose is seen as a priority for business, the big challenge is to ensure more business leaders define the real purpose of their business, and identify how they are going to achieve that purpose,' observed Professor David Grayson, director of the Doughty Centre at Cranfield. "By developing clearly defined strategies and identifying new, disruptive approaches now, businesses can better ensure success and relevance in the future.'

Future leaders identified the core returns on prioritising social purpose as more engaged employees (54 per cent) and increased innovation (53 per cent), while more than three quarters of CEOs (78 per cent) said it offers relevance to the next generation of customers.

To bring such ideas to life requires a different kind of personal commitment, a desire to connect with others, moving beyond a purely intellectual grasp of the issues raised to achieve a sense of understanding and compassion for the situation and needs of others. As we have seen, this is far from easy and requires a large dose of courage. As any leader will recognize, the challenge of sharing a purpose across a large organization in a meaningful way is not be underestimated. Done highly interactively, such statements of purpose and values can leave a tangible legacy which can guide an organization and engage its people over multiple generations.

The Guardian Media Group for example have a statement of purpose and values which is extracted from an article by former editor C P Scott written in 1921.The article is recognised around the world as the ultimate statement of values for a free press. Among the many well known lines are the assertions that 'Comment is free, but facts are sacred', that newspapers have 'a moral as well as a material existence' and 'the voice of opponents no less than that of friends has a right to be heard'. Extracts from the editorial are now used as part of the company's statement of purpose and values: 'Fundamentally it implies honesty, cleanness, courage, fairness and a sense of duty to the reader and the community.'

In light of the power of such an outlook the old corporate notions of rapidly cascading values, printing them on posters and briefing individuals through mass training sessions not only seems out of kilter; it is not going to break through potential levels of scepticism both inside and outside an organisation. Instead, adopt a much slower process that really engages people, potentially using the five principles of a purpose-driven business to enable people to raise questions about the company, its products and services, its dealings with customers and the way everyone works with each other. Perhaps the acid test is the degree to which new and tangible possibilities can really be opened up in the products and services of the business and the way such activities are developed.

This slower approach which seeks to reimagine what growth can mean in a resource constrained world has to some extent been adopted by B&Q, a FTSE 100 UK business, which is looking at every single product in its portfolio and replacing them one at a time with a more sustainable alternative (see Green et al, 1998).[9] It is a brick-by-brick process that builds confidence and engages everyone within the organization in what they are working towards. It is an approach that differs markedly from the more common 'hoopla' that accompanies organization leaders launching a new mission or set of values. It is an approach that demands a high personal connection between individual leaders and everyone in the organization. It is an approach that necessitates a great deal of listening and connecting with employees, customers and communities about what matters most to them. It is a process that

FIGURE 3.3 Five principles of a purpose-driven business

 a blueprint for better business

Five Principles of a Purpose-Driven Business

Honest and fair with customers & suppliers

- Seeks to build lasting relationships with customers and suppliers
- Deals honestly with customers providing good and safe products and services
- Treats suppliers fairly, pays promptly what it owes and expects its suppliers to do the same
- Openly shares its knowledge to enable customers and suppliers to make better informed choices

A good citizen

- Considers each person affected by its decisions as if they were a member of each decision-makers own community
- Seeks and provides access to opportunities for less privileged people
- Makes a full and fair contributuion to society by structuring its business and operations to promptly pay all taxes that are properly due

Has a purpose which delivers long-term sustainable performance

- Operates true to a purpose that serves society, respects the dignity of people and so generates a fair return for responsible investors
- Enables and welcomes public scrutiny of the alignment between stated purpose and actual performace

A guardian for future generations

- Honours its duty to protect the natural world and conserve finite resources
- Contributes knowledge and experience to promote better regulation to the benefit of society as a whole rather than protecting self-interest
- Invests in developing skills, knowledge and understanding in wider society to encourage informed citizenship

A responsible and responsive employer

- Treats everyone with dignity and provides fair pay for all
- Enables and welcomes constructive dialogue about its behaviour in keeping true to its purpose
- Fosters innovation, leadership and personal accountability
- Protects and nurtures all who work for it to ensure people also learn, contribute and thrive

demonstrates that a leader and an organization respect those that they work with and upon whom they rely to deliver. However, for such an approach to work, to appear sincere and not simply to look like the latest round of corporate public relations, it must reflect something significant to the individual leader. These are questions we will explore in more detail in the following chapters.

Conclusion

Developing a sense of purpose for an organization can seem daunting at first. Indeed, to really understand what purpose means is a leadership commitment that requires considerable thought, courage and resilience. Unlike many business activities the gains to be achieved are not short term in nature and are based on a desire to connect an organization to the real needs of the world around it. For many leaders it will represent a significant departure from the narrow shareholder-only focus that they have followed thus far in their business careers. This, as we have seen, is one of the factors that has resulted in many leaders ending up with a divided life and their businesses becoming divided from the rest of society.

Therefore instead of supporting what academics Birkinshaw *et al* (2014) both 'pro-social and profitable goals', it is advocated that we adopt of a different and more integrated approach, something we have called *serving the common good*. 'Businesses that see themselves as a crucial part of a rich and intricate tapestry of interrelated goods that make up the overall good of societies in which they operate can genuinely hope to build trust and the kind of relationship with the rest of society that they need to operate well'.[10] This approach to purpose seeks to benefit shareholders and society at one and the same time, recognizing the interlocking nature of society and business, acknowledging that you cannot have successful business in a failing society and you cannot have a sustainable society if business is failing.

Developing fresh insights into how such an integrative purpose can best be achieved will undoubtedly require great creativity and collaborative efforts. However, in taking this potentially more difficult perspective, a business leader is more likely to deliver long-term sustainable performance by producing goods that are truly good and services that truly serve, ensuring that companies are embedded in society and personally leading a more integrated and rewarding life.

However, there are considerable hurdles that lie in front of leaders considering embarking on such a 'purpose journey'. Shareholders need to be carefully managed, employees need to be included and inspired, society needs to be won over. None of which will happen overnight. During this period of transition developing and following such a purpose represents a risk, one which needs to be managed with great care, skill and judgement.

We will return later to this aspect of embedding purpose into an organization to show how the logic of common good can find its way deeply into the connected psyche.

Set out below are a series of practical actions that will enable a business leader to develop and connect to their organization purpose in practice.

Eight steps to reconnected leadership

So far this chapter has encouraged a reflection on the nature of purpose, why it is important, how other organizations have used purpose to energize their organizations and how leaders can think about purpose in different ways.

However, working with purpose effectively within a business or a senior leadership team can only be effective if the leader and each member of his or her team is also prepared to connect with this important agenda in an honest and personal way. (Rather than treating it as an intellectual exercise).

The section below sets out a guide for leaders to use to initiate the process of reconnecting through purpose with their team and with the wider organization.

Step 1: Reconnecting to purpose: Leadership actions

1 Take time to personally consider how much your organization mirrors the expectations laid out in the five principles. Consider how you would like it to be and capture the key areas that you believe could make a difference to your organization and where your organization could make a difference. Such 'thinking' work can be conducted alone but can also be supported by working one-to-one with a person who you can trust who has an outside knowledge of the business and who can gently highlight some of the challenges your organization may face. Having completed the exercise it is often best to allow those thoughts to be ruminated on, over a weekend or a week, before returning to the topic and writing down some things that you would personally like to see done differently. If you have got to this stage and are feeling comfortable with the review then:

2 Present the challenge to your team. Explain that you would like them to go away and have a similar period of reflection. Agree to meet

again in a few weeks to discuss. Encourage the team to come and talk to you one-to-one if there are any items that they would like to reflect on with you.

3 Conduct a broad, open and high-level conversation with your colleagues about the five principles, about the benefits and challenges of adopting this course for your organization. Look to reach agreement that it is a path worth investigating further without trying to jump to working out in any detail what the five principles mean for your organization.

4 Set time aside for your team to conduct a review of the five principles with a view to arriving at a draft and high-level version of your purpose. This may well take more than one exercise. However, remember that it is not about the specific answers you arrive at, at this stage, but about the broad direction you are going in. One analogy I use when teams are going through this process is to think of it as a craft process of 'throwing a pot' rather than an industrial process of putting something in a moulding press – and out comes a perfect answer. Like potters – this process can take a lot of work and patience.

5 Once you feel you have created something that truly reflects both the history of the organization and its aspirations about the future, then this 'internal' perspective needs to be connected with the other sources of insight. Sessions need to be conducted with customers led by you and members of your team to get a sense of what they see and what they expect. (Some organizations may wish to start by asking their employees, customers and suppliers what they think. Use this input as a means of awakening the top team into different ways of seeing the company and its purpose). The simple act of going through this process will be valuable for the team and will take dialogue to a different level. It is important to go through the process personally rather than having a team doing it on your behalf because this is about experiencing first-hand others perspectives. It is the start of the process of connection.

6 At this point many teams would get a skilled communications person in to help craft the feedback into a form of sharp words that can then be briefed out, with key words put on large posters around the organization. As we have discussed, irrespective of how much hard work that has gone into the exercise up to this point, it is better to

keep the connections open. So rather than follow the traditional path, you and your team now need to open up the discussion to the rest of your senior management group. Sharing why you felt it was time for the organization to look at its purpose, what you are hoping to achieve and why you need their time. They need to go away and personally reflect on the five principles in the same way you did, and then have the opportunity to contribute back what they think the business response should be to the five principles.

7 The next step is not a fast roll-out to the rest of the business. Instead it should focus on practical actions that leaders can take in their parts of the business. Such tangible activities could, as we have discussed, include looking at the product portfolio, it could consider people policies, it could consider the information which is provided to the customer. The aim of this stage is to allow people to internalize what you have discussed and shared, and to start a different dialogue within the company. This phase could also include going to meet other people from very different backgrounds to foster connections that will help alter perspectives within the business. The point here is that you want this work to last.

8 Now having had time to well and truly soak in what the purpose of the organization should be – is it time to take the new agenda to the rest of the organization. Again, this needs to be carefully thought through. The less slick and the more experiential and connected it can be the better.

9 This is the end of the first phase in developing an inclusive purpose. Now conduct a gap analysis between the purpose you are developing and how you (and as wide a range of people as possible in focus groups) think the organization is working compared to the purpose.

10 Use the outputs of this to present an honest appraisal of the business as it is and the business you want to create to all the people in your organization. Use it as a basis for facilitating dialogue. How you encourage other people from inside and outside the organization to contribute to the dialogue will be a test and will demonstrate the degree to which you and your team are starting to bring purpose to life within your company and reconnecting with the world around you. We will explore how you can develop this dialogue in subsequent chapters.

1 3rd Annual Core Beliefs and Culture Survey, Deloitte Consulting, April 2014

2 Business Success Through Serving Society, Blueprint for Better Business Conference, October 2013

3 www.tata.com – Governance section: Values and Purpose

4 Shoshana Davis, It's a contradiction to help people be healthier and sell tobacco products, CBS News, 5 February 2014

5 *ibid.*

6 From a blog by Michael Lee Stallard, President, E Pluribus Partners, www. michaelleestallard.com, 23 May 2014

7 *ibid.*

8 Royal Society of Arts Lecture Series, 2012

9 George Marshal, Director of the Climate Outreach Information Network: Radical activism has a role in speeding up corporate change, *The Guardian*, 31 January 2013

10 Helen Alford, Dean of Social Sciences at the University of St Thomas Acquinas, Rome, in discussion with the author, 2014

Step 2: Building reconnected boards

Positioning: The six leadership practices

In this and the next five steps, we will consider how leaders who have reconnected with their core business purpose can apply this new outlook in establishing different and better connections across all their key constituencies, from colleagues to customers to communities.

FIGURE 4.1 Reconnected leadership model: Building reconnected boards

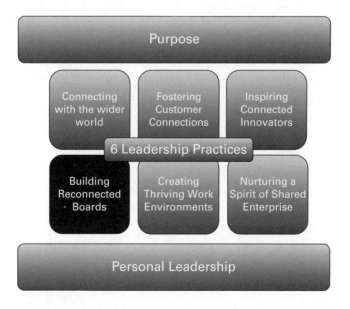

Critical points of connection occur where process, attitude and capabilities are brought together by leaders to deliver better outcomes for business and society. They happen in the way leaders connect with customers or how leaders help to foster innovation or where leaders unite a diverse workforce. These practices tend to be grouped into 'hard activities' such as systems, structure and process or so-called 'soft activities' like people skills, behaviour and culture. Yet the reality is that these two outlooks are intertwined, embodying two sides of the same coin, fused into what I have called *leadership practices*. Such practices reflect the 'habits' of leaders and their organizations. Often captured in procedural manuals but sometimes not written down at all, they are the 'givens' and are instead found lodged deep in corporate memory, often more powerful for being stored in shared human data banks. However, like all habits there are sometimes bad corporate ones, which get in the way of rather than enhance connections and like bad habits they can often be hard to break.

Our focus in this and the chapters that follow lies in those leadership practices which forge connectivity, beginning with the practices of the reconnected board.

Introduction

The nexus point for all connections should be the leaders sitting around the board table. However, as we saw in Chapter 1, increasingly boards can be cut off from the information necessary to anticipate changes occurring in volatile markets. The business then needs to be reactive or 'agile' as the consultants prefer to call it.

The way boards and top teams work is therefore one of the most important practices within any business. Anyone who has worked with a less than effective board will tell you that if things are not connected at the top, forging connections through the business is always going to be a struggle. A renewed effort is therefore required to reconnect a board with a far wider set of constituencies.

In this chapter, we will lay out the three fundamental issues boards will need to address to achieve this reconnection. First, we will consider the critical issue of board legitimacy, where boards get their legitimacy from, and how board legitimacy can be rebuilt. Second, we will consider the changing nature of board accountability and how this can be sharpened to more accurately reflect board members' true responsibilities. Finally,

FIGURE 4.2 Three elements of a reconnected board

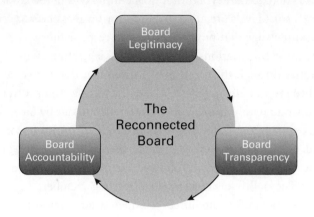

we will consider how leaders can work through their boards to improve transparency.

Power and legitimacy

According to *Forbes* magazine, the 2,000 largest companies in the world account for $38 trillion in revenues and $2.43 trillion in profits and in 2012 employed 87 million people.[1] The world's largest corporations are the powerhouses of our economy. They are giants and have a massive influence on the flow of global trade and, in equal measure, a profound impact on people's lives and the environment. They are colossal in both size and reach and it is worth pausing to reflect on their sheer scale. For example, in terms of GDP equivalents, Walmart is bigger than Norway; GE is bigger than New Zealand; Exxon Mobile is bigger than Thailand; and Nike is bigger than Paraguay. Using these GDP calculations, the ICBC Bank in China should soon be getting its invite to the G20 summit.

The sheer scale of these businesses underlines just how much we have come to rely on them and explains why society is right to expect that such power be exercised responsibly. By operating responsibly in the interests of all in society, business leaders retain the legitimacy they need to make important and difficult decisions at pace without being encumbered by bureaucracy or shackled by onerous legislation. However, such freedoms require that business leaders maintain the highest standards in all that they do, standards that go far beyond simply operating within the law. As we saw in Chapter 1, trust levels are at record lows for business because some have failed to acknowledge that power comes with responsibility.

To date, most corporations have sought their legitimacy by discharging responsibilities through the creation of formal board governance processes that have been repeatedly augmented over the past 25 years. Over 80 countries now operate within frameworks originally laid out by Sir Adrian Cadbury in his eponymous report. However, research by Professor Jeffery A Sonnenfeld (2002) has shown that those boards in US companies where malpractice had taken place, all followed the accepted standards for board operations: 'They all had independent directors; members showed up for meetings; they had audit committees, compensation committees, and codes of ethics were in place; the boards weren't too small, too big, too old, or too young. In fact the research revealed that there were no broad patterns of incompetence or corruption. They *all* passed the tests that would normally be applied to ascertain whether a board of directors was likely to do a good job.' In other words, it wasn't the technical or governance structure or representation around the board table that was the problem. This raises a host of questions, not least of which is why traditional governance codes do not seem to be making the difference that we might have hoped for.

The sources of board legitimacy

Throughout this chapter I will contend that a board's lasting legitimacy cannot simply be developed through attention to governance process and that it needs to be augmented through a board's connections with what is happening around it, both inside and beyond the boundaries of the business.

Earning legitimacy requires visible leadership of a kind that reflects shared aspirations. By so doing, leaders are tapping into a deeper code, which connects the way people believe that everyone should behave towards one other. The presence of such unwritten codes explains why people feel uncomfortable when they see leaders in power doing things that, while they may be technically 'allowed', go beyond what we believe we have a reasonable right to expect. In Japan, such codes started to be formally incorporated into business life from as early as the 17th century. One element of this development was the concept of *Kyosei*, a Confucian idea that literally means 'working together in life' or cooperative living. It represents a connection and symbiosis, beyond conventional business thinking of markets,

profits and laws, with a comprehensive aspiration for justice and cooperation in society. The code describes what is expected of a business leader
or member of a board and seeks to temper individual and organizational
self-interest through concern for common goods and for more basic rights
in a just society.

Within wider Confucian thinking, the authority of the board is therefore
based not only on their technical proficiency, which is how they tend to be
evaluated in the West. It is also based on the way members personally exemplify a code of conduct in which each leader works, together with customers,
colleagues and communities, to achieve harmony. It is a very different way
of thinking about the life of a board and the role of non-executive directors. Stripped back to its most basic level, it captures whether the board has
behaved with honour toward an employee, customer or community member.

From a Confucian perspective, a person can only be considered to be a
jūn zǐ – a superior person or leader – if they behave in line with this code.
Leaders must therefore demonstrate that they 'love and care for their people, understand their needs as human beings, and live and act according
to righteousness'. If the ruler lacks such benevolence and acts inhumanely
towards his or her subjects, he or she runs the risk of losing their legitimacy
as a leader or, as the literal translation puts it, they may 'lose the Mandate
of Heaven' or the right to rule (Bass and Steidlmeier, 1998). Sergiovanni and
Starratt (2002) observed that this 'Mandate' was a 'moral authority derived
from the obligations and duties that followers feel as a result of their connection to widely shared community values, ideas, and ideals'. The question
that the *Kyosei* approach poses is: if leaders are not embodying and modelling these ideal patterns of behaviour in the way they think and act, why
should people follow them? It's a question that leaders in the boardroom
hardly ever ask themselves.

CASE STUDY   Canon – Japan

One organization that has embraced *Kyosei* principles is Canon,
the Japanese camera and imaging company. Canon adopted *Kyosei*
formally as its corporate philosophy in 1988, after 50 years of operations,
during which time these ideas had become a touchstone of how it conducted
business. For the board at Canon, *Kyosei* envisages a society in which 'all people
can live and work together in pursuit of the common good'.[3] When launching
The *Kyosei* principles, Ryuzaburo Kaku, Chairman of Canon, (1997) described the

philosophy as being at the heart of the company's future development with 'the aim of contributing to global prosperity and the well-being of humankind'. These were regarded as 'big ideals' by many commentators and by others as removed from the realities of corporate life. However, 25 years later Kazutada Kobayashi, CEO of Canon's Indian division, described *Kyosei* as 'an integral part of Canon's corporate culture, because everyone in the company as a public entity within society and expected it to contribute to the realization of a better society through sound and fair business activities'. Kobayashi observed that:

> Unfortunately, the presence of imbalances in our world in such areas as trade, income levels and the environment hinders the achievement of *Kyosei*. Canon therefore strives to resolve those imbalances, [it is our view that] a truly global company must foster good relations, not only with their customers and the communities in which they operate, but also with nations and the environment.[4]

According to Kobayashi: 'leaders must bear responsibility for the impact of their activities on society'. The development of these ideas over a 25-year period has helped to achieve its global reputation in precision electronic equipment manufacture, while also creating a unique place to work in which some of the best technical staff in the world can thrive. Canon also prides itself on having a minimal impact on the environment. The examples of *Kyosei* in practice are reflected in everything that the leadership of Canon does, from its partnership work with suppliers to the way it builds its offices. The board actively convey the sense that everything that the organization does must be seen to reflect its interconnectedness and to that end the board have been instrumental in bringing together other organizations who are also looking to embrace *Kyosei* to create true partnerships particularly around technology and environmental innovation.

CASE STUDY   Timpsons – UK

A number of examples where leaders are role modelling different kinds of relationships within their organizations and with the wider community can be found in companies which are family owned.

Timpsons in the UK is an interesting example of such a family run business. It is a shoe-repair chain in Britain, owned by John Timpson and his family, with 800 stores and a turnover of approximately £100 million. The Timpsons leadership team's style is highly distinctive. A great deal of autonomy is given to small teams working in individual stores. John Timpson CBE and his son, James, personally visit shops up and down the country on a regular basis and work on the simple philosophy that 'If you treat people well, it is blindingly obvious that they will do a good job' (Timpson, 2010). The company still has a final salary pension scheme in place and owns holiday homes for workers, while colleagues get their birthdays off and bonuses for exceeding targets. Perhaps one of the most interesting commitments made by Timpsons is its programme to employ ex-prisoners in its stores. What is significant is the level of responsibility and trust that Timpson places in their people, who come from some of the most difficult and excluded backgrounds with past records that others would not entertain. Leadership teams like Walmart for example conduct significant background checks on people before employment, to search out previous criminal records, because they believe that people with past history cannot be trusted. By contrast John Timpson shows a huge amount of confidence in people who have come out of prison, who not only deal with customers, but also all the cash and profits for their stores. It demonstrates an extraordinary faith in the dignity of all people and this respect is repaid in the commitment of Timpsons' colleagues. What is significant here is that the board of Timpsons are demonstrating through their actions that they respect people from all backgrounds. This has a huge impact throughout the company, generating reciprocal commitment by colleagues and embodying the kind of moral authority that is lacking from so many modern boardrooms. However, to make such an approach work, board members need to become not only connected with the purpose of the business but also far more visible within their organizations than is the norm currently dictated by board practice.

The personal example set by John Timpson is also reflected in the observations of Vineet Nayar, the former CEO of HCL (Nayar, 2010):

These connections do not come from retreating to an offsite meeting [with your leadership team], rather they are shaped by leaders walking the same roads as the people in frontline roles, so that people can see by their actions what they stand for. In large organizations this requires a willingness to collaborate with lots of people on what the future for the company might look like. It is by its very nature an iterative dialogue, not a series of top-down decisions. It takes longer and it is messy but it connects people to ideas in a powerful way, building commitment because people believe they have been asked, and not sold to.

These examples illustrate that a greater sense of legitimacy is promoted by a board of directors when it takes time out to not only make connections within the organization by sharing their personal philosophy but also to show that taking the time to encourage others in the company and beyond to embrace these outlooks is a key role of all board members and not just the chief executive. It also highlights that the most powerful tool a board director has is that of personal example. However, for many board leaders this raises significant challenges, because the one thing that few directors have enough of is time.

Why better board connections require greater commitment

The approach set out by John Timpson and Vineet Nayar requires a huge commitment in board time. However, many non-executive directors typically only commit a day and a half per month to their board obligations. Andrew Kakabadse of Cranfield University believes that this makes it almost impossible for non-executive directors to truly fulfil their responsibilities, because of the limited amount of time they dedicate to any one business. In his research, which is discussed in his book *How to Make Boards Work* (2013), he highlights that issues of governance almost inevitably cannot be picked up in that amount of time, and he points to changes in Australia, where a limit has been set for the number of board appointments a non-executive can take on in order to encourage directors to spend more time getting to know their companies.

Building on these insights we could imagine that fostering deeper understanding, by walking the floor, meeting customers and suppliers, can only happen if non-executives were limited to a much smaller number of board appointments, freeing up their time so that they can spend around five days per month within any organization, using the increased time commitment to connect more directly with customers, employees, suppliers and the community. If board members spent more time in their organizations, they would no longer have to rely exclusively on information filtered through the CEO or CFO's office. They would be in a better position to act as a voice of all stakeholders and guardian for future generations, and in the process become more visible in the business.

As we saw in Chapter 1, it has often been through a lack of connection between the boardroom and the shop floor that inappropriate practices have been able to develop. These same disconnections also explain, as we will see later, when fresh shoots of innovation struggle to grow through the undergrowth within many businesses, because people are not clear what the board really wants to see. By improving their connections, board leaders visibly demonstrate that they are stewarding a business's long-term interests and by engaging in this way the board enhances its legitimacy. This is particularly true of non-executive directors for whom this push for greater connectivity to a business beyond the boardroom would have the biggest effect. It may have the side benefit of increasing the requirement for more non-executive directors, as it would reduce how thinly spread some of today's non-executives are. This may in turn encourage businesses to consider an even wider pool of candidates for non-executive positions. The fees would also have to be reassessed, as undoubtedly would the way we hold boards to account when things go awry.

The fiction of 'board accountability'

Most discussions about board accountability come wrapped in the language of corporate governance and compliance. However, as we have already seen, the fact that good governance exists is no guarantee that a board is effectively discharging its accountabilities. Why is this? There is no doubting that accountability matters, but it seems today to be typically understood in a narrow and technical sense. Targets are set in a very precise, almost legalistic way, largely to ensure there is little ambiguity when it comes to evaluation. However, this has served to remove the element of judgement that a leader would have previously used to assess performance in the round. Today, if something cannot be measured, by and large it doesn't get managed. But that is not to say that these matters have no value – far from it. It is often this retreat from the use of judgement that contributes to boards losing track of what really matters.

Furthermore, this tendency towards the use of very specific goals is increasingly – and sometimes intentionally – being used by corporate lawyers as a defence to show that a chain of command did not lead all the way to the top. To illustrate this point, when Credit Suisse was found guilty in the United States in 2014 for helping clients avoid paying tax, they were fined $2.5 billion dollars by the US Department of Justice. However, even though hundreds of people were involved and, as the US Attorney General put it, the conviction made the bank a 'convicted felon', none of the senior directors of the bank were sent to jail or disbarred or sanctioned in any way. The question we must ask is: What happens when the people in charge don't carry accountability for what happens on their watch? What is this doing to levels of trust between society and business – let alone to the fabric of society at large?

What we know is that it is having a profoundly corrosive impact on the public's trust in our major corporate institutions and is washing away the sense that anyone within an organization should be held personally responsible for their actions. As we see increasingly in many areas of public life, the sense of shame that used to exist when people were found to have fallen short is rare; people know that there will be bad public relations to deal with but that those headlines will blow over, especially if helped on their way by the corporation's public relations team. All this positioning has left people confused about what to believe and has regrettably created an environment in which some of those at the most senior levels can start to feel somehow disconnected from or even above the consequences of their actions, leaving either junior staff alone when they are caught in the spotlight or the inanimate organization itself as the sole perpetrator of events. As we saw in Chapter 1, the reality now is that many organizations factor in the risk of things going wrong and set aside a budget for paying the fines that eventually arise from time to time. Even though organizations can be fined and can have their reputations tarnished, it is difficult for most ordinary people to fully equate such consequences with the accepted notions of justice and so, the legitimacy of business leaders continues to decline.

This, I would suggest, is affecting our sense of what being accountable actually means. It is eroding our own understanding of where the boundaries lie between right and wrong. However, in some sectors of the economy, there is a dawning recognition that something is awry. For example, in the aftermath of a series of hospital scandals, the UK Minister for Health set out his expectations: 'There needs to be a sharper focus on corporate accountability for failures – who let it happen, how the conditions were created that enabled it to happen, and holding individuals and boards to account for that failure' (Department of Health, 2013). Martin Wheatley, head of the UK's Financial Conduct Authority, seems to agree: 'We could put up fines three times, five times, 110 times greater – it will not make a difference unless individuals are held to account.' Wheatley holds a simple view that 'accountability is what matters'.[5]

So why in business is the connection between what people do and taking accountability for those actions breaking down? To understand this, we must start with the basic foundations of business accountability – the accountability boards have to their shareholders. According to the accountancy firm Grant Thornton, while boards may be seeking to connect with the investment community, the investment community is proving very reticent about engaging with them. The Office for National Statistics (ONS) reported in late 2013 that the big UK investment institutions, such as Aberdeen Asset Management or Standard Life Investment, who are expected to hold the boards of corporations to account, actually no longer retain many UK company shares. So even if they wanted to call boards to account, they lack the firepower to do so. They just don't have the people to do the work and more importantly, they don't have the votes to make boards sit up and listen. Indeed, the structure of shareholding has changed so profoundly since the early 1980s, the length of time shares are held has dropped from eight years down to less than one year.

Today, most British shares are held by US investors, followed by Europeans and then Asian investors. Likewise, the British have a tendency to invest in US stocks. As a consequence, as economic commentator Anthony Hilton highlighted in the *Independent,* 'at the end of 2012 insurance firms only held 6.2 per cent of UK shares, against 23.6 per cent as recently as 1997. Pension funds, which at their peak in the 1990's held 32 per cent, had fallen back to 4.7 per cent at the end of last year'.[6] So even acting with unanimity and in concert, the two most powerful shareholder groups could typically muster only 11 per cent of the votes. According to Hilton, it would be hard to see 'boards quaking in their boots, if that is the extent of the investors lined up against them'. So shareholders do not have the resources to get involved and, even if they did, it seems that most are actually quite happy to let events run provided the 'numbers' seem to be delivering adequate in-year returns. It would seem, therefore, that any notion we may have had that boards are accountable to shareholders has, while remaining technically accurate, become a practical fiction.

Accountable to a wider constituency

In his book *Firm Commitment*, Colin Mayer (2013), a Professor at Oxford Said Business School, unravels this conundrum further and suggests that boards being accountable to uninterested shareholders means that accountability is effectively delegated to the market. Mayer notes that no one in the current governance framework is really holding the long-term future of the corporation in high enough significance and, as a result, 'share-price becomes the ultimate and indeed only arbiter of success'. As such it is almost a natural consequence for boards to behave in a manner that is increasingly short-termist, doing those things that have the most direct impact on the short-term share price performance.

Do we need a new arbiter of whether boards are discharging their responsibility effectively? Professor Mayer certainly thinks we do and suggests that boards should be connected and held accountable for the delivery of long-term purpose and goals. He considers that an alternative model for achieving this could be via the creation of what he calls the 'Trust Board', which would not be responsible for day-to day-performance, but would have a controlling interest in ensuring that the company acts in line with its long-term purpose and constitution. Professor Mayer highlights the experience of organizations like Tata in India, where the boards of the operating companies report to a Trust, which ensures that the organization remains true to its purpose over time, and is not influenced by short-term share price movement. Sir Dorabji Tata, the son of Tata's founder, explained: 'To my father, the acquisition of wealth was only a secondary object of life; it was always subordinate to the constant desire to improve the industrial and intellectual condition of the people of this country' (*The Tata Way*).

The notion that board members should be accountable to a wider constituency including customers, workers, communities and shareholders and using the yardstick of performance against corporate purpose, offers a route to a more balanced and sustainable outlook. It also links to the notion that boards earn their real authority and legitimacy by doing the right things in the interests of the many and not just the few.

Full accountability requires effective scrutiny

Holding boards to account for the delivery of long-term performance against a core purpose requires a further condition to be in place. Namely, that it is possible for wider society to be able to properly scrutinize the board for its performance against its stated purpose. For this to be done effectively requires a far greater degree of transparency, and indeed honesty with the wider constituency we talked of earlier, so that information is exchanged and insight about what is really happening can be shared.

This is a difficult step as leaders are perhaps understandably troubled that full disclosure would not lead to rational discussions about why a course of action was taken, but rather to the kind of witch-hunt that happens when the press or social media run with a story that is designed to sell newspapers rather than provide a balanced portrayal of all the facts. However, public scrutiny is essential if we are to create leaders who behave responsibly because they feel truly accountable, their decisions must be open to challenge. As the philosopher John Locke put it in the 17th century: 'Any elite, whether commercial, governmental or aristocratic, should experience constraints upon its power' (Balibar, 2013). Such constraints are not possible if people are not aware of what a company is doing and are not able to question the actions that have been taken. True accountability then is about operating in a way that makes it possible for scrutiny to take place. Better transparency could therefore help to redress the power imbalance felt by individuals and the corporations they deal with.

In his book *The Transparent Society,* David Brin (1998) argued that it will be good for society if the powers of surveillance that are currently in the hands of the powerful are shared with the citizenry, to allow 'viewing from below', enabling the public to watch the watchers. Following the leaking of classified security information by Edward Snowden in 2013, it is clear that the internet has unleashed an unpredictable force in which leaders do not always get to decide what gets published when. Leaders are increasingly aware that somewhere in the world 'unwelcome' information about their organization could be released online at any time.

A new culture of candour

The logic follows that, since internet commentary is inescapable, the only way to influence it is to be part of it, to publish everything. Being transparent, opening up, posting material frequently and often is the only way to amass positive links to yourself and thus to directly influence your reputation. A company with no secrets can develop a different level of connection with customers, communities and colleagues, creating a 'culture of candour'. In this new environment people come to trust only those organizations that share everything, even the 'bad bits'. This can range from bad product reviews to the bad customer experiences to bad environmental issues. In a counter-intuitive way, the freedom and access of the internet leaves it up to the viewer to make up their mind and in so doing, they start to apply the same logic they apply to other online connections. There will be good bits and there will be bad bits but in knowing everything, individuals can form their own judgement and are more likely to trust that, rather than a polished reality that a corporation has tried to manage. For most business leaders brought up in the pre-internet era, such a level of openness presents huge concerns. Having spent a lifetime of 'managing the message', letting go of the information to create a more authentic and lasting impression is far easier to say than to deliver on. As Herbert Agar pointed out in *A Time for*

Greatness (1942), 'The truth that makes men free is for the most part the truth which men prefer not to hear.'

However, there is a now a slow dawning recognition of the need to raise levels of transparency in organizations. For example in 2009, as UK City Minister, Lord Myners proposed that the pay and identity of up to 20 of the highest-paid employees at British companies should be disclosed (non-board roles being granted anonymity),[7] Tony Hall, the BBC's new Director General, had his contract appear online along with related documentation, so that the public were completely aware of what he was being paid and the conditions of his contract. In Hong Kong, regulations require banks to list their top earners and in Norway and in Sweden, tax authorities annually release the *skatteliste* or 'tax list', an official record of the annual income and overall wealth of every taxpayer.

Another example of radical transparency is at Unilever who recently teamed up with Oxfam to assess workers' conditions in Vietnamese factories. When Unilever found that conditions in Vietnam fell below the standards that they had set as a board, they recognized that only by being completely open to scrutiny could they learn and develop. Oxfam CEO Dame Barbara Stocking found that the transparency and openness by Unilever required a significant amount of courage, yet proved to be helpful to all concerned.[8]

Groups like Transparency International would suggest that an even more radical form of transparency may yet be required, where nearly all decision-making is carried out publicly and all draft documents and presentations are made available, so that the public can judge what factors were considered when a board was making a decision. Clearly this would not be appropriate for discussions of commercially sensitive issues, but it seems that we are nonetheless at the beginning of journey where the idea that openness is better than secrecy is in everyone best interests.

In public relations there was an old-world saying that you shouldn't write anything you wouldn't want to turn up on the front page of the *New York Times*. This caution and secrecy are being replaced by a new candour which is already starting to appear across the US technology community. According to Clive Thompson in *Wired*: 'Not long ago, the only public statements a company ever made were professionally written press releases and the rare, stage-managed speech by the CEO. Now firms spill information in torrents.'[9] At Zappos.com, the online US shoe retailer, a company-wide wiki lets staff members complain about problems and suggest solutions. Executives work at desks sprinkled amongst the banks of customer-service phone agents. If customers can't find the shoes they want at Zappos, agents are encouraged to point them to other stores. Suppliers are given detailed information about which shoes are selling and how much profit Zappos has made from them. CEO Tony Hsieh says that this approach makes his employees, suppliers and customers more forgiving of everyday mistakes, observing: 'The more they know about us, the more they'll like us.'[10] Of course this new openness comes with potential downsides. The wisdom of crowds can quickly turn into the tyranny of the majority or even the few and the most high frequency tweeters are not necessarily the most representative.

According to Shel Israel, co-author of *Naked Conversations* (Scoble and Israel, 2006), the trick seems to be for corporations to try to behave 'basically like a normal human' and by doing so they can generate goodwill. However, such high levels of transparency and openness in turn demand a different way of thinking about the way decisions are made inside an organization. It points to the need for everyone to have access to *all* the information about the business. In this interconnected and interdependent world, it is logical that people can no longer function effectively if they are not trusted and if they cannot cross the boundaries that they need to achieve their goals in line with the broader purpose of the entire organization. Such transparency has other implications for the way colleagues, customers and communities are all managed. We will come on to explore this theme in more detail in the next chapter.

Speaking truth to power

Having information about a company's performance and plans is one thing, but real connection between those on the board and those on the frontline requires that there is an exchange of views and ideas. In their comprehensive report on engagement in the workplace, *Engaging for Success*, Clarke and MacLeod (2009) identified that one of the most important elements of an engaged workforce is that each person believes their views are heard and valued – that they have a voice. Most leaders understand that they must foster open cultures, and take seriously any suggestions of wrongdoing. But there is a huge gulf between knowing and doing. How many leaders are genuinely prepared to listen to people from every level in their organization? How open are they to criticisms of their leadership and wider organizational practices? How many employees *really* have a voice? What are the channels and opportunities for communication? And what, if anything, changes as a result of speaking up?

Even in an apparently transparent culture, it is one thing to have the information but it is quite another thing to ask difficult questions of senior leaders. 'Speaking truth to power is perhaps the oldest and, certainly, one of the most difficult of ethical challenges because to do so entails personal danger' (O'Toole, 2007). To push back against those in charge takes immense moral courage and may well be too much to ask, or certainly expect, of any one individual, unless the environment makes it much more feasible for that honesty to breath.

This suggests that to go down the path to true accountability requires a far greater connection between leaders and colleagues, an environment in which leaders, in the words of Warren Bennis and Daniel Goleman: 'would do well to reflect on their own receptivity to suggestions, alternative points of views, and others' opinions'. Such leaders will need to possess the virtues of humility, inclusion, service to others, and respect for people (Bennis *et al*, 2008).

Paradoxically, the risks of speaking truth to power are particularly acute for those in professional services firms – the lawyers, accountants and consultants who are the very 'gatekeepers' charged with providing business leaders with unvarnished assessments and warnings and objective advice and counsel. These professionals know that the fastest way to lose clients is to tell them news they don't want to hear. This is especially true when the news is that the CEO's behaviour is at the root of the company's problems. To move this issue forward constructively, leaders need to tap into the motivation for creating an open and honest environment, given the time, challenges and personal development issues it raises.

In the private sector, change will not occur until corporations consciously begin to select, train, develop and reward leaders who listen. Yet, in a continuing study of top managers in large corporations, research found that executives are far more often selected for their proven ability to compete with their fellow members in the C-suite than for their demonstrated teamwork. This reward system encourages the hoarding of information, which then leads to testosterone-fed conflict. Changing that system is the responsibility of boards of directors, the people who have the ultimate responsibility for choosing leaders.

Truly independent boards must not only provide a much-needed check on executive ego but also provide a voice for people within and beyond the organization, creating a positive source of objective truth to power. So boards need to create the situations in which opportunities to hear it like it is can occur. This brings us back to the earlier points in this chapter about visibility. It also means that boards may need to find different and more imaginative ways of curating conversations between various parties. A curated conversation enables connections to be made, but avoids the free-for-all that sometimes occurs in online 'discussions'. Events can be curated online by independent organizations, which ensures that all the points are raised but also provides an opportunity for a corporation to respond and explain its position. The objective of such sessions is that they are seen to be open explorations of issues that are either raised by the action of an organization or by the concerns of a community group. Early examples of such curated conversations are evident in news outlets like Guardian Media. These conversations explore the degree to which an organization has been honest with customers and suppliers, whether it has treated employees with dignity and respect, whether it has acted as a good citizen or been a guardian of future generations. The conversations use 'journalistic' process to gain input from all parties, particularly people and groups who directly experience what a company does, and uses these sources to promote and facilitate a more informed dialogue. The discussions between groups goes on to examine differences of perspective in a structured and mediated way. Mediation is provided by an independent third party, regarded by all parties as someone who can be both an objective expert and facilitator of open dialogue. This form of structured curation over time is designed to foster greater awareness of what is really happening, why and what could be done differently in the future. Having fostered a greater connection between a business and its hinterland, what then becomes critical is the way in which the leaders of the organization use the dialogue to inform how they adapt their personal leadership behaviour and practices moving forward. To date, such discussions have tended to be focused on generically themed issues rather than specific organizations.

Taking such a path also means that non-executive directors must be open to dissenting voices, whether they be customers or suppliers or indeed representatives of employee groups like trade unions. It is perhaps interesting to note when the successful luxury car brand Jaguar Land Rover was acquired by the Tata group from India, they managed to secure a partnership with Unite the Union based on an understanding of the long-term future of the operation and a commitment to investment and jobs. This level of openness and partnership had been something which was previously problematic. Without a willingness to provide this kind of forum for real discussion on a broad range of matters, boards will have only a partial understanding and view of reality. What is undoubtedly difficult for many leaders to acknowledge, is that there is a both an information and power imbalance at play in most workplace situations, and that even if information is made available, the ability to both analyse and challenge the course of action that a leader is set on is always going to be difficult. To illustrate the point I spoke with documentary television makers in the United Kingdom who were looking for suppliers to the UK's grocery sector to comment on the pressure they were put under to cut costs and some of the actions they had to take as a consequence. The programme makers were unable to find any food manufacturers to make a comment, because they were frightened of the repercussions that would ensue. How this power imbalance, between large companies, suppliers, customers and staff is addressed is one of the bigger issues facing any leader who wants to reconnect and develop a level of trust inside and beyond their organization.

A new kind of non-executive director

So far we have discussed the degree to which legitimacy of leaders and boards can be enhanced where they act in the interests of all the constituencies; where they use this perspective to ensure transparency of information to all sources of information; and where, through their own increased visibility, they provide greater opportunities for people – be they customers, employees suppliers or communities – to speak truthfully to those running large organizations and to question the decisions that are being made, which have a direct baring on their livelihoods. For non-executive directors to be able to connect in this way would require a change not only in the amount of time that they spend with each company that they work with, but also a change in the scope of their fiduciary responsibility so that they can bring a far broader perspective to the board table and use this insight to better hold the organization to account. However, there is one final step that may be required to fully restore the legitimacy of boards: how directors are held to account when things go wrong.

Consequences

For some, the only way forward to restore full accountability within business is to give the courts more powers to prosecute and fine organizations for any illegal actions carried out in the name of the organization. Some believe making such powers of redress easier will curtail improper corporate behaviour across all sectors. However, as we saw earlier, simply creating the ability to fine a corporation for the misdeeds of its staff or indeed imposing larger or punitive fines, has to date only resulted in corporations making bigger accounting risk provisions.

Something clearly needs to change in the way large corporations consider the consequences of their actions. This point was graphically illustrated in the case of a recent newspaper scandal in the UK. It involved a 13-year-old girl, Amanda 'Milly' Dowler, who had gone missing and was subsequently discovered to have been murdered. While the investigation was under way, *News of the World* journalists managed to hack into and electronically access Milly Dowler's phone and listen to voice messages.

It took nine years for Milly Dowler's murderer to be caught, tried and convicted. Within months of that conviction, news reports revealed that journalists from Rupert Murdoch's *News of the World* had illegally listened to voicemails left on the missing girl's cell phone during the police investigation. For the British public, this was an outrage too far. In the subsequent Leveson inquiry into the behaviour and conduct of the British press, considering this and other cases, News International owner Rupert Murdoch was asked to account for the behaviour of the people on the newspaper he owned and ran. His defence was that he had put too much trust in his key lieutenants but he himself knew nothing; likewise his son James, who had been Chairman of News Corporation operations in Europe and Asia, could apparently not be expected to know every detail of the operation; and Rebekah Brooks, Chief Executive of the UK newspaper arm, claimed that she had managed the organization in a way that relied on the 'good judgement' of her staff.

The general sense from those watching the proceedings was that this apparent lack of knowledge wasn't good enough. It served to illustrate the absence of board accountability and highlights why there has been such a rapid deterioration of trust in our leading corporate institutions. There is a serious risk that prominent business leaders seen to be 'getting away with it' creates a wider culture in which everyone in an organization considers it fair game to bend the rules.

Ignorance and the doctrine of command authority

Isn't it time for us to consider a different test when considering the accountability of leaders in our organizations? If not then how will we get them to connect fully with the consequences of their actions?

In the Second World War, General Tomoyuki Yamashita was regarded as one of Japan's most accomplished military commanders. As the war progressed towards its final chapter, Yamashita's troops were besieged in the Philippines by General MacArthur's army. Under attack through 1944 and 1945, the Japanese Army committed many horrific acts. Immediately after the war, Yamashita was captured and put on trial in Manila. The prosecution conceded that he had neither ordered nor committed these crimes. However, he was found guilty and became the first person to be charged with an 'omission' by failing to discharge his duty as a commander – 'to control the acts of members of his command' – even though he did not directly know what they were doing. Subsequent cases at the Nuremberg tribunals were unanimous in finding that a lesser level of knowledge than actual knowledge may be sufficient for a commanding officer to be held responsible.

The subsequent Geneva Conventions and other trials that followed Yamashita have developed this doctrine further, yet the notion of command authority has yet to pass across into the commercial world. Perhaps if leaders were to think about their role in creating cultures where individuals feel it is acceptable to hack phones, encourage tax evasion, rig currency rates or overlook safety considerations, then such actions would be less likely to occur. As a starting point, we must begin to change our expectations of non-executive directors to become more connected and engaged in their organizations, to be the conduit for all constituencies and to ensure, on behalf of others who do not have a voice, that truth is spoken to power and that executives are held to account against the long-term purpose of an organization and not simply the short-term share price performance.

Conclusion

This chapter has looked at the immense power held by today's boards, including economic power that for the largest corporations is now bigger than that of many nations. We have argued that such power can only be legitimized if leaders are seen to visibly embody both the values of the organization and also crucially reflect those values which the whole of society would aspire to. To do so we explored the need for board members to become far more visible and connected within their business and the communities they serve. This would require individual leaders to spend more time getting to know the issues faced by customers, employees, suppliers and community alike. By getting more directly involved, they will change the way they view situations faced by their organizations and society. They may also start to change as leaders as they become more connected to the realities of the environment in which their business operates. (We will return to the theme of personal transformation in Chapter 10). We have also explored how, in the internet age, this new appetite for openness and transparency can enhance a business leader's connection with the real interests and concerns of customers and suppliers.

This advocated approach requires a far greater degree of solidarity to be demonstrated between those who choose to lead and those who follow. As we have shown through this chapter, it is only through strengthening their connection with others that leaders can demonstrate this, behaving in a manner Confucian philosophy would describe as *jūn zǐ*, or 'superior persons or gentlemen'. However, for boards to reconnect with all their constituencies, board leaders must begin to demonstrate that if a corporation does transgress, they will hold themselves to account for their own actions and the actions of their people. From where we stand today, this seems like a daunting path to go down, but it may be a small price to pay if business leaders are to develop their position as stewards of the economy.

Over time, it should be possible to reposition the role of non-executive director towards becoming a 'Guardian of the Future of the Company'– its people, customers, communities, suppliers and shareholders. Substantially increasing the visibility of non-executives should, over time, help to give them a different kind of authority in the organization – as the people who are there to uphold the purpose of the business. When moral authority is established, it can have a profound impact on the effectiveness of an organization. Leaders can rely less on external controls and more on norms and values. They can start to reduce the level of direct supervision as employees feel duties and obligations to act and perform in a certain way and can become self-managing. Taking and developing this perspective can help to rebuild the legitimacy of the business in the eyes of society at large. To this end, we will close this chapter with a number of leadership actions that could help to accelerate this transition to a reconnected board.

Eight Steps to reconnected leadership

Step 2 – Reconnecting the board: Leadership actions

1 Non-executive directors must better connect with their organizations and increase time spent with employees, with customers and suppliers. This could be achieved by, for example, limiting the number of commercial boards on which a non-executive can sit to a maximum of three.

2 For non-executive board directors to represent a broader constituency they need to visit 'frontline operations' and produce independent reports on their findings. This requirement should be included in a new code of practice for non-executives. This could include meeting customer panels to hear direct feedback on real experiences. Non-executives could also visit suppliers on a regular basis, including visits to subcontracted operations and 'overseas locations' to see the reality of operations.

3 As an intermediary step, and to move faster in the direction of creating board level connectivity, the establishment of an advisory board could be considered. This can be a group of individuals from a broader demographic and background who can provide insight directly on everything from community to technology developments. This could provide an accelerated way of getting a more diverse voice heard around the top table.

4 The trend of smaller and smaller boards should be reversed. While the efficiency of small boards cannot be doubted, having a truly representative and diverse set of voices from both within and beyond the company means that there needs to be more seats at the table, not fewer, such that non-executives can engage in real challenge.

5 To foster an environment where individuals at all levels start to feel that they are trusted with critical information about performance, all board financial performance should be shared with everyone in the business and employees should be educated in how to interpret the information. While this has been attempted in some places, it usually ends up being a limited exercise of briefing unintelligible information to people in a hurried fashion, rather than a genuine attempt to disseminate meaningful data.

6 Making it possible for people from the frontline of a business to have a voice at the highest levels is not easy to achieve in a meaningful way. Creating forums where people are not just presented to but involved directly in problem-solving formats to tackle real challenges is one way that these efforts can move from platitudes to a practical reality that people can see working in the organization. To have longevity such efforts have to become a practical way of moving the business forward, otherwise after a while busy leaders just cancel them from their diaries. Re-examining the role of trade union representation should also feature here.

7 Non-executives could meet directly with employees on a face-to-face basis in 'employee-meets-the-board discussions', without the presence

of executive directors. These meetings would not be about pay-bargaining, but would discuss broader issues affecting the business. Like an AGM, this could be called an APM – The Annual People Meeting – where tough issues and challenges are brought to the floor and given the airtime they need. The credibility of this forum would hinge on the level of action that occurs. There will be those who feel that such activities would only serve to undermine 'Management' but giving a voice to employees is difficult and new process need to be explored.

8 In many global organizations it is difficult for some leaders to identify with anywhere as 'home'. This 'floating' nature of top teams makes them less likely to connect with any community, never mind all communities in which the business operates. One action a board could take is to determine that they will treat one place as their 'home' community. Reflecting this commitment, this would be the place where senior leaders would get directly involved in schools and social activities. Without this anchor, so many leaders actually never end up as part of any community and have no sense of how the company is experienced outside of its immediate activities.

---

1 *Forbes* Business Magazine 10th Annual Global 2000 Survey, 18 April 2012
2 Corporate Governance Review, Grant Thornton, 2012
3 Promoting CSR activity through a corporate philosophy of Kyosei, Sustainability Report, Canon, 2014
4 Bushra Ahmed, OneWorld South Asia, March 2013
5 Jill Treanor, Increasing fines will not change culture, *The Guardian*, 21 March 2013
6 Anthony Hilton, Shareholders can't hold boards to account, *The Independent*, 21 September 201
7 Heather Stewart and Jill Treanor, Lord Myners wants City to name its top earners, *The Guardian*, 23 September 2009
8 Dame Barbara Stocking in conversation with the author, October 2013
9 Clive Thompson, The see-through CEO, *Wired* Magazine, March 2007
10 *ibid*.

Step 3: Creating reconnected work environments

05

“ *We have a responsibility to create the conditions for people to lead a life they can value.* (AMARTYA SEN, INDIAN ECONOMIST AND NOBEL LAUREATE)

Introduction

We discussed in Chapter 1 how the apparent cost-effectiveness of modern operating models has led many leaders to think of employees merely as means of achieving their business objectives, losing sight of both the 'human dimension' of work and the connection with people in it. We saw how increasing numbers of people feel that they and their work are treated like components in a fragmented global supply chain. Yet, as the management guru Peter Drucker observed in his book *The New Society* (1993): 'Every study of workers shows that they consider the social function of work as the most important one before and above even the fulfillment of their economic demands.'

This mismatch has led to a decline in the sense of connection people feel between the work they do and the organization they work for. It should therefore come as little surprise to find levels of employee engagement and trust declining to record lows, while stress levels are up as people struggle with uncertainty over the future of their jobs, while skill gaps and talent pipeline shortages are a growing threat to every major developed economy in the world.

In this chapter we will consider the need to fundamentally change leadership outlook and practice, shifting from a view of people as just another 'resource', to respecting them as individuals who are part of a community, both inside and beyond work. In this way we can identify the steps needed to create reconnected work environments.

FIGURE 5.1 Reconnected leadership model: Creating thriving work environments

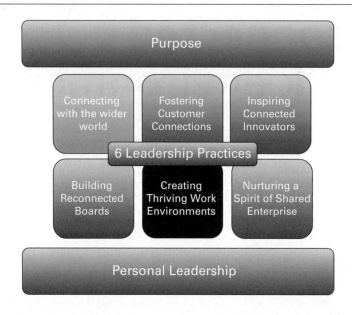

We will explore how leaders can reconnect with colleagues by focusing on three key issues:

1 How can leaders forge a stronger sense of identity and belonging?

2 How can leaders better connect with their people through improved organization design?

3 How can leaders create inclusive environments where the whole workforce can realize their potential?

In Chapter 1 we saw the extent to which people are increasingly disconnected from their work. In developed countries individuals find themselves running hard to keep up with the demands of work and life but not having the time to enjoy it, while people in the developing world aspiring to western luxury are forced to abandon much of their cultural heritage and forgo their dignity to buy a piece of that vision, if not for themselves then for their children.

For some business leaders this may not seem like a primary concern. After all it is difficult enough to relate to people at work, without having to see the tasks that they perform in this wider societal context. However, as we discussed earlier, people are not commodities and cannot be reduced to purely commercial needs and wants. Work has always played an important

role. It has given people a sense of belonging; it has helped to provide structure and identity; it has given people the opportunity to become all that
they can be by assuming responsibility and taking charge of things that can
make a difference. In this way, work has contributed to people having an
increased sense of dignity and self-worth. Work has also enabled people to
realize their potential, to stretch themselves and to collaborate with others
to do more than they could ever achieve on their own. Work has created a
sense of meaning. Work, then, is important – far more important than just
the job we do or the career people have.

In this chapter we will discuss how leaders can create more reconnected
environments to help people to be both more of 'their whole selves' at work
and in turn to offer more of themselves to the work of the organization. The
first area we will consider is the importance of creating a deeper sense of
identity and belonging.

Identity and belonging at work: Lessons from terrorism

One place we can surprisingly find some insights about identity and belonging is in the US Centre for Homeland Defence and Security, specifically
in their use of a framework for understanding the behaviour of terrorist
suspects. Known as social identity theory, this approach was developed in
the UK by two sociology professors, Tajfel (1982) and Turner (1982). It
has plotted how people adopt the norms, beliefs and behaviours of fellow
group members and how, in so doing, they distance themselves from people
considered to be outside their group. This pattern develops irrespective of
whether or not the views and attitudes are rational. They gain their validity
because they are the values and behaviours of a group that is important to
an individual. This is a powerful idea in the context of our review of work
environments because it identifies that the connections between people can
be woven together to build not only enhanced group cohesion but also significantly enhanced motivation.

Social identity research has shown that groups have a fundamental need
to provide their members with a positive social identity and do so by establishing a positively valued distinctiveness from other groups. This, in turn,
improves group cohesion and productivity. The research found that people
who join terrorist cells often do so without a strong desire to follow a particular 'cause', rather because they want to be with people they feel affinity

with. This affinity can occur because people are a similar age or from a similar background; not necessarily because they initially feel an attachment to a terrorist ideal. However, as the members of a group spend time together, sharing experiences, they begin to form and operate in accordance with their own norms and customs and they also look to accentuate this distinctiveness, developing a sense of pride about who they are and starting to think and describe others as being less like and often of less worth than themselves.

'Successful' groups look to reinforce these points of distinctiveness, through their achievements and through the stories they tell themselves about who they are. We can see the stories these groups tell in the amateur videos posted online, showing groups of young men going off to fight in Syria or elsewhere. The bonds within a group are further strengthened by higher levels of personal support and reciprocity, such that individuals start to feel honour-bound to conform to behaviours that are expected, and feel a distinct sense of shame if they cannot do so, or fall short of the group expectation. These connections therefore become very powerful sources of motivation for the people in the group, providing incredible sources of energy, direction and cohesion. Clearly these forces can then be applied in incredibly destructive ways, but they can be applied as a force for good.

CASE STUDY   Create: A social enterprise to help people get their lives back

An example of the latter can be found in the case of a non-profit social enterprise restaurant in the UK. Here, Director Gary Stott applied both Tajfel and Turner's thinking to help individuals suffering extreme social exclusion regain a sense of purpose and meaning in life in order to re-enter the workforce and re-build their lives. According to Stott, the critical challenge was not training people to obtain new skills, but rather to help people re-form their sense of who they are; to see themselves as valuable human beings who have lives with meaning. Rediscovering those aspects of their humanity is not about putting people through a training process; instead it requires careful assimilation. Fragile people with difficult behaviours start to slowly open themselves up to new role models and colleagues who are offering genuine support, not from a position of power or authority, but as co-workers. This reconnection with people with different outlooks is critical. It starts a process of shifting the individual's identity away from the groups they have up to now spent time with, towards individuals and groups who they would aspire to be like. Reflecting on the outstanding success of the programme which ran successfully between 2006 and 2012, Stott observed:

> We have worked hard to create the right (psycho-social) environment for people, within which they can form relationships with other colleagues, develop a sense of personal mastery and confidence in the work they are doing and receive coaching support from others when needed. The development of a new sense of identity from seeing yourself as a former drug-user, whose friends may well still be living that kind of life, to seeing yourself as a trainee chef, is a huge shift of outlook and a really difficult transformation. It can take between three and six months to become embedded, such that a person feels that this is who they could be. Developing a sense of pride and identification with the work group and what it stands for is absolutely key.[1]

The insights from Tajfel and Turner's work shine an interesting spotlight on all groups and all kinds of institutions. From a negative perspective, it highlights the trap of leaders only ever hiring people in their own image, becoming an old boys' club or falling victim to discriminatory practices and blocking people from entering an organization. However, it can also highlight the power of social identity to shape constructive behaviours, successful outcomes and a stronger sense of who we are and what we are capable of. The most successful leaders understand that if they can create situations within their institutions where leaders at every level role model the highest standards and set the highest expectations, then the wider social group will do all that it can to keep those standards in place, without having to be forced to act in this way. As such these then become self-regulating features of the organization.

Without these self-regulating features defining 'what we do and how we do it', leading any group becomes a far more difficult task, demanding higher levels of explicit direction, supervision and control. As we saw in Chapter 1, the implications of not fostering the right 'behavioural expectations' leads to a need for continued layers of management and organizational hierarchy which exist largely to oversee the work standards of others. Much of this remains in place in many organizations, despite sweeping advances in computer and communications technology, because leaders have not helped to forge a strong enough sense of identity. We will return to this point later in the chapter.

We can also see the positive effect of this approach where successful school leaders foster a positive sense of identity and belonging within groups, such that students provide their own internal competition over what is expected, effectively becoming self-regulating. As a consequence, the role of teachers becomes one of raising aspirations rather than supervising the collection of homework. Strangely, we see exactly the same effect in gang cultures where young people, deprived of other institutions to identify with, find solidarity and reciprocity in the gang culture, which provides much-needed structure, pride, a sense of belonging and identity in their lives. It is the honour and support provided by individual members of these gangs that make them so difficult to penetrate, as we saw in terrorist cells. As British sociologist David Gauntlet observed in the aftermath of the London riots in 2011: 'Identities are not given but are constructed and negotiated.'[2]

Without this collective sense of who we are and what we stand for, individual efforts to raise performance can drain away like water through sand. The thing that captures and pools these efforts is the sense of collective identity. Yet, as we have seen earlier, we seem to be actively moving away from any form of group identity, as hourly paid teams are disconnected from the organization into temporary or agency labour groups and management tasks are broken out into projects performed by skilled freelancers or outsourced. This fragmentation is verging on a disembodiment of what we once thought of as an organization. It makes it increasingly difficult for organizations to form cultures that are unique, or to create a level of pride within a company that people feel is worth fighting for.

These frontline experiences are reflected in the strategic development of business over the long term. Arie de Geus, the Dutch management academic and former Shell Executive, conducted a review of the characteristics of organizations which had extended their longevity beyond 100 years, while retaining their unique corporate identities. Within 27 such organizations, De Geus (1999) observed two sets of common characteristics. The first was a strong sense of community and collective identity around a common set of values – a community in which all members knew they would be supported in their endeavours to achieve their own goals. The other characteristic was openness to the outside world and tolerance to the entry of new individuals and ideas and, consequently, a manifest ability to learn and adapt to new circumstances. For this model to work, it required that people form stronger connections with each other, creating a sense of shared belonging and identity united by a common sense of purpose. We will see in later chapters that developing stronger connections, through a cohesive sense of identity, can be particularly important where high levels of creativity and service are required.

How then can leaders forge stronger connections and create powerful identities, which help to pull people together? One possible route is through what organization theorist Etienne Wenger (1998) describes as 'communities of practice' – a web of relationships and self-generating social networks. Wenger explains that people achieve a joint purpose through the pursuit of a common practice, shared ways of doing things and relating to one another. Over time, the resulting work becomes a recognizable bond among those involved. Such practices are marked out by their self-generating network of communications, within which Wenger highlights three features: mutual engagement of its members; a sense of joint enterprise; and a shared repertoire of routines – tacit rules of conduct and knowledge. As Fritjof Capra observes in his book *The Hidden Connections* (2003), these interactions create a 'boundary of meaning' and within that a sense of belonging and identity occurs. Capra goes on: 'It is crucial for leaders to understand the interplay between the formal designed structures and the informal, self-generating networks.' The tacit knowledge and skill that is built within and across these boundaries of meaning are often unspoken and rarely written down, but they are frequently where much hidden value resides. In light of these insights, a leader's role moves from one of being in control, to being the person who helps to connect the group: to help it connect around a common sense of purpose, to help it to establish high standards and expectations and to help people to connect with one another and to those outside.

While leaders can focus on broader ways to foster such communities, the small things can also make a huge difference in a work environment. We now know that people who work in close proximity can more quickly resolve issues and are better at sparking and spreading ideas. This happens easily in small companies but can become far more difficult in larger organizations. Marissa Mayer, CEO of Yahoo ordered an end to remote working as part of a new era of collaboration, explaining: 'To become the absolute best place to work, communication and collaboration will be important, so we need to be working side-by-side.'[3]

The approach taken by Mayer recognizes a simple truth, that in activities like eating with each other at lunch time, we get to discuss both work and non-work issues. Not only does this provide opportunities to develop a better understanding of each other, it also weaves a complex web of relationships and meaning, which in turn, helps build greater cohesion and faster decision-making. This then is where we will find the reconnected leader in the future, helping a group to forge a sense of identity and meaning and making connections both across and beyond the organization.

From the soft power that comes from the social connections between people and communities, we turn next to the way work is organized, considering how harder structures within and beyond organizations can be developed to foster greater connectivity at work.

Organization and work design: Reconnecting leaders to the frontline

Ensuring leaders are connected to people throughout their business is essential to building thriving environments. However, it can be difficult to achieve in large organizations where people rarely see senior leaders. In such environments it is easy to understand how the connection between senior leaders and what is happening on the frontline can be lost. Recent scientific research has shed light on this issue.

Known as the Dunbar number, it indicates that the brain's capacity for storing information on other people is 150. It is our connection capacity. This 150-person relationship limit has proved to be the unseen number throughout history shaping the maximum size of early village formations and the size of divisions within the Roman army. Within the 150 frame, everyone knows what everyone else is doing, people can operate with high levels of autonomy and become highly effective at setting and sustaining standards and effective norms of operation. Beyond 150 communications become far more complicated and other modes of co-ordination become essential.

CASE STUDY   Gore-Tex

It was with this in mind that Gore-Tex, the clothing and materials manufacturer, set about consciously shaping an organization to build effective relations between people. Each of their production units contains no more than 150 people, a size chosen so that every manager and leader can know every person. All decision-making is done through self-managing teams of 8 to 12 people including hiring, pay and projects allocation. Significantly, the CEO is elected by the staff. Rather than relying on a command-and-control structure, current CEO Terri Kelly believes, 'It's far better to rely upon a broad base of individuals and leaders who share a common set of values and feel personal ownership for the overall success of the organization. These responsible and empowered individuals will serve as much better watchdogs than any single, dominant leader or bureaucratic structure.'[4] Terri Kelly observed in an interview in 2010 that: 'The very act of having hierarchical structures and leaders who stand in the centre or under the spotlight making all the decisions, actively takes responsibility away from people.' Externally

Gore-Tex feels that giving the impression that leaders always know what is best, always have to have the answers, presents a distorted and damaging picture of reality, because the knowledge really exists within the organization itself. According to Terri Kelly the first design flaw that many organizations fall into is supporting the myth of the all-singing, all-dancing, all-powerful leader. Gore-Tex believes that this flawed thinking needs to be addressed first, so that small autonomous teams can feel that their decisions will not only be valued but also utilized for some greater good for the organization. Central to making this kind of change happen is therefore how a leader views their role and their comfort in giving up power to the team. The Gore-Tex outlook is linked to a general principle of subsidiarity in which people are allowed to develop by being able to contribute to making decisions at all levels. In such environments leaders do not create dependency because decisions are not unnecessarily reserved to higher levels in the hierarchy. People are given the freedom, and support where necessary, to take on the risk of decision-making and to have a voice in their work, thus fostering innovation, creativity and a sense of shared responsibility. Needless to say it takes a very different kind of leader who can say that they are not there to make all the decisions, rather to be there to be the architect of the overall system. 'Gore's philosophy holds that the ultimate measure of leadership is the ability to develop strong "followership" and the extent to which others seek an employee's advice and knowledge on important decisions.'[5] This peer-driven approach ensures that leadership at Gore is earned, not appointed and underlines the direction of travel highlighted in Chapter 1. It highlights the degree to which leaders need to become far more connected to the wider workforce if they are to earn their respect. We will discuss this outlook as part of a wider reflection on leadership in Chapter 9. This level of openness requires a great deal of courage but it does foster a far higher level of community and the interdependence within Gore-Tex's operating units.

CASE STUDY Morning Star

Morning Star, a US fresh produce (fruit and vegetable) company, is another such organization that has sought to remove boundaries within its business. Its stated goal is to create a company in which all team members 'will be self-managing professionals, initiating communications and the coordination of their activities with fellow colleagues, customers, suppliers, and fellow industry participants, without receiving direction from above.'[6] Every person at Morning Star is a colleague in a web of multilateral commitments. Nobody is the boss and everybody is the boss. In this environment everyone has to do whatever needs to be done.'[7] At Morning Star, nobody uses the term 'empowerment' because this assumes that authority trickles down, that power gets bestowed from above, as and when the powerful see fit. In an organization built on the principles of self-management, individuals aren't given power by the higher-ups; they simply have it. Personal mission statements for every employee are the cornerstones of Morning Star's management model and employees are responsible for acquiring the training, resources, and cooperation needed to fulfil their mission.

Flatter management structures are critical for business success because they help people to connect directly to rapidly changing environments. Firms organized around small, autonomous teams are much more nimble than large hierarchies, making it easier to respond to change. Innovation is fostered as there are fewer layers of management for an idea to progress through and because many innovations can simply be implemented as people have greater control of their day-to-day environments. Rather than being held together by layers of management and management control systems, organizations are united through a sense of shared purpose.

CASE STUDY   Zappos

Another organization that is adopting this philosophy is US online shoe retailer, Zappos. Tony Hsieh is the CEO who aims to put employee and customer happiness at the centre of their organization philosophy. They have scrapped hierarchy and job titles altogether. Everyone is now a partner with an agreed duty to support others whose work relies on their actions. Zappos have branded this managerless system 'Holocracy' a comprehensive practice for structuring, governing, and running a managerless organization. It replaces today's top-down predict-and-control leadership approach and has instilled what it refers to as a system for rapid evolution in the businesss's core processes – something that is essential when a business is growing as fast as Zappos' online operations have. All power vests in the constitution or core purpose of the organization. According to Hseih, the basic question everyone must have at the forefront of their minds is whether what they are doing is working in line with the long-term purpose of the organization. If it isn't, the tensions this creates should then provide the basis for constructive dialogue about how things need to be improved. Everything is organized around this explicit purpose. This allows what Hseih refers to as the 'emergent behavior' of the whole system, without being controlled by either a single heroic leader or even the collective group. The holocracy governance process is not governance 'of the people, by the people, and for the people' – it is governance of the organization, through the people, for the purpose. It enables the organization to find and express its deepest creative capacity, by putting the search and practice of purpose at the heart of everything they do. The system demands a great deal from everyone in the business. It rejects the normal parent–child relationships between leaders and colleagues and instead says that everyone has responsibility for resolving the issues within their power to resolve. It requires a huge amount of maturity from individuals in the business and consequently Zappos invests heavily in selecting and training people through, for example, three-day pre-hire bootcamps, to ensure that anyone joining is suited to the unique Zappos environment. The demands it places on leaders to focus on fostering connectivity between colleagues and with the customer are at the heart of the leadership role in the organization.

New organization design requires a connector-in-chief

In 2004, psychologists Deci and Ryan demonstrated why such radically different structures work. In their US study, workers who had greater autonomy in their decision-making felt greater satisfaction, performed better at their jobs and had lower levels of depression. The researchers observed: 'Human beings are inherently motivated to grow and achieve and will fully commit to even uninteresting tasks if their meaning and value is understood and they have a sense of control over what they are doing.' Similar analysis has been carried out across other countries with consistent results (Grouzet *et al*, 2005).

In a number of technology environments these ways of working are developing further into what are becoming known as 'Worknet' organizations. They have grown up to mirror the looser connectivity of the web. Worknets are interesting because they increase competitive advantage through the collaboration of small and agile self-directed teams, made up of people who are not part of the organization but are nonetheless connected by a common purpose and values. It is the nature of the work that determines the best way to organize. Such network-centric structures are smart ways to respond to complex and rapidly changing environments. Leaders in these environments do not attempt to control people; rather their focus is on establishing a connection amongst everyone in the group through a strong and consistent purpose, while fostering ownership of issues at, or as close as possible to, the frontline of the operation. All these organizations foster problem-solving through open, transparent debate, which is made possible because of their demonstrable respect for everyone.

A number of organizations are now using this approach to open up the way they work, for example Automattic, who build and support WordPress, which provides the platform for about 20 per cent of the world's websites. It only employs a few hundred people, who all work remotely, with a highly autonomous and flat management structure. Commenting on the implementation of initiatives such as those at Zappos, Andrew Hill observed: 'Self-organization does not mean ditching structure all–together or getting bogged down in consensus decision-making, and companies run big risks if the attempt to implement self-government in one go.'[8] The emphasis has to be on changing the role of leaders to become 'connectors-in-chief', with an equal emphasis on coaching frontline people to take on the responsibility for problem resolution and inter-group working. This is a complex transition to navigate.

There is much we can still learn from the often-maligned Canadian Professor Elliot Jaques (1956 and 1964) about the levels of responsibility people can be expected to take on effectively. Jaques believed that there was a requisite level of structure in any complex organization and contested that a limited level of hierarchy was not only inevitable but also essential to the health of organizations and to the people in them. Jaques is at odds with many contemporary management thinkers who contend that hierarchy is bad per se. His belief was that there needed to be a natural stratification of companies based on the time horizon of decision-making and identified four different levels linked to these decision-making time horizons. He proposed that production line workers need to focus on what is happening minute-to-minute, hour-to-hour and day-to-day; without this intense focus, details would be missed. People who sit on the boards of organizations were, in his view, the only people with the insight to look at what lay ahead over the next five years, ensuring that the organization was ready for whatever lay around the corner; those individuals should be sweating those details. In between were people who can plan week-to-month and from month-to-year. This did not mean that frontline workers could not have valuable insights about innovation and the way customer expectations are changing, in fact, in the Jaques view of the world, that level of problem-solving is exactly what you would expect people to be doing. Following this logic, employees should be given the autonomy, decision powers, tools, information and, above all, freedom to act, to make the decisions which were best placed to act upon.

Many large organizations today have approximately seven or eight layers between those on the senior leadership team and the frontline. The less efficient can have upwards of 12. Every leader at every level wants to demonstrate that they are adding value or providing necessary checks and balances to the decision-making process. However, without clarity on the decisions that can and should be taken at each level, these layers lead to involvement by leaders in situations where they are, quite frankly, not needed. As we saw in Chapter 1, recent estimates show that there is now one manager in place for every six people in the workforce. It suggests that rather than providing outstanding support, leaders are involved in hands-on 'doing'. Such micro-management helps to explain why the biggest single contributing factor to the workplace stress is management behaviour. According to Professor Gary Hamel management has become the most inefficient of activities. The more management layers there are, the more people will return to a default position of passivity, particularly if there are people around (leaders) who offer to take problems away from them.

As we have seen, there is an alternative: if leaders start the design of their business with the intent that they will connect with rather than control people on the frontline; if they ensure that their people have the maximum amount of responsibility designed into their roles; if technology, process and structure are there to support that people-centric goal. Providing all the people on the frontline are working towards a common purpose, we will see radical shifts in productivity and creativity. Another proviso, to which we shall return later, is that leaders must change the way they personally operate by connecting with people as coaches and facilitators, not as controllers and managers. In this way we open up the potential for organizations to really work in a way that enables people to not only assume their fullest responsibility but also increase the capacity for them to assume their full potential. In the next chapter we will explore what else a reconnected leader can do to help their people reach their potential and perform at their best.

Connected talent environments: The power of many

We will start with an examination of what a 'connected talent environment' could look like. During the 12th and 13th centuries Venice became the dominant force in European trade. In their analysis of this success, Acemoglu and Robinson (2012) highlight the way Venetian society was crafted to become the most highly interconnected and inclusive environment in Europe:

> Inclusive economic institutions are in turn supported by, and support, inclusive political institutions [which] distribute political power widely in a pluralistic manner and are able to achieve some amount of political centralization so as to establish law and order, the foundations of secure property rights and an inclusive market economy.

Conversely, extractive political institutions that concentrate power in the hands of a few reinforce extractive economic institutions to hold power. Acemoglu explained in an interview that their core point is that countries thrive when they build political and economic institutions that 'unleash', empower and protect the full potential of each citizen to innovate, invest and develop.

The success of Venice was based not on its geographical location, but rather on creating an environment in which its people could flourish, through an inclusive system of social mobility called *La Commenda*. This system paired those at the top of society – the holders of great wealth – with those at the start of their careers. This enabled wealthy gentry to sponsor up-and-coming ships' captains who would complete long and dangerous voyages around the world in pursuit of rare goods and riches. This approach was marked out by the connections between the Venetian businessman who would risk their money and the ship's captain who would risk their lives. Furthermore, on the ship's return, the businessman and the captain would split the proceeds 50–50. The linkages highlighted by the Venetian experience between a flourishing economy, open business, inclusive culture and thriving environments are so often overlooked yet are all essential for producing sustainable growth. We will explore in the following chapters how leaders can reconnect with their people and create such thriving environments.

The lessons from 12th-century Venice can provide some powerful insights for our current issues, and contrasts sharply with McKinsey's concept of *A War for Talent*, which encouraged corporations to hire in only A-star names, and has led to vast swathes of the workforce feeling that they somehow no longer make the grade Yet, as we saw in Chapter 1, it still has a hold on much corporate thinking about how people should be developed. Our reality suggests a different approach may now be required.

We know that the skills people need today will be considerably different to those necessary by 2020. In China, for example, huge efforts are being made to close the skills gap, but even their vast 'ant tribe', which is the name the Chinese give to the millions of graduates the country is producing, cannot cope with an estimated shortfall of 24 million graduates and technicians which are forecast by 2020. The skills gap will cost China an estimated $250 billion and have a huge impact on its growth and GDP.

Google believes that we are only at the beginning of what it calls a 'slow dawn' in the next era of what technology can do and what will be available.[9] One statistic captures the opportunity and challenges that await us. Over the next five years, the number of hand-held smartphones and devices will expand from around two billion today to around five billion. That amount of connectivity of people and ideas will unleash levels of creativity and demand that are almost unimaginable. It is clear that talent demand in this new environment will continue to outstrip supply and inhibit growth unless we do something differently. Progressive organizations will therefore need to be able to flex and adapt in order to realign themselves so that their entire organizations become talent academies. They must constantly leverage all talent pools, foster the exchange of talent and encourage collaboration between themselves, academic institutions and small entrepreneurial companies. Such a highly dynamic form of talent management will connect all the people within an organization through a continuing learning agenda and will connect the company with external organizations that are learning new and different things. This capability to 'grow your own' talent and 'grow with others' will become a key determinant of future success. Those organizations that believe that everyone has talent and invest in closing the skills gaps as an continuing business activity will reap huge benefits in terms of employee loyalty and commitment as well as having a workforce that is more prepared to learn and adapt as new challenges come along. Such progressive organizations will connect and collaborate with talent rather than fighting over it.

If this is the future, then what of today's approach to talent? As we have seen, it is increasingly clear that current talent strategies are not working. According to recent US data, 20 per cent of top talent typically leave an organization within a year of being identified as top talent; 46 per cent of all new hires leave the organization within their first 18 months, with the cost of replacement estimated by some sources as being up to 150 per cent of first year's salary. Getting the talent agenda right is clearly a pivotal element of all successful business strategies. However, many western companies have relied on being able to easily hire the talent they need, when they need it. This period is coming to an end, for while hiring on demand created huge flexibility, it has also exposed business to significant risk as the availability of the 'right skills' is becoming far less certain, and even when you know what the skills are for today, you can be pretty sure those requirements will change very soon. The notion that leaders can keep churning through staff in an attempt to replace and upgrade is an approach that is running out of road.

Perhaps one of the central problems is how disconnected the view of 'talent' has become inside major organizations. Often viewed through a separate talent process, the conventional talent grid can create a sense that there are elite groups of special people. As we saw in Chapter 1, such language effectively disenfranchises the majority of people inside a business. How can leaders move talent practices from being a separate set of activities run by the human resources function and reconnect them to what the business is fundamentally about? This starts with revisiting basic questions like: Does every person matter? Do leaders nurture people to achieve their potential and develop as human beings? Do leaders give a fair chance to people from all backgrounds, including the underprivileged? These are difficult questions for any organization, but they offer far more than a narrow window on talent development, which blights so many organizations and instead provides leaders with opportunity to create environments which foster the common good by helping people to bring more of their potential into reality. Some leaders are making strides to create a far more inclusive approach to talent development.

CASE STUDY SAP

One such business is SAP, the German computer software company, which has recognized that promoting education and training is one of the best ways to improve its long-term performance and address the problem of chronic youth unemployment, an issue affecting the technology industry as a whole. This long-term commitment has seen SAP working with the World Bank to start to address the scarcity of skills on the African continent, with the aim of developing world-class IT and business capability. The initiative called 'Skills for Africa' is part of SAP's long-term aim to give Africa's youth an opportunity to play a role in contributing towards future economic growth and infrastructure development. In Kenya, for example, Kenya's Information and Communications Technology Board and Multimedia University of Nairobi have committed to delivering professional training and providing official ICT certification to 100 university graduates. SAP's commitment to developing people is farsighted by any standards. In 2013, it announced that it would recruit hundreds of people with autism because people with autistic conditions have a unique talent for information technology, particularly in problem identification in software code. SAP said that by 2020, 1 per cent of its global workforce of 65,000 employees would be people with autism. The company said it believes that 'innovation comes from the edges, and only by employing people who think differently and spark innovation will SAP be prepared to handle the challenges of the 21st century.'[10] These initiatives build on SAP's foundational commitment to growing its own talent, with apprentice-style academies in sales and engineering already well established around the world. This outlook also applies to leadership development and includes a unique alternative to traditional volunteering: providing paid, short-term assignments in emerging markets for emerging leaders who help solve business challenges with non-governmental organizations (NGOs) and growing entrepreneurs. The most successful leaders are those who understand the global economy, are on the cutting edge of innovation and can effectively collaborate with people from a wide range of backgrounds and perspectives.

CASE STUDY   Wipro and Tata in India

Such progressive approaches to talent development are also highly evident in India, which has perhaps one of the most progressive approaches to skills development anywhere in the world. Two of India's leading technology companies, Wipro and Tata, invest heavily in skills development. They assume that people will arrive with skills gaps and see it as their job to invest in them and close those gaps. This is markedly different to the prevailing logic that exists in many UK and US firms, where the typical expectation is that people must come 'job-ready'. Wipro and Tata recognize that there is a common good to be achieved by developing people. It is good for the future of their firms, but it is also good for the communities in which they operate. At Wipro's training centre, they can accommodate 4,000 people per day and offer a catalogue of voluntary and mandatory training courses to improve technical, communication and leadership skills as employees move up the corporate ladder. Tata has created a six-month training programme covering everything from engineering and technical skills to teamwork, leadership and other soft skills. Tata states: 'The training enables youngsters from less-privileged background to be as good if not better than those from elite universities.'[11] It also makes them very loyal to the company. This approach isn't just about creating opportunities early on in people's careers. There is a clear sense that growing people from within creates a mindset that everyone in the company has talent and is valued. By promoting internally, the promise that people will have the opportunity to grow and develop is realized continuously. Such approaches connect leaders throughout an organization because of the shared experience that people encounter during their development. This hidden network is hugely powerful, knitting an invisible thread into the organization, which people identify with and can pull on. So much of this kind of development has, as we discussed in Chapter 1, disappeared between the 1980s and the 2000s, leaving a huge gap particularly in technical talent pipelines.

Coaches can foster a growth mindset

In our reflection on Venetian commercial history discussed earlier, we saw how high levels of inclusivity led to people from 'lowly' backgrounds aspiring to become members of the ruling elite. This system nurtured by members of the Venetian leadership group, who personally put their own time and money into bringing the approach to life, provides a good example of what connected leadership looks like in the arena of talent development and demonstrates how a culture of inclusivity can work to create a dynamic and vibrant enterprise. However, it also shows how important it is to create an environment in which people believe with good reason that the wider organization wants them to develop and that it is worthwhile stretching themselves, and taking risks, because they can see that real opportunities do exist for 'people like them'.

Developing the sense that opportunity and growth are possible within an organization is a critical role for a connected leader and forms part of creating what eminent US psychologist Carol Dweck (2012) has called a 'growth mindset'. Her analysis has shown that individuals who believe they can continue to learn, and that their capacity for learning is not fixed, are more likely to take on and try new and adventurous things, to stretch themselves and to grow. If leaders shut down this willingness to take on and try new things by, for example, undermining employee confidence, they ultimately shut down the likelihood that an organization will continue to thrive.

Given how people will continue to need to acquire new skills throughout their careers, this is perhaps the most important attribute we can look to develop in people. Leaders can engender this mindset by creating environments in which employees are encouraged to keep taking on new tasks, new roles and new learning, where they can see that with the support of their leader they can continue to progress.

This then, is one of the most critical connections and explains why leaders who build strong coaching environments help to shape the character of an organization. Another element of the coaching that leaders can provide comes in the nurturing of what US psychologist Angela Lee Duckworth (2013) calls 'grit'. Grit is doggedness, which shows through in people's willingness to tackle and – critically – stick with new challenges for long enough to see that they are making progress. Duckworth's research has proven that this doggedness, rather than any innate sense of inborn talent, is a far better indicator of whether a person will succeed and go on to master a subject than anything else. Duckworth measures the level of development on a grit index, and has now shown that grit is a far more accurate predictor of future high school grades than IQ level.

Leaders who connect with their people by demonstrating commitment as active coaches send a clear signal into the 'subconscious of the organization' that employees can continue to progress if they continue to work at things. This is a very different signal to the ones spread by organizations whose pressing short-term needs for talent are most often met by external hiring. This approach can unintentionally communicate that hard work, sticking at things and sticking with the company aren't highly valued and can unwittingly contribute to people thinking that their careers may be better developed elsewhere.

In contrast, the potential benefit of leaders operating as effective coaches has been highlighted at Google. In the research, based on 10,000 observations, Google's Project Oxygen aimed to identify what the best managers at Google are doing to develop teams that perform better, are happier and have better retention rates. The conclusions were summarized in 'Google's Rules', which consists of a set of eight good behaviours. Number one on the list of attributes was coaching.

CASE STUDY   Grant Thornton–UK and International

Grant Thornton have worked hard to shape a distinctive presence for themselves in the highly competitive and increasingly concentrated market of global professional services and accounting. Often pitched against the so called 'Big Four' accounting firms, Grant Thornton have looked to differentiate themselves by focusing on their ability to unlock their clients potential to grow. In doing so they have made a virtue of their positioning in supporting mid-market clients, those dynamic companies who still have the ambition, space and capacity to grow rapidly. They have also crucially recognized that if what they offer is going to feel different for their clients, then it has to feel different for their people. They have therefore created a Centre for International Coaching Excellence, based out of the UK, bringing together themes of personal well-being and mindfulness to create a cadre of over 100 Director- or Partner-level coaches, who are now deployed throughout the firm to bring the best out of their people. Their approach has helped to improve decision-making at every level of the firm. By equipping leaders to think more deeply and broadly they have enabled their people to build the confidence they need to achieve results in an increasingly complex environment. The level of commitment to this transformational change is marked, and all the coaches at Grant Thornton are accredited to internationally recognized standards (something that is rare inside most firms).The approach has been adopted by the UK, US and Canadian firms' boards and is now being rolled out around the world. It is perhaps interesting to note that such holistic approaches to leadership including mindfulness are emerging throughout the business world, where leaders from visionaries like the late Steve Jobs to sophisticated technocrats like Mark Carney, the Governor of the Bank of England.

Conclusion

In Chapter 1 we saw how disconnected employees have become as a result of working within organizations with all-time low levels of engagement and trust. We compared how we work today with the historical case study of Venice's creation of a fully inclusive society within its city state. This

TABLE 5.1 The reconnected workplace

Attributes of a Reconnected Workplace	Actions
Ensure people feel included	Sending clear signals that people's ideas from all sources are valued and acted upon.
Foster a strong sense of identity	Raising intrinsic levels of motivation, by designing jobs with greater opportunities for mastery, autonomy, purpose and relationships.
Encouraging people to take more responsibility	Creating new operating models which can only function without managerial intervention. Reducing unnecessary managerial decision-making, and removing layers.
Creating real opportunities for people	Celebrating role models who have risen through the organization.
Nurturing a mindset of Growth and Grit (resilience)	Regularly helping people to move into new roles or projects which are new and difficult – providing support through coaching.

highlighted how a combination of inclusivity, identity, internal talent progression and a system of reward sharing can create a truly dynamic and thriving environment.

However important these components are, they will only make a difference between a normal workplace and a thriving environment if they are congruent with the way leaders lead, something we will come back to in more detail in a later chapter.

For now it is worth highlighting three essential ingredients:

- First through the behaviour of leaders and the extent to which they are prepared to relinquish power, by enabling people to make more of the decisions about things which effect their work and their interaction with colleagues. In doing so our conception of the modern leadership changes to become that of 'connectors-in-chief', the people who encourage, recognize and shares ideas across and beyond an organization. The importance of this activity cannot be underestimated in our interdependent world, as renowned social biologist Edward O Wilson's explained in his book *The Social Conquest of Earth* (2012): 'It has been the complexity of our social interactions and our ability to master them that has led to the success of the human race.' Indeed these features 'have caused our brains to develop and evolve in the way they have'. In concluding his book he cites an 'iron rule' of nature and performance: 'Selfish individuals will beat altruistic individuals but altruistic groups will always beat groups of selfish individuals.' Wilson adds: 'Humans are the only species that form communities that contain multiple generations and where, as part of a division of labour, community members sometimes perform altruistic acts for the benefit of others.'

This point is reinforced further by Ezio Manzini one of the world's leading experts on sustainable design, and the power of collective approaches. He has to this end created his own Slow Labs, in New York City, where slowness describes an expanded state of awareness, accountability for actions, and richer spectrum of experience for individuals and communities. It celebrates local, close-mesh networks of people and industry, and draws upon cultural diversity, and the open sharing of ideas and information to arrive at innovative solutions.[12] In these ways interestingly both Wilson and Manzini are reflecting that to be successful in this new era leaders must create organizations which are open and interconnected and must be completely reconnected themselves if they are to make this possible.

- Second, leaders must adopt a fresh outlook on how they think about the management of people in their organizations. They must begin with a view of people as people, not as assets or resources, but as individuals with homes and families and backgrounds and futures – individuals who are colleagues but are also part of wider communities with wider responsibilities. Ultimately leaders will only be able to make meaningful connections if they understand the desire of individuals to commit to something bigger than themselves and recognize that work provides a way for people to feel a sense of belonging in their lives. Leaders carry a special responsibility in shaping these environments, experiences and endeavours.

- Finally, leaders have a unique responsibility to conserve, celebrate and develop an organization's corporate memory. Such memories exist in the minds and collected experiences of people who have worked within an organization over many years. Much of this history is oral and while it is sometimes written down, its power comes from the people it resides in. Such memories can provide organizations with a kind of societal conscience, by reminding 'us' of who we are and how we should or should not do things.

When people no longer stay in an organization for any length of time, such memories are inevitably lost and with it the power leaders have to nurture a deeper 'conscience' about what is right for a company. Reconnected leaders value the part such connections play in creating sustainable environments, which help people to grow as moral as well as intelligent communities. Developing talent from within and encouraging it to stay for the long term is a crucial role that reconnected leaders play in making this happen.

We will now consider some specific actions leaders can take in order to turn these themes into practical realities.

Eight steps to reconnected leadership

Step 3 – Reconnecting through the workforce: Leadership actions

1 *Growing your own is the best way to grow a strong and cohesive culture.* To maintain constancy of purpose, leaders need to have a deep understanding of the philosophy of the organization from the roots up. This requires greater commitment to the development of people than in the majority of organizations who hire first and develop later.

   It is perhaps interesting to note that UK government departments recognize that they simply cannot compete for talent on the basis of salary scales alone. They therefore have one of the largest youth entrance programmes in the country and put considerable effort into developing career paths and moving people across departments of government. There is much that could be re-learned in business by paying more attention to these grassroots practices. Having the best youth entry scheme into your organization is the critical first step to developing your future leaders. Growing your own talent is also a way of growing and strengthening a company's ethos, whereas the constant stream of external hires can only ever dilute the concentrate.

2   *Create role models – living cement!* To create a strong sense of identity, leaders can develop internal cohesion by making a special effort to identify different people at all levels of the organization who exemplify progression up the internal route and embody the organizations purpose and desired leadership behaviours. Too often the 'stars' of the organization become the latest big signing from the outside. Instead, selected homegrown individuals can role model what 'good' is, acting as 'living cement', holding the organization together. They are invaluable. How many people do you know personally in your organization who are like this and how many did you promote and develop?

3   *Make the whole organizaton a talent academy.* In contrast with other assets, which only depreciate, employees are the only assets which can appreciate over time. Sadly, we have come to think of development only in terms of upward progression. Not only is this unrealistic for the majority, it is also highly demotivating for them.

    Leaders can create an alternative environment where everyone is working to achieve personal mastery in what they do. In the retail industry, it is possible to have annual awards for the best butcher and fishmonger of the year, but this is also possible in every line of work. It is important when doing this that such approaches do not become 'talent' shows; rather they should be looking for individuals who are learning and mastering their jobs. This sense of mastery also has to mean something practical for people. It has to mean less direct management control and more freedom to operate so that individuals on the frontline can develop a real sense of being responsible for what they do. It is one of the biggest forms of respect we can show anyone. The highest respect we can offer is for individuals at all levels to have the opportunity to give back to others at work, by using their skills not only in doing their jobs but also in skilling up their colleagues. By taking this kind of approach a leader can create a talent academy across the whole workforce rather than in an isolated training room.

4   *Become a coaching organization.* One of the most important roles leaders can perform is to create connected work environments to enable individuals to take responsibility and become self-directed decision-makers. These decision-making skills can be enhanced by

equipping everyone in the organization with effective problem-solving skills supported by the right tools and information.

If this were easy then no doubt many more organizations would have gone down this path. It is a three-stage commitment, requiring a system in which individuals can attain personal mastery in the jobs they perform; in reducing the number of managers because individuals do not need that level of oversight; and by upskilling leaders to act as coaches who can manage these difficult transitions and critically help to build the confidence of colleagues to take the steps necessary to assume these responsibilities. But it cannot stop there. This is not about simply having leaders skilled as coaches. The company must become a coaching organization: embodying a coaching ethos in all that it does; nurturing a growth mindset; having a stretching performance process; equipping leaders to bring the best out in people; and fostering the shared sense of identity and powerful role models we discussed earlier.

5 *Monitor stability in the workplace.* Many organizations monitor sickness absence and labour turnover, but to create a connected work environment people literally need to stick together. The surest signal that this is important is to have it not only as a top three metric that is measured by the board but far more importantly it should be become something that a leader asks about whenever he visits the frontline. If leaders want to demonstrate that they care about their people, one of the best ways of doing that is to ask about who has left in the past months and to find out why. It quickly becomes apparent that a leader regards any such unplanned loss as a loss of experience from the business, it starts to humanize the company and communicates that there is a direct concern about individuals. This is easy to set up but difficult to deliver consistently over time. However, once others start to copy role model leaders and start to take an interest in why people have left, they will also start to take actions to reduce the things in the environment that make people want to leave in the first place.

Stability can also be achieved by encouraging people to build up social as well as economic networks. These are the ties that often help to bind people together.

6 *Everyone has got talent.* As we discussed earlier, having a system which signals that there are maybe 5 per cent of the workforce who have got the special 'whatever it takes to get on', is likely to alienate

the other 95 per cent of people. Recent research on talent distribution has questioned the validity of bell distribution curves for plotting talent in organizations. The reality is that performance in an organization is distributed far more like a long tail. The challenge therefore is to create environments in which everyone has their performance raised. Focusing on the broader environmental issues we discussed earlier is one way to achieve this. However, one of the simpler things that a leader can do is to ensure that a variety of different people are chosen for projects and exciting initiatives, not just the same faces. As we will see later, getting teams to innovate and excel is all about getting the right mix of talent and experience and not just those that are 'brightest' but lack the ties back into the business. This kind of approach also helps initiatives get accepted more quickly across an organization.

7 *Radically redesign jobs and reduce the number of management layers.* With the advance of technology we are getting to the stage where people in front line jobs can take on complete self-management of their tasks and responsibilities. Unlike the approaches still taken by some leaders, who see delayering as a direct cost reduction exercise, to create a connected workforce leaders start at the opposite end of the process. They start with the individual who is doing the job, asking how we can build roles around people that are truly rewarding, that allow individuals to take on maximum responsibility. That ensures there is the opportunity for people to see the outcomes of their work and to take a sense of pride in what they do, to contribute to decisions over how the work gets done and to review how the team is performing rather than being reviewed.

While much of this has been talked about for some time, new technology now means that the tools are there to equip people in new ways. In the process it creates the opportunity for people to take a real sense of ownership so this isn't just a question of taking out layers. This is a radically different way of thinking about work and valuing people. It's the kind of practice that made it possible for Richer Sounds, the UK-based electronics retailer, to compete with the surge to online and the commoditization of the industry. Rather than headcount reduction, it starts with job enhancement and it reflects the way most people would choose to work.

8 *Create networks of interest to foster long-term agility.* If a leader can consciously look to connect a person into a business in multiple

ways, these connections can help to speed up innovation and service across a business. One way to do this is through the creation of communities of interest. These bodies don't work when they appear superficial and do not produce tangible benefits for an individual. However, if the community of interest is genuinely developing best practice that can be shared more widely, people will want to be part of it. This success will also demonstrate that there is another level in the organization beyond 'just getting the job done today'. The more people can be encouraged to get involved in these networks, the more likely that an organization will become fluid and porous enough to share ideas and become more agile in the process.

1 Gary Stott, Director of Create, in discussion with the author
2 A2 Media, How is the identity of youths constructed by the press? December 2012
3 Jenna Goudreau, Back to the Stone Age, *Forbes* Magazine, 25 February 2013
4 Tim Kastelle, Hierarchy is overrated, *Harvard Business Review*, November 2013
5 Claire Zillman, The case for employees to pick their CEO, *Fortune* Magazine, July 2014
6 *ibid*.
7 Gary Hamel, First let's fire all the managers, *Harvard Business Review*, December 2011
8 Andrew Hill, *Financial Times*, 6 January 2014
9 Matt Brittin, Managing Director, Google UK, speaking at an Odgers Berndtson Summit in March 2014
10 SAP to work with Specialisterne to employ people with autism, SAP Press release, May 2013
11 Sarah Fister Gale, NewsWorkforce Webinars – India, workforce.com, April 2013
12 Ezio Manzini, SlowLab.net and www.desis-network.org/authors/ezio-manzini

Step 4: Nurturing a spirit of shared enterprise

06

Introduction

In this chapter, we will look at how leaders can use connections to forge a spirit of shared enterprise, where a true sense of common ownership and accountability are combined to inspire and foster innovation and lasting commitment.

FIGURE 6.1 Reconnected leadership model: Nurturing a spirit of shared enterprise

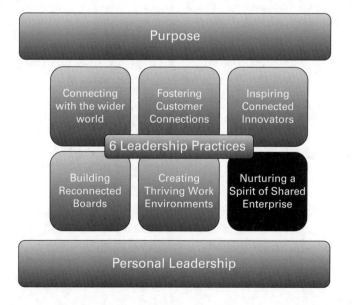

We will consider whether the leadership practices being utilized by many of today's leaders to inspire and motivate their people are, in reality, creating largely transactional relationships, which contribute to the growing sense of fragmentation inside and outside organizations. We will also reflect on how we think about and measure the work of enterprises and discuss how this is contributing to dysfunctional short-termist behaviour. These perspectives then need to be set against an alternative vision which considers how leaders can ignite a positive spirit inside their organizations, how this can be fuelled by inducing a greater sense of shared endeavour and how all these energies can be brought together to build an enterprise full of vitality. But to begin, let us first consider the phrase 'spirit of shared enterprise' in a little more detail.

Spirit is derived from the Latin word *spiritus* meaning 'breath'. It can also mean the right action for the right reasons and putting heart and soul into something. Spirit can extend beyond the ephemeral to more concrete notions of doing things in a spirited way, with vigour or vitality or a sense of fun, as in high spirits. Spirit can also capture a collective sense of meaning, as in the French *esprit de corps* with its notion of loyalty to each other, 'team spirit' or the German *zeitgeist* capturing the 'spirit of the age'. So spirit is a vital ingredient for any organization to capture. It is often what we sense when we walk into a successful business.

Sharing is a basic element of human life, responsible for strengthening social ties and ensuring well-being. Sharing infers that we need to cooperate with others because we recognize that when operating alone we have limitations. We also recognize limitations in others and, in the act of giving and receiving, discover something of our shared humanity. The success of sharing is dependent on the degree of reciprocity we demonstrate and engender and implies a degree of taking on board and valuing the opinions and contributions of others. Sharing creates a far greater plurality of thinking in an organization, which is crucial for innovation, as we shall see later. Sharing also opens our thinking to the notion of stewarding limited resources for others, implying a degree of responsibility for the collective good. In so doing, it surfaces a need for solidarity with others and discourages purely self-interested decisions.

Enterprise is the most concrete and worldly of the words used in our phrase. It is the place where ideas, creativity and action converge, where energy and resourcefulness are found and where things happen.

If we consider all of this in light of the leadership crisis and employee disconnection outlined in Chapter 1, we might reasonably argue that whatever we are doing is not generating a 'spirit of shared enterprise'. Poor employee engagement scores and low trust in leadership are good indicators that the spirit of shared enterprise has been leaking out of our organizations for some time.

Throughout this chapter we will explore how leaders can rekindle this shared spirit and reconnect everyone to the purpose of the enterprise. This is essential if we are to enhance the compatibility of our organizations with the way the world is changing around us – from business being seen as distinct and separate from society to a position in which business is regarded as more integrated and embedded, fitting within our broader ambitions, recognizing that organizations can only succeed within successful societies.

In this chapter we will therefore consider how future leadership practices can better align and support the creation of a shared approach to success and build a more inclusive and sustainable enterprise. Through the course of the chapter we will also reflect on the degree to which fresh approaches to motivation can help our enterprises and to that end we will evaluate how leadership can better align issues of performance measurement, pay and ownership. First, however, we must put our current discussion in its wider context by reflecting on how we got here.

Context

After the stock market crash of 1929 and the Great Depression that followed, the Roosevelt administration sought to reframe the role of business in society and positioned business leaders as 'New Economic Statesmen', playing a stewardship role in society beyond the strict confines of their organizations. This consensus lasted for almost 50 years, during which time the pay gap between the highest and lowest was halved – a period which has come to be known as 'the great compression'. This period also coincided with some of the most impressive economic growth rates in the 20th century. In other words, it was part of an approach to economics and business that synthesized economic and social good.

The 1980s saw this compact fracture following the oil crisis and a growing sense that the West was stagnating and falling behind the rest of the world, notably the Japanese. Fresh thinking sought to reposition the role of executives not as stewards but as hard-driving entrepreneurs, who needed to be greatly incentivized and completely aligned to the expectations of shareholders through a relentless focus on shareholder value. A new model for business emerged, shaped by three fundamental assumptions:

- individuals are self-interested maximizers;
- talent is a scarce resource, which needs to be rewarded accordingly;
- individuals respond well to contingent rewards (bonuses), so performance systems should be designed to put significant amounts of pay at risk, to motivate individuals to overachieve.

Over this 30-year period, these assumptions have become hard-wired into leadership thinking and practice, leading to something of a silent revolution in the relationship between executives and their employers. Old contracts have been torn up. Out has gone an orientation towards collective efforts, stewardship, job security, promotion from within and a secure retirement; in have come individual achievement, risk-taking and an obsession with shareholder value. Yet these modern pay-for-performance systems, with their focus on narrow short-term measures, now seem to be badly broken. There are serious questions as to whether the current performance formula can continue. As John Plender put it: 'As long as incentives are at odds with ethical requirements, common decency will be a minority pursuit. Scandals are inevitable. And as the gap between bankers' pay and that of executives outside the financial system grows ever wider, business leaders lose moral authority, and the case for enlightened capitalism is devalued.'[1]

If this then is the current state of affairs, how can we develop an alternative approach that will inspire and engage employees and rebuild trust with customers and communities alike? We will consider through the rest of this chapter how leaders can rethink their approach, framed by the goal of creating a shared spirit of enterprise. We will start by exploring how we have come to think about what it takes to motivate people and how we must expand our outlook if we really want to reignite a spirit of shared enterprise.

The changing psychological contract

In an effective organization, the workplace becomes a thriving community infused with a commitment to quality, creativity, and compassion. By contrast, the symptoms of repressed spirit show up in low morale, fear, turf battles, high absenteeism and turnover and chronic health problems.

These problems occur in part because the 'psychological contract' between organizations and their employees is changing. In many instances, employees no longer feel they can bring their whole selves to work, because the 'self' they are being encouraged to express is one which is discordant with their deeper need to do a good job, to collaborate with others and to make a meaningful contribution. Let us briefly examine how this deeper psychological contract is being corroded. The intense focus on bonus arrangements that is found in many modern organizations can send the wrong message to individuals about 'what matters round here' and may actually 'demean and degrade' the intrinsic value of the work itself, according to Harvard philosopher Michael Sandel (2012). So it is easy to understand why some senior executives talk about feeling they have 'divided selves' – the person outside work living in tension with the person who does whatever it takes to compete and survive in the work environment. Unfortunately, a divided sense of who we are is not beneficial for our physical, mental or spiritual well-being. The recent surge in senior executive burnouts, for example, is testimony to the pressure that living a divided life can cause.

The extreme shift in the 1980s to a pay-and-performance focus initially created a self-preservation culture amongst leaders. They quickly came to understand the price of failure, as boards removed people who weren't delivering. Indeed, recent statements on corporate governance have argued that one of the key functions of the board and non-executive directors is to hold executives to account in this way and to exit them quickly if they are not delivering. Research by Dikolli, Mayew and Nanda at Duke University (2011) has shown that for each negative quarterly performance, the probability of CEO turnover increases by between 18 per cent and 36 per cent. According to research by Kaplan and Minton (2008), over 75 per cent of CEOs in 1998 would be gone by 2003. The job of the CEO had clearly become increasingly precarious. Meanwhile, senior executives came to understand what was expected of them, what it took to over-deliver and how to ratchet up their rewards. They had to stop being 'company men', start taking dispassionate decisions about their businesses and place a total emphasis on shareholder value – something that the City and Wall Street would easily understand and like. In the process, the connections between senior leaders, their organizations and the world beyond became broken. This emphasis on narrow, short-term performance clearly has direct implications for the kind of spirit that gets engendered in many organizations. People have learned a number of unwritten rules and, despite their better instincts, can see that true long-term commitment is not what is really valued. Of course it is never expressed in this way, and will instead be discussed as something like 'the need for agility'.

While this outlook is eroding spirit, it is also potentially directly damaging business performance. It is almost impossible to evaluate the performance of senior leaders over short time horizons, to disentangle what they have done from general market trends, to decide whether their contribution has not only moved the dial, but also made a lasting difference. Harvard Professor Mihir Desai observes (2012): 'Short-term goals do not allow us to differentiate between luck and skill.' This all adds to the argument that excessively high executive pay is not related to the real individual contribution that any human being (executive or anyone else) can make. The way such short-term goals are set and managed also corrodes trust – another important foundation of spirit within a business.

Evaluating the performance of people within organizations is not new. However, since the 1980s these reviews have moved from informal to formal to mechanistic to legalistic processes. As this has happened, discussions have shifted from ones based around honesty and judgement to ones founded on contract. Performance contracts embody the degree to which boards expect individual executives to be single-minded in getting the job done – almost whatever it takes – and go some way towards explaining how risk-taking is (unintentionally) encouraged by focusing executives on significant financial rewards for hitting narrow targets. This, in turn, reduces the intrinsic trust and motivation involved in just doing a good job. Indeed (as we shall see later) research has shown that these heavily incentivized packages reinforced through performance contracts can actually encourage people to cheat the system.

Many management performance contracts can also incentivize individuals to be 'less responsible' by increasing profits or share price in shorter time horizons than may be prudent, leading them to do things which may not lead to the long-term success of their organizations. This kind of asymmetric risk can be shown to be at the heart of a number of governance problems in business, because the remarkable wealth that is obtainable simply by influencing short-run outcomes can inevitably distort an executive's outlook (Desai, 2012). To some extent, this has already been acknowledged through the introduction of 'claw-back' provisions.

Yet the risk imbalance remains. As John Authors of the *Financial Times* recently highlighted, individuals can still earn life-changing amounts of money, risking the future of their organizations, without risking any of their own money. Setting narrow goals in combination with high incentives, along with a culture that pursues those goals to the exclusion of all else, can lead to individual managers adopting logical but unethical behaviours. We have seen these practices in areas ranging from banking to healthcare: hitting only those targets recorded in performance management reviews and ignoring other critically important activities (such as overall patient care); distorting recorded results simply to ensure targets are hit; or rigging market rates to guarantee profit performance and bonus payouts. Gaming the system may not be a wholly conscious activity but it is certainly far more widespread than we might have imagined. Gaming has turned an old truism on its head – from 'what gets measured gets managed' to 'what doesn't get measured doesn't matter at all'. We will return to this later in the chapter. This approach to performance management produces the opposite spirit to that which is intended. By offering very large rewards for over-delivering against very narrowly based, short-term results that are managed through a highly formal contractual relationship, organizations and their leaders are unintentionally creating a spirit of low commitment, low responsibility and low trust. What then, is the alternative? How can leaders connect with employees in a way which creates a more constructive force in the workplace and a deeper sense of meaning and fulfilment?

According to Deci and Ryan (2000), there are three components necessary to build a deeper kind of intrinsic motivation:

1 *Mastery* – the belief that we have the ability to influence important outcomes.

2 *Relatedness* – the experience of having satisfying and supportive social relations in the workplace.

3 *Autonomy* – the experience of acting with a sense of choice and self-determination.

These three factors combined can not only raise productivity, but also build creativity and improve happiness, collectively known as 'Self Determination Theory'. The research and analysis completed by Deci and Ryan show that if leaders want to reignite the spirit within their organizations, they need to ground their approach in the basic human need to develop our skills and capacities, to act of our own accord, and to connect to others and to our environment. Indeed we do our most creative work when we feel that we are acting according to our own will towards goals we find meaningful. Deci and Ryan found that rewards such as prizes and money were not only less effective than behavioural psychologists had long supposed, but under some circumstances could actually *diminish* people's feelings of engagement and motivation.

Given these insights into what truly motivates individuals to give of their best at work, it is perhaps surprising that a stronger connection has not been made between current pay and performance systems and the potentially corrosive impact they could be having on overall workplace motivation, health and stress. While there are undoubtedly many factors at play, employee engagement has been on a constant downward path for some time, hitting all-time lows in the United States in 2012/13. According to the annual Gallup Survey of employee motivation, over 70 per cent of all employees now claim to be disengaged or highly disengaged from their work.[2] Given what we now know about the potential impact of current approaches to pay and performance management, perhaps we should not be too surprised at this result?

In summary, while modern performance management may produce short-term results, it erodes the qualities that are essential for building an organization that can produce long-term sustainable results. The next dimension we will consider is the degree to which current leadership approaches foster collaboration and sharing and how leaders might enable employees to share more effectively in the workplace.

Individualism and insularity

Individualism has become the predominate wisdom of our time. This is manifested in public life and in our rights as consumers to absolute freedom of choice. Choice is a good thing. So good that it is almost regarded as an end in its own right, even when the choices on offer are of limited significance. Choice is manifest everywhere, from fashion to lifestyle, healthcare to schooling. Sitting on our own, with a Kindle or iPad, listening through our headphones to our own music selection, while reading our own curated selection of news stories, this individualized society has brought distinct (yet isolated) benefits.

This individualistic outlook on which much of life is now based has been swallowed whole and vigorously applied inside most organizations. With it, as we saw in Chapter 1, has come the rise of individual career plans, personalized and flexible benefits schemes, personal performance targets and individual bonuses. But has this individualism been a good thing for organizations, for their performance, for their relationship with employees, for their impact and contribution to the wider world? After all, aren't organizations by their very nature supposed to be collectives of people who come together to achieve more than they could ever under their own steam?

According to influential organization thinker and MIT Professor Fred Kofman, in his book *Conscious Business* (2006), a 'conscious business seeks to promote the intelligent pursuit of happiness in all its stakeholders. . . [to] produce sustainable exceptional performance through the solidarity of its community and dignity of each member'. So community in business clearly does matter, but its place has been usurped to a large extent by our obsession with the individual.

James Gorman, who became CEO at International Bank Morgan Stanley shortly after the 2008 crash, thinks we are in need of a rethink on the culture in his industry. He observes: 'We need to change the perception that it's the individual that's the hero.'[3] Such hero cultures are, however, deeply engrained in many companies, with individually tailored pay and performance systems cascaded to every level of management reinforcing, in the words of Professor Kofman, 'a level of individualism which has created much of the unintended dysfunctional, toxic siloed working and interdepartmental conflict which are regrettably common in many organizations today'.

Executive pay is perhaps more than any other factor exerting a distorting influence on leadership thinking and is contributing to a more general disconnection between business and society. Respected management thinker Sumantra Goshal (2005) has argued that such individual financial incentives have become the 'enemy of virtue' by attracting the 'self-centred narcissist' to the executive ranks. Goshal's view is that this approach undermines the sort of social capital that corporations should be encouraging amongst their employees: the motive to reciprocate, the desire for social approval and to work on intrinsically rewarding tasks. John Doerr, an outspoken Silicon Valley venture capitalist puts this even more colourfully, making a clear distinction between: 'Mercenary managers motivated by the lust for making money, and purpose-driven managers driven by the desire to make meaning.'[4] This is a view supported by commentators and academics alike, as Jay Lorche the American academic observed: 'Pay systems have been central to a radical shift that has taken place in the nature of organizations over the past 25 years, their purpose and the way we regard them.'[5]

The sense of individualism is reinforced when senior leaders are regarded by many as self-seeking individuals, chasing big bonuses and maximizing personal gain from an economic system with a growing gap between winners and losers. It seems to many that the inexorable rise in top pay is out of control, out of sync with the rest of society and out of line with any objective sense of fairness.

As we saw in Chapter 1, the gap between those at the top of the 'hourglass' and those at the bottom has been accentuated as a disproportionate slice of the pie has been taken by a small number of leaders at the top of business, while those on the frontline have seen their pay levels stall. It is creating barriers in the workplace and reducing any sense of solidarity or feeling that 'we are all in this together'. This cannot by any objective standard be good for cohesion, morale or motivation, particularly where everyone is expected to work hard but a minority are getting handsomely (and disproportionately?) rewarded for their efforts. Without the sense that we all contribute and we all have a stake in the outcomes, there is a growing risk that the fabric of business and society will start to come apart at the seams. At its worst this approach also produces organizations that display an increasing level of insularity, suffering a kind of corporate myopia.

The new connected era therefore presents fresh dilemmas for leaders. How can we build a focus on long-term performance without letting our grip on today's deliverables slip? How can we encourage more collective endeavour without sacrificing personal ownership? How can we bring to life our network of obligations while keeping things simple, clear and transparent? Developing an alternative approach to pay, measurement and motivation will not be a simple proposition.

However, the tide is beginning to turn. We will examine one approach, which is attracting growing interest, and demonstrates the difference between work environments which are structured around atomized and individualistic relationships to one which is built around sharing; the employee ownership model. This approach has proved to be successful in several different countries around the world. It creates a direct and tangible connection between employees and the organization in terms of share ownership. However, it is also apparent that the decision to distribute ownership to employees is but one reflection of a desire by these organizations to ensure employees have a voice in the business's direction and are seen to play a critical role in sharing in the long-term success of the enterprise.

Employee ownership

As we discussed earlier, one of the biggest disconnects between leaders and their people is diverging pay levels and fragmenting workforces. In their book *The Citizens Share* (2013) Blasi *et al* set out a bold proposition. Rather than a small percentage of people at the top having their incomes tied to the business through generous share programmes, could progressive leaders open up that opportunity of company ownership to all of their workforce? The authors' view is that this route ensures that everyone reaps the rewards of economic growth by owning a piece of the firms that employs them. It is an approach that is already popular in the technology sector where many companies offer this kind of plan such as Google and Microsoft. Christopher Matthews noted in *Time* that this kind of broad-based capitalism presents a route for leaders to reconnect everyone in an organization ensuring that everyone has the opportunity to participate.[6] It may well be an idea whose time has come as there are a growing number of firms across the globe that are demonstrating that this can be highly successful for all parties. However, there are some organizations that have taken the idea of employee ownership and associated workplace democracy to a different level. We will explore some of these cases now.

CASE STUDY Publix – USA

The grocer Publix is the largest employee-owned firm in the United States with $27.5 billion in sales and an employee-owned fund controlling 80 per cent of the company. *Forbes* journalist Brian Solomon describes Publix as a Walmart slayer, as it is one of the few retailers that have been able to withstand the power and might of the retail behemoth.[7] Publix is noted for its high standards of customer care and for developing its people from the shop floor. Its president is Todd Jones, who started out as a bagger 33 years ago. Those who may think that employee ownership is only about treating employees well should note that Publix is the most profitable retailer in the United States, with better margins than Walmart, Kroger and Whole Foods. All employees with more than a year's service and 1,000 work hours receive an additional 8.5 per cent of their total pay in the form of Publix stock. According to Publix, a store manager who has worked at the company for 20 years and earns $100,000 would typically have around $300,000 in stock and another $30,000 in dividends. What is also significant about Publix is that the route to those levels of reward are completely transparent. Publix almost exclusively promotes from within and every store displays advancement charts showing the path each employee can take to become a manager. According to *Forbes'* Brian Solomon: '58,000 of Publix's 159,000 employees have officially registered their interest in career advancement.'[8] It is this combination of ownership of a real stake in the business with opportunity and a sense of inclusion which generates such high levels of commitment. Publix now has over 1,000 stores and works through these to partner with local communities to support education initiatives in pre-school children. As a consequence, the company is ranked number one in the United States by the Centre for Corporate Citizenship in Boston. However, Publix believes that it is the way employee ownership helps them to engage with their people and the impact that this has which is most important. Publix grants shares of a store-specific bonus pool every 13 weeks. The exact amount varies, but typically 20 per cent of quarterly profits go into that larger pool; 20 per cent of the pool is then paid to the store's employees. When competition opens up across the street and sales are impacted, employees are impacted. This provides a huge point of social connection for everyone within the organization. As a result collaboration is highly valued and Publix teams communicate to get projects accomplished and to learn what is working well in other stores.

CASE STUDY   The John Lewis Partnership – UK

In the United Kingdom, employee-owned firms already contribute more than £30 billion each year to the UK economy, equating to approximately 4 per cent of GDP and this is growing at 10 per cent per year. The UK retailer John Lewis Partnership has pioneered the employee ownership model since 1929 and now has 91,000 partners who all have a say in how the Partnership is run, as well as an equal percentage share in the profits. The organization is brought together not only by its pay structures but also because all are given a voice in running the firm, which is central to the principles of co-ownership. John Lewis's ownership structure was established by John Spedan Lewis, whose father founded the business in 1864. He signed away his ownership rights in 1929 to allow future generations of employees to take forward his 'experiment in industrial democracy'. His ideas are set out in the company's constitution which has at its heart the idea of establishing a 'better form of business'. The constitution states that 'the happiness of its members' is the Partnership's ultimate purpose, recognizing that such happiness depends on having a satisfying job in a successful business. It establishes a system of 'rights and responsibilities', which places on all Partners 'the obligation to improve our business in the knowledge that we share the rewards of success'. The Constitution defines mechanisms to provide for the management of the Partnership, with checks and balances to ensure accountability, transparency and honesty. It established the representation of the co-owners on the Partnership Board through the election of Partners as Directors (Elected Directors) and it also determines the role of the Partners' Counsellor.[9]

According to Zoe Wood, retail correspondent for the *Guardian*: 'Partners share in the benefits and profits of a business that puts them first.'[10] John Lewis's constitution also lists a formal mission to maximize the happiness of its staff. The power structure involves a staff council – for ideas and complaints to filter up to the board – and a weekly magazine where staff can air their views about policies and management, anonymously if they choose. According to Wood: 'staff earn the same as shopworkers at rival chains – but the year-end bonus is a significant top-up. Its directors, on the other hand, are paid substantially less than their boardroom counterparts at businesses such as retail chain Tesco'. According to Tracey Killen, Director of Personnel at the John Lewis Partnership: 'The great strength of the partnership's model is that employees have a real stake in the business. . . co-ownership allows the partnership to take a long-term view, because we do not have to answer to external shareholders who are usually seeking quick returns.'[11]

CASE STUDY   Eroski – Spain

The employee ownership model is also thriving in the Spanish retail sector, where Eroski is the biggest unit within Spain's Mondragon cooperative group and the world's largest worker cooperative. It employs 80,000 people in Spain and around the world. Based out of the Basque region, they have survived the severe recession in Spain partially by being more flexible and by sticking together. This connection between leaders and employees is referred to as a spirit of solidarity. When times are bad, the workers decide to cut wage costs themselves and as owners of the company they also forsake dividends. Eroski has recently agreed another round of wage reductions in which workers' incomes will drop by 5–10 per cent. But unlike other companies, where wages are cut while executive pay soars, leaders at Eroski are taking the biggest cuts. Indeed, pay structures at Eroski are tied to the ideals of co-ownership; this is everyone's company and it means that senior leaders have their pay capped at eight times the lowest-paid worker.

Mondragon has not been immune to the economic downturn and austerity in Spain and has had to make closures at one of its manufacturing units Fagor. However, its exports have surged by 10 per cent to €4 billion in 2011/12. Eroski's story highlights that while employee ownership does not remove people's normal anxieties in tough economic times, it does promote a sense that everyone is in it together with a connected spirit throughout the enterprise. One of the things that has made Eroski and its parent company unique is that, as we set out in Chapter 1, it has a clear sense of purpose based on humanistic principles founded on Catholic Social Teaching and values.

These are based around *cooperation*, where everyone acts as owners and protagonists; *participation*, which means that everyone is involved in making key decisions and heightens a sense of ownership across the organization; *social responsibility*, which it achieves by means of the distribution of wealth to all employees based on a principle of solidarity; and *innovation*, focusing on constant renewal in all areas. Once again this structure is supported by very high levels of employee participation through groups called *challas* (chat groups) made up of about 30 people at a time. These forums get to discuss issues that will then be voted upon at the general assembly. The participation rate ranges from 75 per cent to 95 per cent, which is incredibly high by any standard. However, at the heart of Mondragon's approach to engagement lies a commitment to employee education, which starts with all employees but is also spread to members of the community and other partners. Mondragon undertakes this level of educational commitment so that everyone in their organization understands the underlying ethos of the organization and can therefore collaborate more effectively with each other. It enables everyone to connect at a meaningful and long-term level rather than just in the completion of today's tasks. What is clear is that the Mondragon philosophy about business permeates into a whole way of life.

CASE STUDY Arup – UK

In 1946, engineer Ove Arup set up a consulting engineering business in London, with businesses operating across Europe, North America, Africa, Australasia and South East Asia. Arup has grown to become the firm behind some of the world's most iconic and environmentally sustainable buildings, from the Sydney Opera House to London's 'Gherkin' tower. The business is distinctive for many reasons. At the heart of much of this is its guiding philosophy and the way it has been established as a trust for the benefit of its employees and their dependents, with all employees receiving a share of the profits on an annual basis. The organization believes that the combination of this core philosophy or purpose and its ownership structure allows it to have a strong convictions about the projects that it undertakes, which sit alongside their other commitments to clients and commercial objectives. They believe that the result is a business that is clear-sighted about its priorities and its role in society. Central to its guiding philosophy is a sense that what it does is connected to society and the wider world at every level. In the words of the Arup founder in 1970: 'our lives are inextricably mixed up with those of our fellow human beings... there can be no real happiness in isolation'. Arup recognized that the firm's strength lies in its distinctive values, independent ownership and genuine quality and integrity in all its dealings with clients and other stakeholders. This has led the firm to employ a healthy and eclectic mix of talented people with very different perspectives from many cultures. In 2011, following a period of rapid international growth, Arup gave a key speech which sought to reignite employee commitment and passion for the company's distinctive values – the focus of this speech was 'connection'.

These case study examples highlight the value of employees being connected to the organization and to each other. They illustrate how sharing not only in the rewards but in information and decision-making can create a real sense of collective ownership not only for addressing the immediate challenges that the business is facing but also for its longer-term purpose. This cohesion and high level of employee engagement is in stark contrast with more conventional organizations that rely on narrow financial incentives and superficial efforts to engage with their employees. While creating such a sharing environment clearly represents a significant commitment from the leaders within a business, it could be offset against the short-term engagement agendas that undoubtedly cost many organizations a huge amount but have such limited results. This section also highlights that when people feel bound together they are ready to accept and share hardships, as well as looking to share in the benefits when they arise.

Having considered how leaders can foster a real spirit and energy through giving employees a great share in the business, we will now consider how this renewed energy can be more effectively focused on the outputs of the enterprise.

Enterprise

Most enterprises are managed for mediocrity, unable to sustain performance over the long term and even less able to manage difficult transformations.

(Scott Keller and Colin Price in *Beyond Performance*, 2011)

This section will look at two important ways in which leaders need to rethink their approach to enterprise: how they define their enterprise's areas of focus and how they set the timescales over which the work of their enterprise is measured. Both of these factors are critical in determining how leaders create a shared spirit around their business and achieve long-term sustainable growth.

Bad profits

We saw in the previous chapter how most organizations are managing the performance of individuals in a narrow and short-term way. This is equally true of the whole enterprise. Few leaders differentiate between shareholder return measured only against financial criteria and the ability of an organization to renew itself and to sustain exceptional performance over time. Such a narrow focus can have disastrous effects on the enterprise, leaving what Fred Reichheld and Rob Markey (2011) described as 'brand liabilities'. This occurs where a business is making profits while leaving customers disgruntled, where profits are creating liabilities which will have to be repaid one day.

As Reichheld and Markey observed:

> Whenever a customer feels misled, mistreated, ignored or coerced, then profits from that customer are bad. Bad profits come from unfair or misleading pricing. Bad profits arise when companies save money by delivering a poor customer experience. Bad profits are about extracting value from customers, not creating value. When sales reps push overpriced or inappropriate products onto trusting customers, the reps are generating bad profits. When complex pricing schemes dupe customers into paying more than necessary to meet their needs, those pricing schemes are contributing to bad profits.

Based on this analysis leaders would be well advised not to pay out bonuses if they believe they are being achieved in a 'non-sustainable' manner. Yet this has rarely occurred, at least until recently. This is partly because leaders are often poorly equipped to distinguish between what is and isn't sustainable, as this requires an ability to take a much longer view and to better understand the external impact of an organization's actions.

However, Scott Keller and Colin Price have made an attempt to capture a broader and deeper base for understanding sustainable performance, through the concept of 'organizational health'. They have researched over 500 companies and 2,000 leaders to demonstrate that robust organizational health can ensure a business is 2.2 times more likely to produce better than market average earnings before interest, tax and depreciation (EBITDA), than a business managed purely in the traditional way.

Unilever's CEO Paul Polman has also sought to encourage other leaders to reconnect what they do with the world around them by using a broader measurement framework. Polman recently discussed his proposals at the World Economic Forum and observed:

> We remain convinced that businesses which address both the direct concerns of citizens and the needs of the environment will prosper over the long term. This thinking lies at the heart of the Unilever Sustainable Living Plan. As the thinking becomes embedded in our business, there is increasing evidence that it is accelerating our growth in ways that contribute to positive change in people's lives.'[12]

Two examples of putting this thinking into practice can also be found in the work of the German organization Puma and in the emergent approach of 'B Corporations' in the United States.

CASE STUDY   Puma – Germany

Puma has taken these ideals and perhaps gone further than any other commercial organization to evaluate what it does as an enterprise and the impact this has. In 2011, Puma published their first environmental profit and loss (EP&L) account, which connects the business with all its environmental, social and economic impacts – including fair wages, working conditions, job creation and tax contributions. Puma's aim is to give a true picture of the cost of producing its goods in terms of the natural resources used and the environmental impacts of its operations, from raw materials through to the retail transaction. This approach offers a real insight into the environmental consequences of commercial decisions and at the same time highlights the potential commercial consequences of natural resource shortages. Puma believe that without measuring them, wider impacts cannot be managed or reduced. Their approach offers a real insight into the environmental consequences of commercial decisions and highlights the potential commercial consequences of the environmental realities unfolding around the world. Jochen Zeitz, Executive Chairman of Puma concluded: 'The approach we have taken has been indispensible for us to realize the immense value of nature's services that are currently being taken for granted but without which companies could not sustain themselves.'[13] The groundbreaking Puma approach gives us a sense of what understanding the full impact of our business activities really involves and presents a clear insight into how leaders can help employees, suppliers and customers connect in a different way with the business.

CASE STUDY   B Corporations – USA

A different but equally radical approach is offered by the US-based
'Benefit Corporation' (B Corporations) movement, which is aiming to
reconnect the meaning of success in business to success in society. This
sector is comprised of organizations that are purpose-driven and create
benefit for all stakeholders, not just shareholders. With over 900 companies
in over 60 countries now registered as a 'B Corporation', this growing idea is
encouraging all companies to compete not just to be the best in the world, but
also to *be* the best for the world. This powerful connection enshrines wider
stakeholder consideration in the articles of incorporation and is perhaps the
most innovative element of the B Corporation model. While this may be a
response to a particular set of US legislative challenges, there is no doubting
that it is a movement that is catching people's imagination. The approach is
designed to attract more 'patient' capital and has led to the establishment of a
separate investment rating method based on input from big investment houses,
including Goldman Sachs and J P Morgan Chase. B Corporations have provided
an effective umbrella for connecting the purpose and measures of some
leading companies in the US to a broader set of targets than narrowly defined
shareholder returns. The challenge for leaders is how they translate the energy
that is clearly released by people involved in the B Corporation movement into
mainstream corporations, which are all ultimately responsible for creating the
common good.

A marathon not a sprint

Alongside the need to develop a deeper and broader focus on the true purpose of our organizations, leaders can also look to make better connections
with employees, customers, suppliers and shareholders when they frame
their enterprise's aims as a marathon and not a sprint.

Interestingly, the extreme focus on short-term performance was initially
enabled quite mundanely through the introduction of the humble computer
spreadsheet in 1979. The spreadsheet turned what had previously taken 20
hours of work previously into a 20-minute exercise. It revolutionized the
way numbers were to influence business and created a new breed of 'analysts'. These analysts no longer needed to complete long apprenticeships or

to talk to people on the frontline to understand how the job got done or the issues that were involved. With all the information they apparently needed at their fingertips, they could remain detached and were soon supporting bankers to tell boards and CEOs how they could run their businesses to deliver better returns on their investments.

Alongside the new tools that appeared in the early 1980s, businesses also adopted a powerful new ethos. Harvard Professor Clay Christensen (2013) suggests that this approach has now been raised to the level of a 'New Seminary of Finance' where the high priests are the business schools, private equity partners and investment managers, who have taught us to measure goodness as the maximization of profit over short timeframes.

These metrics generate an intense focus on quarterly capitalism. As a result, company leaders become obsessed with short-term delivery and almost inevitably lose their connection with wider and longer-term concerns.

In an article in the *Harvard Business Review* in 2014, Dominic Barton (Global MD, McKinsey) and Mark Wiseman (President of the Canada Pension Plan Investment Board) argue this focus is counter-productive, observing that: 'companies are less able to invest and build value for the long term, undermining broad economic growth and lowering returns on investment for savers'. They, like Christensen, identify the main source of the problem as 'the continuing pressure on public companies from financial markets to maximize short term results'. Early in 2013, McKinsey and the Canada Pension Plan Investment Board (CPPIB) conducted a survey of more than 1,000 board members and C-suite executives around the world to assess their progress in taking a longer-term approach to running their companies. The results were stark:

- 63 per cent said the pressure to generate strong short-term results had increased over the previous five years.
- 79 per cent felt especially pressured to demonstrate strong financial performance over a period of just two years or less.
- 44 per cent said they use a time horizon of less than three years in setting strategy while 73 per cent said they should use a time horizon of more than three years.
- 86 per cent declared that using a longer time horizon to make business decisions would positively affect corporate performance in a number of ways, including strengthening financial returns and increasing innovation.

- 46 per cent of respondents said that the pressure to deliver strong short-term financial performance stemmed from their boards who expected their companies to generate greater earnings in the near term. As for those board members, they made it clear that they were often just channelling increased short-term pressures from investors, including institutional shareholders.

The implications for current practices of leadership are clear. We are spending too much time and effort measuring the wrong things and looking for results over too short a timeframe to such an extent that we are not only destroying true value over the longterm, but also failing to adequately consider the consequences of this performance in anything other than the narrowest financial terms.

Colin Price, author and leader of McKinsey's worldwide organization practice, estimates that on average at least 40 per cent of leadership time is spent on driving day-to-day numbers and ensuring things get executed 'feeding the beast', leaving insufficient time to focus on issues of renewal and regeneration.[14] The problem with the current metrics is that they directly impact issues like the development of people or expenditure on disruptive innovation, which only pay off in 5 to 10 years, whereas efficiency improvements are designed to pay off in one to two years and create greater capital returns.

Wise investment is contingent on having measures which connect the focus of leaders in organizations with the wider concerns of society and ensure that the performance of the company is likely to be successful over the longterm only if leaders are contributing to the common good. The tide may at last be starting to turn in the right direction. People in some surprising places are making connections between a broader set of long-term measures and sustainable and successful business performance. In a letter to investors, by the Chairman of the extraordinarily powerful Blackrock Investment management company, Larry Fink said: 'Companies that Blackrock invests in should be primarily focused on achieving sustainable returns over the long term, and a long-term strategy for growth was the most important thing needed for Corporate Governance.'[15]

The shift from narrowly defined short-term performance criteria to a broader-based outlook that doesn't reward the production of bad or easy profits over long-term organizational health is a slow process and requires the foresight shown by leaders like those at Puma or Unilever to make a start, to fully understand their impact and to get everyone in their organization thinking about how their companies can impact the common good.

Conclusion

Throughout this chapter we have considered how current approaches leading major enterprises have become overly narrow and short-term-focused. We have reflected on the way this approach to management has unconsciously served to sever many of the ties that inspire and bind employees together. We have suggested that an alternative model is available for leaders who wish to create a connected enterprise, which creates a strong spirit in a firm by considering the intrinsic motivation people get from doing good work and having a sense of autonomy. We also considered how this could be supported in working practices. We then looked at how people could be brought together by having both shared goals and a shared and transparent way of sharing rewards. Finally we looked at the way we think about the nature of the organization and the importance of developing a more holistic approach to measuring an enterprise's activity.

However, it is only as these three dimensions of spirit, sharing and enterprise come together that we can start to see the potential for a different dynamic in the way we run our organizations, where everyone feels like they are in it together. In the chapters that follow we will consider how this new-found spirit of shared enterprise can make a huge difference in our communities, with our customers and in how the organization creates a different future for itself. Before moving on to this, let us consider some practical steps that leaders can take to create a shared spirit of enterprise.

Eight steps to reconnected leadership

Step 4 – reconnecting through shared enterprise: Leadership actions

1 *Create a long-term focus.* Link all discussions on targets to the work on purpose, set out in Chapter 1. Ensure that each area of measurement links directly back to one of the five principles of a purpose-driven business. However, while these specific measures can be used as milestones to evaluate progress, they should not be used in a mechanistic or box-ticking way.

   The board's non-executive committees should retain the right to final evaluation of performance based on a wider assessment of company progress the degree to which the company is contributing to the common good and promoting the dignity of individuals. This movement away from performance contracts to an evaluating overall progress will be a major step for boards and senior leadership teams.

Remove and replace all short-term incentive programmes with a longer-term approach (Recent research by Patterson Associates, a US remuneration specialist, has observed that a shift is already starting to take place, and fund manager Fidelity is one of the key movers pushing for a move to long-term incentives, saying that it would vote against any organization that is not making this move.[16])

Such long-term bonus payments should be held by the company in shares for a minimum period of a decade. This would allow the full consequences of earlier leadership decisions to materialize and impact not only on the value of rewards but also change the outlook of leaders about the decisions they make.

2 *Create shared ownership.* Performance reviews should focus on whether an individual has delivered their commitments and obligations, which in turn would determine whether an individual could participate in a company-wide shared profit scheme. However, the quantum of investment in the Share Trust should be determined by the performance of the whole organization, reinforcing the sense of interdependence in the company and with other key partners, with little or no impact on the level of bonus an individual can earn. For such a system to generate honest efforts and eliminate coasting by some people, the performance reviews need to be highly transparent.

3 *Introduce share trusts.* ALL employees should have a meaningful stake in the long-term success of the company. This is essential if we are to create networks of shared obligations, ownership and enterprise.

4 *Create inclusive environments.* Establish ratios for differentials between senior leaders and frontline employees. These should be published with a clear rationale and voted upon at the AGM. Institutions responsible for corporate governance should set expectations for what best-practice ratios look like, with organizations required to 'comply or explain' (why they exceeded such guidance).

---

1 *Financial Times*, 10 June 2014
2 State of the American workplace, Report, Gallup, 2013
3 Michael J Moore, Bloomberg News, November 2010; and *Balancing Me and We: Why we must change our work culture*, The Work Foundation, January 2013

4 Great companies are led by missionaries, not mercenaries, speech by John Doerr (Partner at Kleiner Perkins Caufield & Byers) at Wharton Business School, March 2000

5 Jay Lorche and Rakesh Khurana, Towards a new paradigm for executive compensation, Harvard Law School Forum on Corporate Governance and Financial Regulation, May 2010

6 Christopher Matthews, Can employee owned companies reboot the economy? *Time* Magazine, November 2013

7 Brian Solomon, The Wal-Mart slayer, *Forbes* Magazine, August 2013

8 *ibid.*

9 John Lewis Partnership, Constitution, updated version, January 2014

10 Zoe Wood, The John Lewis Model, and what others could learn from it, *The Guardian*, January 2012

11 Tracey Killen, interview in *Management Today* Magazine, 2007

12 Paul Polman, Volatility and uncertainty, the new normal, www.unilever.com, April 2013

13 Jochen Zeitz, speech at The Princes Accounting for Sustainability Project, 15 December 2011

14 Colin Price, The principles of organisational renewal, interview on YouTube, January 2011

15 *Wall Street Journal*, 21 March 2014

16 Remuneration Report, Patterson Associates, 23 February 2014

07

Step 5: Connecting with the wider world

> *You cannot wake a person who is pretending to be asleep.* **(SUDANESE PROVERB)**

Introduction

Our world is now more interlinked and interdependent than at any time yet as we have discussed leaders remain relatively narrow in their outlook. This chapter will explore how large corporations can move beyond old models of corporate social responsibility to channel their core business activities in ways which improve the common good while delivering sustainable profitability.

As we have seen, many organizations try to do good, or to compensate for any negative impact of their core business activity, by investing a percentage of profits in corporate social responsibility programmes. These activities started out in well-intentioned ways but are now met with growing cynicism. According to a report by The Kellogg Institute at Northwest University in Boston massachusetts (Lys *et al*, 2013), such efforts may be wasted as companies who engage in corporate social responsibility (CSR) do not perform any better than those who do not. However, the report also wryly notes that financial analysts can often give companies who are spending more on CSR a higher stock rating, in the belief that businesses must be performing well to justify using some of its profits being used in this kind of way: 'CSR is what rich companies *do*.' Such cynicism is perhaps useful in highlighting the flawed nature of the whole corporate social responsibility movement and demonstrates that most companies still inhabit a divided universe in which there is core business activity and then a separate team working on CSR pledges.

Needless to say, very few of the initiatives launched under the CSR banner, no matter how laudable, appear to make much of a long-term impact to sustainability. The Sudanese folk story at the introduction to this chapter relates to our present position because it nicely captures the sense that despite our knowing that there are far bigger issues that lie before us in terms of the environment or social cohesion, as business leaders we have thus far chosen to pretend that they do not hear or understand them. Yet as we have discussed in earlier chapters, this is only because we have accepted that we can continue to live a divided life. Once we see our purpose and the purpose of our business as being about serving the common good, then we can begin a process of thinking differently about the issues.

We need to start by rethinking how we understand these challenges. For example, if we consider that the world's population will grow from 6 to 9 billion by 2050 and that, alongside this, consumption per head is forecast to double, we will see demands on the planet going up three-fold, to unsustainable levels. Throughout this chapter we will therefore reflect on the interconnected nature of business, through its supply chains, through its relationship with customers and through its presence in the community and will consider how reconnected leaders can help to create better and more sustainable solutions to the difficult challenges which lie ahead. Doing so will challenge leaders to reinvent how they grow in a world of finite resource.

FIGURE 7.1 Reconnected leadership model: Connecting with the wider world

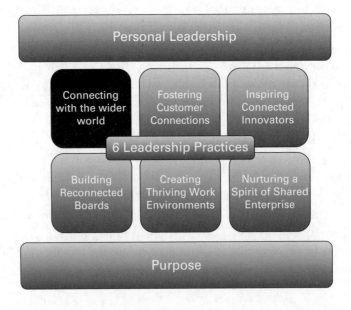

Leaders thinking differently

To arrive at a different answer we need to reconsider what we mean by sustainability and whose responsibility it is. The organic food movement provides an interesting example of what we would like to think of as a big success in the fight to reduce pesticide in food production. It has been in operation for over 40 years and has worked tirelessly to educate consumers, yet today less than 1 per cent of all global food consumption is 'organic'. The approach is laudable but it is not having a big enough impact on results in anything like the timescales that are needed. It highlights that simply relying on consumers to change their habits is not going to move us to where we need to be from an ecological sustainability perspective.

If consumers cannot produce the answers we need on their own, then governmental action may be part of the answer, but the leaders of the world's biggest corporations will have to work collaboratively with governments if any real progress is going to be made, particularly given so much of life is now enabled or protected by large corporations. This is therefore a leadership issue, not for consumers or consumer groups, but for the companies who produce our products and for the retailers who sell them to us.

Analysis by the World Wide Fund for Nature (WWF) shows that there are just 500 companies that control 70 per cent of the key commodity sales in the world. The list of key commodities covers everyday products like sugar, wood, cocoa, palm oil, soya beans and cotton. In fact the top 100 companies alone control 25 per cent of the trade. James Clay, who is responsible for what WWF describes as their business transformation agenda, argues that the leaders of these 100 organizations could change the world if they were prepared to think about how the whole of their supply chain is working.[1] This is what we described in Step 1 as being within the sphere of developing a purpose in which a company is both a 'Guardian for Future Generations and a Good Citizen'. It also requires leaders to become great collaborators across their industry sector, working directly with competitors in roundtable settings to come up with solutions that are right for people and planet. This requires leaders who are capable of looking at the agenda in a way which is bigger than their own firm and acting in the interest of the common good. In doing so leaders, according to WWF's James Clarke, will need to treat certain issues as being 'pre-competitive'.[2] Despite their ground-breaking thinking the WWF has had to run the gauntlet of other NGOs, which say that the partnerships it has struck with industry to get involved in finding lasting solutions are far too cosy. Nonetheless, its approach to facilitating dialogue with industry presents a glimpse of what a group of reconnected leaders can do.

Changing the way we manage production

Globally, people are using about 25 per cent more natural resources than the planet can replace. As we saw in Chapter 1, although advances in technology have helped people to produce things more efficiently, the benefits have been swamped by ever-higher levels of consumption by affluent western economies and the growing middle classes in the developing world. Given the challenges we face, we have entered an era in which leaders must rethink the way things are made. How we can all do more with less will depend on leaders making radical connections between the resources they use, the way they operate, and the wider world. In the following case studies we will see how leaders are bringing innovative thinking to redefine how things are made.

CASE STUDY Mars

One example of an organization that is thinking about their sustainability in a truly long-term way is Mars Incorporated. They want to stay in the chocolate business, not just for the next decade but for as long as possible. However, they have realized that current cocoa production methods are less than efficient, with only 25 per cent of cocoa plantations producing over 70 per cent of the cocoa yield. They have therefore begun a long-term investigation into cocoa DNA to identify which factors are influencing yield. The findings of the research study are being published online so that as many researchers or companies as possible can start the process of looking at the problem and hopefully help to identify a solution to the cocoa yield problem. If they get this right, Mars will be in a position to increase yields to meet forecast increases in demand without having to increase the amount of land space that cocoa production requires – land that should either be preserved as natural habitat or used for other domestic crop production.

CASE STUDY DyeCoo, IKEA and Nike

Actively setting out to find innovative solutions requires planning, some risk and long-term commitment. By 2025 there will be a further 1 billion people on the planet, at which rate – as we have discussed – the growth of the earth's resources may struggle to support everyone's basic requirements for food, water and heating. IKEA's leaders recognized that it needed to accelerate both the rate of innovation and the level of impact it was having on environmental matters so it created a separate innovative venture capital arm called 'GreenTech'. Its remit was to search the globe to find cutting-edge ideas and help them scale up more quickly through the use of its IKEA venture-funding arm. Managed like any other business investment stream, GreenTech has specific areas of focus, from water usage to energy efficiency to green home design.

The textile industry is one of the largest consumers of water and most of the world's textile suppliers are located in Asia. The scale of the industry's activity in the region can put pressure on the availability of clean water and contribute to environmental pollution in the discharges from manufacturing processes. IKEA identified an organization called DyeCoo, based in the Netherlands, which had invented a process to remove the use of water in the dyeing process and eliminate the risk of effluent discharge, a known environmental hazard. IKEA's investment was in partnership with Nike, one of the largest garment manufacturers in the world, with a significant number of plants in Asia. Through this partnership, IKEA is helping to speed up the development and availability of the technology. Nike's Vice President of Sustainable Business and Innovation, Hannah Jones, said IKEA's role in DyeCoo textile systems represented 'an exciting step in cross-industry collaboration. A key objective is to scale the technology to benefit consumers, business and the environment [through the] accelerated development of more sustainable materials and manufacturing processes.'[3] What is perhaps most significant about this work is that it is not a one-off, but forms part of a coherent strategy to use innovation and partnership, often with small start-up organizations. It is connecting IKEA at multiple levels to issues in the environment and, in the process, to small start-ups and business collaborators in other sectors like NIKE who share similar environmental ambitions. It demonstrates that these extended connections can be a very powerful point of leverage for the benefit of the organization and for wider society at the same time.

Changing the way we manage people in global supply chains

We saw in Chapter 1 how the risks associated with managing supply chains have escalated as operations have been outsourced and off-shored to developing parts of the world. The scope for people being exploited remains high, with incredibly poor worker conditions, wages and rights being a feature of many less developed countries. While the State has a duty to ensure human rights are protected, this becomes an almost impossible task if corporations do not also respect and actively participate in the application of these rights. Leaders can ignore these issues or they can connect and engage in them and by doing so, can take a lead in respecting the dignity of individuals and transforming the conditions of work and ordinary lives of people everywhere. In the following case studies we will see how leaders have made such deeper connections count.

CASE STUDY IKEA

IKEA provides another example of leadership team starting to rethink their businesses in a more connected way. IKEA is not perfect and has been heavily criticized in Sweden for its secretive and byzantine tax practices. But there is still much that can be learned about the way in which IKEA's leaders are making valuable connections with challenges facing the communities in which they operate, as we shall see in the following example.

Iqbal Masih was born in 1983 in Muridke, a small, rural village outside Lahore in Pakistan. At the age of four, he was sold into bonded labour for 600 rupees ($12) by his family. The region is one of the biggest handmade carpet-making areas in the world and Iqbal had been sold to a local carpet weaver and tied to a loom and forced to work 14-hour days in order to repay that original debt. Iqbal's work as a small boy involved tying knots in the rugs. The small hands of children were well-suited to this work and as a result the carpet factory owners kept the boys and girls in a malnourished state so that they wouldn't outgrow their work. Mistakes were costly for the carpet owners and children were beaten if errors occurred. Iqbal escaped on one occasion, but was captured and tortured by the owners. Eventually, he was freed by the Bonded Labour Liberation Front of Pakistan (BLLFP). The hideous labour conditions and practices of his factory had left him with a tiny frame and stature, standing less than 4ft tall and weighing less than 60lbs. Yet, with the support of BLLFP, Iqbal started campaigning against forced labour – first in Pakistan, then England and then the United States – and his efforts helped to free hundreds of children from forced labour. Sadly at the age of 12, on a visit back home, he was shot and killed. This was 1995 and though his murder remains officially unsolved to this day, many believe he was killed for his work as activist by the 'Business Mafia' who controlled the Pakistan carpet industry. When IKEA discovered that the factory at which Iqbal was once enslaved was one of its suppliers, it immediately took action. First, it did something that lots of organizations don't do – it looked internally at its own supply chain and began addressing the problem from within, taking all steps necessary to ensure that an IKEA product would never again be created by manufacturers that exploited children. IKEA then solidified a commitment to eradicate the problem at its root. The company partnered with UNICEF to create a programme to help prevent child labour by changing the conditions that led to child labour in the first place, namely: poverty, hunger, and illiteracy. Today, this same programme serves more than 500 villages in India's 'carpet belt', an area with a population in excess of 1.3 million. IKEA has further helped to establish self-help groups for women to create savings of their own and providing them with access to micro-loans, so that tragedies like Iqbal's never happen again. Acknowledging that poverty was often the result of the onset of illness, IKEA and UNICEF also worked with the World Health Organization to establish a five-year vaccination programme in the region, vaccinating almost 300,000 women and children from 3,000 villages in the period between 2002 and 2007.

The use of child labour is a huge global issue and the IKEA initiative only scratches the surface. However, it serves to demonstrate the significant influence that major corporations can have by focusing on core supply chain activities, as opposed to things that are outside their remit. It enables the leaders within an organization to start to directly make a difference beyond the immediate boundaries of their organization and by making a connection helps leaders to understand that issues of poverty, which can directly affect the livelihoods of workers and their families are matters which they should give consideration to. IKEA have learned from their experiences in India and recognized that by connecting directly with issues they can have a longer-term influence on the sustainability of their organization and, in the process, the world around them.

CASE STUDY Nike in China

In 2013 China grew by an amount larger than the size of the entire Turkish economy's GDP. According to James Kynge at the *Financial Times*, such unprecedented levels of growth have stretched the country's infrastructure and led to significant environmental challenges, including air and water pollution. Chinese leader Xi Jinping is looking to create a new vision for the country. In the same way in which the 'American Dream' is seen as an all-encompassing idea which captures the aspirational nature of the country and its people, so the Chinese dream is equally difficult to pin down but nonetheless aims to bring together deep-seated ideals of civilization and civility, great harmony and *Wang Dao* – the 'kingly way', to create a different kind of future for the Chinese people.

One of the biggest challenges this vision faces is structural shortages in domestic blue-collar workers. So China now has an estimated 220 million migrant workers in the country, who are not entitled to housing, health or education subsidies and suffer poor working environments. Nike, an organization that places a heavy reliance on production across Asia, has been severely criticized for its use of sweatshops and child labour. It is working hard to change this, both in terms of the perceptions and the practice on the ground. With this in mind its leadership team has spearheaded an initiative in China called 'Let Me Play', which has formed collaborative partnerships to address the health and well-being of migrant workers in its plants and is supporting the integration of migrant youth into new communities around sport and exercise. These improvements are being delivered in partnership with China Children and Teenagers Fund, which empowers migrant youth. Since 2007, the initiative has reached over 235,000 young people by training teachers in better tuition methods. The Chinese Ministry of Education has acknowledged that the Let Me Play approach is helping to meet the needs of migrant young people. The initiative is a pointer as to how Nike have, by making better connections with workers communities and the People's Republic of China (PRC), underpinned the performance of their operations and also helped to address potential social issues. The key point is that the Nike initiative recognizes that helping address the common good by tackling issues of health and well-being in its workers and the wider community around their plants is the best way to ensure the long-term success of their operations.

Nonetheless, China continues to have issues surrounding the way it manages people in its giant manufacturing facilities and there continue to be problems in the conditions of people who have come to work in the cities from agricultural areas and from outside China. In July of 2014 Samsung, for example, became the latest of the major tech companies to be highlighted for employing child labour in its Chinese facilities.

Changing the way we see our connections with customers

Corporate activities affect the lives of people every day, no more so than in the goods that they sell and the services that they offer. These have a far greater impact than peripheral activities which are added at a later date to corporate social responsibility programmes, no matter how well intentioned. As we saw in Step 1, the degree to which leaders can connect with the real needs of society will influence the degree to which these goods are truly good or services which truly serve. In the following case studies we will see how leaders have made those connections count.

CASE STUDY Centrica – UK

Centrica supplies gas to millions of UK homes. It is an organization that has experienced a high level of customer hostility throughout the recession as escalating gas prices have seen companies making bigger profits at a time when the consumer has been tightening their belts. Having made a number of mis-steps with their customers, they have at the same time established a foundation that gives assistance to old and disadvantaged people struggling to pay fuel bills. Some have seen this initiative as slick corporate gloss. Given the hikes in fuel costs that have been passed on to consumers the approach had perhaps unsurprisingly gained little traction and the help wasn't getting to the people who would benefit most. It was only when Centrica started to see the challenge in terms of their core business activity and turned to their own workforce that they got a breakthrough. It was by talking directly to frontline colleagues that CEO Sam Laidlaw discovered the extent to which the service engineers, who visited millions of people's homes every day to fix boilers and read meters, were already part of the lives of their customers, particularly the old and the infirm, and at a much deeper level than he had previously thought. In fact, it was these service engineers who knew which customers were vulnerable and which would benefit most from the support that could be provided by the foundation. If these insights are possible by extending the connection which already exists between a company and a community, then what can we learn about how leaders can channel other existing 'touch points' within their organizations to better connect with the wider world?

CASE STUDY Unilever – India and Africa

In 1885, William Lever, one of the founders of Unilever, set out to 'make cleanliness commonplace' for people living in Britain's Victorian slums. Lever had strong beliefs and knew that insanitary conditions in the slums of Britain's industrial towns were a blight on the country's prosperity. A grocer's son, Lever worked his way up, eventually building a factory at Port Sunlight and 10 years later Lifebuoy soap was introduced with profits re-invested in a village to house his workers in good conditions and ensure they were fit and healthy for his manufacturing operations. Today the organization, which still bears his name, is looking to make 'sustainable business commonplace'. Few organizations have connected their involvement in the community and their strategy as clearly or explicitly as Unilever. Once again, the work Unilever are doing is seen as central to their operations, rather than a CSR add-on. Under its 'Sustainable Living' plan, the company makes it very clear that all of its business activities are connected back to its purpose. It is now applying the focus which saw it bring basic hygiene to the slums of Victorian Britain, to the challenges of insanitary living in the slums of Africa, India and Asia. Unilever has brought research by major health organizations to the heart of its strategic focus. It has shown that babies are most vulnerable to disease in the first 28 days of life and every year an estimated 3.6 million newborn babies die in the first month of their lives. Furthermore, every year 2 million children fail to reach their fifth birthday because of diseases like diarrhoea. Simple, low-cost health interventions such as handwashing with soap can reduce this figure by up to 44 per cent. Unilever is now on a mission, through its Lifebuoy soap brand, to spread the importance of good handwashing habits across India and Africa. Their aim is to help more children reach their fifth birthdays. The work is being delivered in partnership with NGOs and different governments as Unilever has recognized that it needs to tap into existing on-ground networks and expertise to gain the connections it needs with local people. In Africa, Unilever Foundation partner PSI (Population Services International) and the Millennium Villages Project are helping to adapt its programmes for different contexts.

In Indonesia, Unilever have developed a new partnership with USAID, and the Maternal and Child Health Integrated Programme to reach new mothers and birth attendants with hygiene education. By 2012, the approach had been expanded to 16 countries, with the most significant expansion in Africa, where programmes are now running in nine countries, reaching more than 11 million people. Alongside basic hygiene, the lack of safe drinking water is also a major public health issue, particularly in developing countries, where around 80 per cent of diseases are waterborne. Unilever aims to make safe drinking water available and affordable to 500 million people through its Pureit in-home water purifier by 2020; 45 million people have gained access to safe drinking water from Pureit since its launch in 2005. Pureit is helping to reduce the incidence of diarrhoeal disease by up to 50 per cent. Unilever has worked with a range of micro-finance and NGO partners to improve the affordability of the purifier for those for whom the price remains a barrier to purchase.

The connections which Unilever has been able to create through this work, with both its own people and with the people in deprived countries, has the power to be transformational for both the local communities who receive the benefits and for individuals in Unilever who are working on these initiatives. Unilever have made a powerful connection with its own people who feel that their core work is serving the common good while connecting directly with communities in some of the most disadvantaged places on earth. They are also growing the business. It is a powerful combination and many Unilever people, having seen what is possible, are now hungry to get involved in more of this work. Unilever's challenge is to be able to channel these energies to keep and to keep the connection across all the work it does. It is a good challenge to have.

Unilever is adapting its business models to connect business and social goals, demonstrating that organizations need to become highly innovative to build business around common good. The Unilever example started with business attempting to connect. However, society is also now trying to connect with business.

Changing the way we see our relationship with the communities in which we are based

Large corporations by their very nature operate in many towns and cities, often covering the globe. As we discussed in Chapter 1, this can result in business leaders feeling like nomadic tribes, constantly on the move, somehow removed from all communities, and increasingly rootless with an affinity to no place and no one. It explains why so often large corporations are described by the public as faceless, as people sense the disconnection and feel that there is no one they can identify with. Yet businesses still have roots, through their offices and factories but largely through their employees, who unlike leaders never 'relocated' and are very much part of the community where they were born, raised and now work. Leaders can do a great deal to build on these links and forge greater connectivity by understanding the social value which the core activities of their organizations can bring. By doing so leaders can transform their businesses from assets under management to become hubs around which thriving communities can grow.

CASE STUDY   Morrisons – UK

In the West, concerns continue to mount over the divide which exists between the affluent few and the excluded many, not least of which is the growing numbers of unemployed young people who are still excluded from work. In the United Kingdom, the Salford Docks area just outside Manchester was once one of the largest docks in one of the most successful industrial cities in Britain. Today it stands idle and retail and entertainment outlets have replaced most of its booming factories. Between the dockside redevelopment and the city of Manchester lies one of the most deprived areas in Europe, the Ordsall estate. It is a blackspot on an otherwise successful story of city regeneration and its continuing problems have led some to believe it will always remain a problem area. It is a mixture of 1960s box-kit housing and the remains of Victorian slum buildings, housing families who have not worked for three generations. It has consequently become a focal point for drugs and crime.

In 2010, the Morrisons retail business announced that it was going to build a supermarket on the boundary between the Ordsall estate and the highly impressive Media City, set on Salford Quays. Local residents wanted the supermarket to ensure it gave at least half its jobs to the people from the estate. But people on the estate had lost not only the specific skills they might need for jobs at Morrisons, but equally importantly they had lost the habits of work and the confidence which goes with it. The problem was, there were no jobs to gain experience in, so people were trapped in a 'Catch 22' situation: without experience they couldn't find work, and without work they couldn't get experience. Through a partnership with the local council and with the input and leadership of the community, Morrisons created a real work environment through the establishment of a small social enterprise and training centre. With the combined focus of local education, the local council and the business, 80 per cent of jobs in the store were indeed filled by people from the estate. It provided a huge lift to the people from the community and was a crucial step in changing the area's perception of what it could achieve. It also gave the store a headstart in building a relationship with potential customers in the local community because everyone knew someone in the store and customer service was built in. Once again, we see in this example that what is good for the community can also be good for business and vice versa, provided that business leaders make those connections.

For Morrisons and the local council it was a glimpse of how true partnership connections between large corporations, social enterprise and government could create breakthroughs. Equally importantly, it started to open the eyes of the leaders to the significant difference they could make to their local communities – not through special community projects, but by re-engineering the hiring process to help people find a route to meaningful work inside their business. The power of this kind of connection has now been enshrined in British legislation. The Social Value Act requires that any government contract consider the social impact of awarding the work as well as the financial aspects. Britain is a world leader in the development of social enterprise start-ups and the potential now exists to help these organizations to scale up. However, as in the case of green innovation, it is going to be a very slow road for these enterprises to achieve any scale if they do not connect with larger corporate partners to obtain the support and access to funds that they so desperately need.

CASE STUDY Danone – France and Bangladesh

Muhammad Yunus is an acclaimed social pioneer and author of *Building Social Business*. He highlights the need to re-imagine and re-engineer businesses which focus first on creating social value and in the process open up new markets where before none would have considered them possible.

Back in the 1970s Bangladesh had just gained its independence and was in a terrible way. The war of independence had left the country in ruins and this was compounded by floods then famine. Muhammad Yunus recounts the story of seeing a woman who needed to borrow the equivalent of 5 cents, to buy bamboo to make crafts she would then sell. The moneylender, through his interest rates, effectively put the woman into a kind of debt bondage, forcing her to sell all her products through him. The poor did not qualify to receive loans from the banks and could not break out of this cycle. By 1976, Yunus started to give out small loans, allowing people to repay the loans to him in very small weekly amounts; eventually the Grameen Bank ('village bank') was created. Today this concept of micro-finance or micro-credit has spread around the world, dedicated to meeting the unserved needs of the poorest people.

In his book, Yunus talks about his concept of social business: 'The biggest flaw in our existing theory of capitalism lies in its misrepresentation of capitalism, human beings engaged in business are portrayed as one dimensional human beings whose only mission is to maximize profit. Humans supposedly pursue this economic goal in a single-minded fashion. This is a badly distorted picture of a human being. As even a moment's reflection suggests, human beings are not moneymaking robots. The essential fact about humans is that they are multi-dimensional beings. Their happiness comes from many sources not just from making money'.

His views are a long way removed from CSR: Yunus has observed that 'CSR is a department of a company that by maximizing profits might set aside some money for the local community, to promote the idea that the company is a good neighbour. By contrast a social business is directly devoted to changing the economic and social situation of the poor, or to creating some other social (or environmental) improvement in the world. A profit maximizing company might devote 95 per cent of its resources to producing profits and 5 per cent or less to making the world a better place. A social business devotes 100 per cent of its resources to making the world a better place.' In some regards Yunus's vision is not dissimilar to the ideas set out in Step 1 about the development of a purpose for the common good. The only difference is that a purpose-driven leader understands that a sustainable business is one which can only survive in the long run if it is creating good for the whole of the community. Nonetheless there are significant lessons that can be found in Yunus's experience.

Yunus rose to prominence through his groundbreaking work in establishing the micro-finance model of banking in Bangladesh. He took the idea to everyone who would listen to him and one of those was Franck Riboud, Chairman and CEO of Groupe Danone in Paris. Danone agreed to create a joint business selling Soki Doi Yoghurt to the children of Bangladesh. The key for Yunus was that the yoghurts would be fortified with nutrients that the children badly needed, as 49 per cent lack basic iron, calcium and zinc, causing poor eyesight and problems with immune systems. The aim was that the yoghurts would be affordable for all. Through a joint venture Grameen Danone opened its first factory in 2006 – a small and efficient plant, near the city of Bogra. It started to produce products for sale in 2007 but sales did not go well. After consulting with the Grameen staff and local NGOs, they discovered that the network of Grameen ladies whom they had hoped would sell the product had not been sufficiently involved. In Bangladesh, everyone is connected to everyone else, and without this community support, particularly when talking about door-to-door sales, the project would fail. Sales immediately improved when a local manager was appointed to lead the Grameen Danone initiative. Today Grameen successfully sells its yoghurt in the cities of Bogra and Dhaka through a network of 1,600 shops, and has opened up a new operation in Chittagong.

The experience of Grameen Danone demonstrates that making a complete connection between community and company is not easy, but that it is possible to create a business that delivers a vital social need and makes money. It is a far cry from CSR and other forms of corporate philanthropy but demonstrates how, through these kinds of connections, all businesses can create social value. It shows how connecting corporations with the community and with local suppliers can transform supply chains to deliver commercial advantage and change the value that is delivered to the broadest section of society. It is transformative for business, for the communities they serve and for the people inside organizations, who rediscover a greater sense of personal meaning and value.

There are thousands of small innovative social enterprises that have sprung up over the past decade. Few have grown to sufficient size to have impact beyond their local area. In part this is because they lack the expertise, infrastructure or investment to deliver at scale. This is exactly what large corporations could provide by establishing innovative partnerships like the ones initiated by Yunus. One such example is Snact. They started up because they saw that despite millions of people in Britain being affected by food poverty, tonnes of perfectly edible food were getting thrown away every day. Their mission is to turn surplus food into edible snacks. Operating out of east London, Snact makes 'fruit jerky', small snacks made of fresh fruit that has been blended together and dried out into strips. Every morning, its founders scour London's wholesale fruit markets to buy 'surplus' food that would otherwise be destroyed or sent to landfill, just because it is too ripe for shops, or simply the wrong shape or size. In an interview with the Telegraph, co-founder Ilana Taub commented 'Literally tonnes of perfectly good fruit gets thrown away in the UK before reaching shops.' She estimates that 80 per cent of the fruit thrown away by markets every day is still edible. By using food that is delicious, nutritious and safe, Taub could help major food retailers and producers to make their supply chains far less wasteful, turn waste products into fun food and help combat national food poverty.

These examples illustrate that organizations and leaders can connect far more closely with their communities and with issues facing the environment than previously imagined. They show that it is possible to combine the disciplines of business with a different ethos to create significant social value. These practical examples demonstrate that we can make life better for millions of people today, by rethinking our business models and reconnecting ourselves and our business in the process. What is central to this thinking is that these activities arise not out of side activities or as a proportion of profits, but out of a re-examination of core business activity. It also highlights the power of helping business to connect to the unspoken needs of future generations, an issue to which we shall now turn.

Legacy

'Society is a partnership between not only those who are living, but between those who are living and those who are yet to be born.'

(Edmund Burke, 1790)

A paper by Rupert Read, produced for the UK Think Tank 'Green House', called for the creation of a statutory body – 'Guardians of the Future' – which would have a right of veto over investments or activities today that might leave a poor legacy for future generations. In an interview in the *Guardian*, Read said that the idea came from the worry that 'the current institutions of government are not future proof'.[4] This may seem a long way off in the world of government and politics, but inside business it is not inconceivable that the independent non-executive directors could have a statutory remit specifically designed to report to the board on the long-term outlook and challenges facing the organization. Indeed some would say that this is precisely the role that non-executives should play in the running of a business. This point was reinforced in 2010 in talks about climate change, when the World Future Council observed that 'on retirement, great leaders voice their regret that they had no time to think, no time to reflect on the consequences of their decisions, particularly with respect to the state of the world they are leaving to their grandchildren'.[5]

Few leaders spend enough time thinking about their legacy – what they will leave behind for the organization, the people and the community they serve. According to Glenn Llopis, a leadership adviser in the United States: 'legacy is not defined at the end of the road but rather by the decisions made [and] the actions taken, throughout the many phases of your career, as you contribute to growth, innovation and opportunity both in and outside of the workplace'.[6] Thinking about your work from a legacy perspective embraces tough reflection. It requires that you evaluate the last 10 years of your career and ask questions about what the next 10 years could look like. By connecting to the wider world leaders can change the path of their business and the course of their long-term legacy.

Conclusion

The 2014 survey of Global Trends by market research company Ipsos MORI found that for the first time people are now pessimistic about the future that lies ahead for the generation of young people who are now reaching maturity. In a survey of over 16,000 people in 20 countries, Ipsos MORI found that 42 per cent of the world's population felt that the future will get worse and only 32 per cent believe it will get better for the next generation. In the UK the number of people feeling optimistic about the future is now only 22 per cent and in France it's a startling 7 per cent.[7] This is true in both the developed and the emerging world. Of the concerns that people have, 73 per cent of people feel that the world is becoming increasingly unstable and the same number fear environmental disaster lies ahead. How can we respond to these growing anxieties about our shared future?

We saw in Chapter 1 how as consumers we increasingly find ourselves absorbed by the objects of our desires, our attention captured by the next purchase or whatever we are looking at or listening to on our mobile devices. In our business lives we have become wrapped up in the constant struggle for competitive survival and advantage. Plugged in to our own worlds but tuned out from everyone else's. These dual obsessions have made us absent minded about the wider world around us. Yet we clearly do not live or operate in a vacuum. There is nothing that business is capable of doing that is not contingent on the communities in which we operate, or the environments that we source materials from or the people that we either serve or rely on.

The challenge we have therefore been exploring throughout this chapter is how leaders can become more mindful of society's changing outlook so that we might not only be more responsive in meeting peoples emerging needs but also better anticipate how our organizations can make a greater contribution for the good of society as a whole and so ultimately produce more sustainable business results.

As the leaders of major organizations we are in a unique position to respond, we can do something about this outlook, we can reconnect. We are in a privileged position to change the path we are on, but only by acknowledging and embracing the interdependent and interconnected nature of the world our business is part of. As we saw in examples at Mars and DyeCoo, leaders can impact our future environments, as we saw at IKEA they can reshape the way supply chains work to make them more humane, as we saw with Unilever and Danone companies can help communities to become healthier. To play this role, however, leaders must first understand their organizations as an enmeshed and embedded part of successful communities and a sustainable world. Leaders must develop their perspectives to see that are not separate from life, 'giving something back' when it seems appropriate, but a fully integrated, inseparable part of whole which will thrive (or not) as a complete system.

Existing supply chains provide one vehicle for leaders to start exploring how they can re-establish better connections, and in doing so, have the opportunity to once again play a role as stewards of the economy, setting standards which benefit everyone and not just a few and influencing market practices which touch everyone, by collaborating up and down the value chain. To this end, we now turn to some specific first steps leaders can take.

FIGURE 7.2   Connecting to the wider world: Influencing the value chain

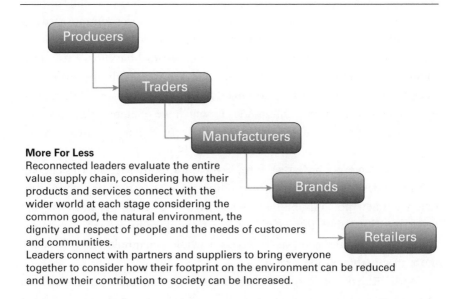

More For Less
Reconnected leaders evaluate the entire value supply chain, considering how their products and services connect with the wider world at each stage considering the common good, the natural environment, the dignity and respect of people and the needs of customers and communities.
Leaders connect with partners and suppliers to bring everyone together to consider how their footprint on the environment can be reduced and how their contribution to society can be Increased.

Eight steps to reconnected leadership

STEP 5 – Reconnecting to the wider world: Leadership actions

1 *Curating difficult conversations with society.* To connect, senior leaders need to move from investment in PR to investing in meaningful dialogue with society by instigating having curated conversations in which a range of constituencies can bring dialogue and perspective, such that all voices are aired but that a balanced perspective is arrived at. The *Guardian* currently runs such forums on issues of the day within its society section. Such meaningful dialogues could be facilitated around the big issues facing business, society and the environment, centred on what your company does. It should be regarded as a process of learning and connecting and is a far broader conversation than conducting focus groups on how you can sell more of a product or deliver a better service.

2 *Establish a venture capital arm and foster partnerships with social enterprise.* We will discuss the issue of innovation in a later section. However, establishing a venture capital arm that can partner with smaller entities, whether they are involved in environmental or social innovation, would provide a mechanism to bring ideas into an organization from different and diverse backgrounds. This kind of venture can involve a mix of the brightest and some of the most experienced to ensure that the best of the organization is getting to connect directly with people who think differently about the world beyond the boundaries of the organization. Use this seedcorn to then establish larger partnerships with local organizations that will develop the capabilities and skills of local people, beyond simply doing a job.

As we saw in the example of Grameen Danone, one of the ways large corporate leaders can reconnect with the world around them is to partner with 'small' social enterprise which is operating on the ground. Such enterprises can help to change the way you run a simple business process, whether that is where you source fair trade food from or how you make engagement with disadvantaged communities an integral part of the way you recruit people into your business.

3 *Review your supply chain.* Take a step-by-step approach to consider all the links in your supply chain and consider the degree to which the practices (whether environmental, people or social) would be acceptable in your core operation. Then ask why they are acceptable in a supplier. Consider how changing your policies in this arena could directly improve the environment of people in developing countries. Getting to know all suppliers, not just a few, is a way of ensuring that you really understand and are connecting with society.

4 *Visit sites within your supply chain.* As part of the formation of deeper connections with the world beyond your operation, visit locations from where you obtain supplies, with members of your team. Develop an intimate understanding of what the impact is on local communities.

5 *Product review.* Establish a product and service review process across all your business. Consider which products can be re-engineered to provide additional benefits to the environment and to deprived individuals and communities, or can be re-engineered from a price perspective to give access to a market which was once beyond the reach of individuals.

6 *Legacy review.* Consider your personal legacy and map out a clear sense of what you would want this to be about in 10 years' time. Consider what percentage of your time you are currently spending creating a legacy you could be proud of. If that is a low percentage because of how busy you are at work, then consider how you could develop a broader perspective on the nature of your work so that it becomes a reflection of what you would like to have left behind.

---

1 James Clay, How big brands can help save biodiversity, TED Conference, July 2010
2 *ibid.*
3 Shelly Banjo, After the flood, *Wall Street Journal*, June 2010
4 Richard Read reported in theguardian.com, posted by Damian Carrington, January 2012
5 Guarding our future: How to include future generations in policy making, World Future Council, 2010
6 Glenn Llopis, 5 ways a legacy driven mindset will define your leadership, *Forbes Magazine*, 20 February 2014
7 Ipsos MORI Global Trends Survey, April 2014

Step 6: Creating deeper customer connections

08

Introduction

In 2013, the *Economist* Intelligence Unit (EIU) conducted a global study of customer relationships, surveying senior executives across 19 different industries. The executives highlighted one single issue above all others as the common denominator: the need to achieve better connection with customers. The *Economist* report concluded that customer intimacy is the new imperative for CEOs and that connecting customers, partners, employees and products is central to improving the customer experience and business performance in the coming years. Yet, despite the recognized strategic importance of customer connection, as we saw in Chapter 1 there have been a series of incidents in all sectors that have eroded the bonds between companies and customers.[1]

Unfortunately, there is still a tendency, when talking about customer connection, to think of it as being about those obvious 'touch points' in call centres or the front desk. In this chapter we will see that customer connection is about the *entire* relationship between a customer and an organization. The customer connection should therefore influence how leaders think of everything that we do in our businesses.

This chapter will examine how leaders can rebuild those connections, mend ties, and create deeper relationships so that business can deliver products that are truly good and provide services that truly serve their customers. We will go on to explore how leaders can renew trust in their organizations by delivering on the commitment to reconnect with their customers at every level.

FIGURE 8.1 Reconnected leadership model: Fostering customer connections

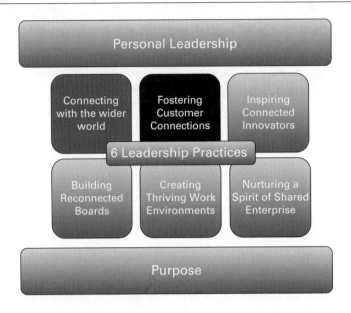

What really matters?

If leadership is going to reconnect with what customers want, it is crucial to understand what is really going to take to make them happy. Far too often the level of insight gleaned about what customers really think about a company and its products remains at a highly superficial level. However, several prominent market commentators have discerned a sea-change in the underlying attitudes of customers across the world.

In an essay entitled *The State of the US Consumer 2002*, Myra Stark of the global ad agency Saatchi & Saatchi wrote:

> It's as though the consumer is asking, 'What really matters? What do I really care about?' In the face of threats to our safety, our way of life and our economic stability, Americans have pulled back from many of the things that seemed to matter in the 1990s – materialism, career, the celebrity culture, the affluent attitude – and are rethinking how they want to live and work.

Daniel Pink, author of *Free Agent Nation* (2002), calls this new seriousness 'the flight to meaning' and observes: 'In turbulent times people get serious about finding meaning.' These attitudes haven't changed in the ensuing decade; if anything, they have become more sharply focused since the crash of 2008.

The work of Martin Seligman (2011), head of the Penn Positive Psychology Centre, reflects the comments of Myra Stark but points us in a different direction. 'So many people build their lives around pursuing pleasure,' observes Seligman, 'when it turns out that engagement and meaning are much more important.' Seligman asserts that happiness is not solely derived from external, momentary pleasures. He uses an acronym, PERMA, to summarize correlational findings:

- *Pleasure* – humans seem happiest when they have this.
- *Engagement* – the absorption of an enjoyed, yet challenging activity.
- *Relationships* – social ties have turned out to be extremely reliable indicator of happiness.
- *Meaning* – a perceived quest or belonging to something bigger.
- *Accomplishments* – having realized tangible goals.

So if making connections, building relationships and finding meaning is the source of real happiness for most people, then surely a better understanding of how happiness works should be a foundation for deepening relationships with customers in the future?

Levels of happiness

Ancient philosophers and thinkers often define happiness in terms of living a good life, or flourishing, rather than simply as an emotion. Similar thinking from faith traditions is captured in the writings of Robert Spitzer, Ron Rolheiser and the Buddhist monk Matthieu Ricard amongst others, and can be summarized into four levels of happiness along these lines:

- Happiness Level 1: *Having it* – derived from acquiring things (immediate gratification).
- Happiness level 2: *Doing or winning it* – derived from achievement (short-term happiness).
- Happiness level 3: *Giving* – derived from contributing (long-term happiness).
- Happiness level 4: *Being* – derived from experiencing meaning (enduring happiness).

The chart shown in Figure 8.2, illustrates how for each level and type of happiness, there is a corresponding level of customer connection. We will go on to explore how understanding the drivers of happiness can provide us with insights in how we manage our connections with customers.

Where we stand on this 'happiness ladder' affects every aspect of life, from our view of success, and quality of life, to human rights and the common good. But isn't happiness too 'fuzzy' a concept to relate to business strategy and what does it have to do with the business of buying and selling things?

At one level, happiness is a proxy for the business phrase 'customer satisfaction'. However, I have intentionally used the 'happiness ladder' precisely because it requires greater judgement and refers in a much more holistic sense to what people may be looking for.

The degree to which our sense of happiness has been shown to have a positive impact on our overall well-being is quite striking when we compare it to other things we know to have a direct impact on our lives. Over the past 30 years, Professor Edward Diener of the University of Illinois has led

FIGURE 8.2 Creating customer connections

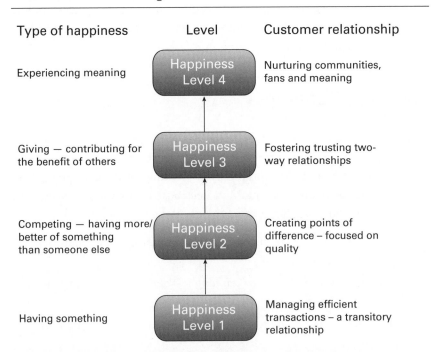

Type of happiness	Level	Customer relationship
Experiencing meaning	Happiness Level 4	Nurturing communities, fans and meaning
Giving — contributing for the benefit of others	Happiness Level 3	Fostering trusting two-way relationships
Competing — having more/better of something than someone else	Happiness Level 2	Creating points of difference – focused on quality
Having something	Happiness Level 1	Managing efficient transactions – a transitory relationship

As we progress up the model – the requirements for efficiency, points of difference, two-way relationships do not disappear completely, they just become far less important than the depth and quality and wider meaning of the connection.

research into how happiness can extend your life. He concludes: 'if cigarette smoking can reduce your life by six years, being unhappy can reduce it by nine!' So what makes people happy is really quite important, especially if as a leader you want to differentiate yourself from your competitors. In the next section we will consider the different routes being deployed by business to connect with customers and how these different levels of connection drive different levels of happiness.

Now let's explore what each of these levels are about, how they influence the customer and what they mean in terms of the connections that leaders can foster and the environments that they can create.

Happiness level 1

'Having it all' can provide a sense of immediate gratification – the first piece of chocolate cake is delicious, the second piece is OK, the third piece isn't great and the fourth piece is disgusting. Having it all it can also leave us ultimately dissatisfied when we realize that we are after all no different than the rest. This sense of dissatisfaction can feel like a dull ache, that we fix over and over when we buy something new. It is perhaps this feeling that acts as the underlying driver beneath our desire to over-consume, and to throw away. In this mode, according to spiritual writer Ronald Rolheiser (1999), we are so overcharged with desire that we find it hard to come to a simple rest. It can lead to a fundamental dis-ease that prevents many people from finding a sense of peace.

As a consequence this kind of happiness is simply the immediate pleasure experienced from having something: owning the latest car or gadget. Happiness level 1 can be intense but is equally short-lived. It is what Professor Seligman more accurately refers to as a pleasure in that it is immediate but it doesn't last.

Customer connection here is all about managing transactions efficiently – it provides the happiness the customer derives from the fleeting satisfaction they get when they acquire something. The customer relationship here is built on the expectation is that they will pay a fair price and that they can trust the product they are buying. Despite the challenges we all face in the 21st century, almost everything in a material sense in western economies has improved significantly over the past 30 years. Yet somehow we remain dissatisfied. One example of this trend is in the automotive sector. Buying a car 30 years ago was still an 'emotional journey' and a hit-and-miss experience as many still had reputations for breaking down, leaking oil, faulty electrics or rusting quickly. Today, cars don't rust, they rarely break down, and they consume less fuel, provide smoother rides, travel at higher speeds, entertain us and keep better control on the road. So why are we not as thrilled by them as we were by the rust buckets of a bygone era?

One answer may be because cars are really all the same now – they have been perfected by engineers and designers who have studied what we like about the drive and look and function of cars. Every quirk and rough edge has been removed and many cars lack any sense of personality. Exaggerating to make a point, perhaps? But here is what the self-declared 'car nerd' Jeremy Clarkson had to say on the homogenization of the car market in his *Sunday Times* column: 'There are fast Golfs and big Golfs and cheap Golfs. There are Japanese Golfs and American Golfs… But they're all Golfs. I can tell the difference between a Ford Focus and a Vauxhall Astra, but that's because I'm a nerd. However, I'm not such a nerd that I don't realize both are actually Golfs.' Admittedly Clarkson was reviewing a Golf at the time, but his final observation in this article perhaps captures the sense of what has happened to all cars. They have become 'me too' objects; we would like to think we are different, but we are all being treated the same. It was 'like reviewing a floorboard', said Clarkson: 'it does what it's supposed to do [but that isn't very interesting].'[2]

This mass standardization hasn't just happened with cars. Mobile phones in the past didn't do everything for us in the way smartphones do today, but they all showed a little of the creativity that had gone into their design. Today, they all look the same – elegant, thin black cuboids, with a bit of steel somewhere on the device to denote or mark the logo of the maker and the ubiquitous shiny screen to swipe. This partly explains the desire of increasing numbers of people to revert to local or hand-made produce; increasingly 'distinctive' means 'better' in the minds of many consumers.

This processing of everything into highly standardized units has happened because the modern practice of leadership – with its standard management practices, common IT applications and homogenized philosophy – is now operating in all major companies in all markets. It should not come as a surprise that if you do the same things as everyone else, you are likely to get the same results. Consequently everything looks, feels and sounds the same – no matter how much the advertising tells you otherwise.

High streets in every city in the United Kingdom look much the same. Every store has been 'optimized'. Go to a shopping mall in Tokyo or Singapore, Prague or Dallas – while the names might be different (or not!) the look and the feel is very similar. Everything has been 'designed' based on millions of hours of research to deliver a perfect customer experience; unfortunately in the process, nearly every ounce of originality has been engineered out. No matter what the customer care gurus say, it is going to be difficult to 'delight' customers for very long when they are bored.

Level 2: Happiness level 2 'doing or winning it' – derived from achievement (short-term happiness)

This happiness is all about ego-gratification: being the best, the fastest, smartest, most esteemed, admired, powerful etc. Happiness level 2 can be a great driver of progress and causes many of us to strive to be better. This is the happiness of comparative advantage – being better or owning something better than others. This kind of happiness results from competition with other people. We see our 'self' in terms of how we measure up to others. It has been called 'the comparison game.' Such happiness can be unstable; failing to win can lead to unhappiness and a sense of worthlessness. Exclusive pursuit of this type of happiness can also tend to oppress others. It can be driven out of a fear of failure, rather than a pursuit of happiness. Nonetheless, it is still pretty short term and causes people to continue to chase the prizes that are involved, unable to get off the treadmill of 'success.'

Leading the customer connection here is all about providing the opportunity for your customer to feel like they can exceed neighbours and friends by acquiring something better. Happiness is derived from 'competing and winning'. For leaders it is often about creating a competitive environment.

The advertising industry has thrived for over 50 years largely on the premise that people competed with each other and gained satisfaction by being able to be slightly different and slightly better than their neighbour. Product and market segmentation evolved to the level of sophistication we see today, in part to reflect the unique profiles of each one of us and in part to cater for this need to be slightly better than the crowd. This is the level where brands occupy so much importance and so much expenditure. They offer the customer the prospect of feeling better and being happier because the brand that they purchase 'makes a statement' that they have more taste or more money than others. Once others are seen wearing or driving these brands it can make the competition to acquire them stronger. Once again the car industry had historically been at the vanguard of servicing this desire for one-upmanship, with its progression from one series to three series to five series to seven series cars. However, this kind of happiness is not sustainable.

Trusting in experiences

Many companies acknowledge the need to establish a deeper connection with customers and the role connection plays in customer attraction and retention. A recent survey by Zendesk (which works with the likes of

Disney, Vodafone and Sony) identified that only 55 per cent of customers would recommend a company due to great service while 85 per cent would warn friends and family if they have had a bad experience with a company and 85 per cent would pay more to get a better service experience. Despite the clarity of the survey data, few organizations have changed the way they choose to interact with customers. In the United States, for example, a staggering $214.3 billion is still being spent on standard advertising (2011), yet only 4 per cent of Americans trust advertising to give them an honest view of the product they are buying.

What customers increasingly do trust is their own experiences and those of the people they know. In fact, 83 per cent say they trust 'independent sources' – people with whom they have a personal relationship – over advertising. So if 'business as usual' is leaving people cold, feeling processed and undervalued, while everyone is wearing the brands that used to be so rare and aspirational, how can a company mark itself out for the future?

This new landscape will be defined by those companies that take the initiative in playing it fair and offering something extra. It is about organizations having real insight into what is in the best interests of customers and reciprocating with their own actions. Companies must be seen to be doing things for other reasons than honouring a service contract or getting an extra sale out of supporting the customer. To foster this kind of relationship, an organization must move beyond the transactional view of service to what Don Pepper and Martha Rogers call a 'trustable relationship'.

In their book *Extreme Trust*, Pepper and Rogers (2012) identify that the minimum standard required by customers in the future will be fairness and anticipation of what customers really need, rather than allowing them simply to buy what they think they want. Many will say this is an unreasonable standard, but it is already happening today. Apple is perhaps one of the best examples of this in practice. If you try to purchase an iTunes recording that you have previously already purchased, they will prevent the sale and tell you that you already have that item in. This shifts the balance of the relationship from being a pure transaction to feeling like a relationship where the company is on your side and isn't just trying to squeeze you for every penny. Based on the understanding that it is this trust which will bring you back again and again, Apple have created their Apple Stores, which are large iconic spaces epitomizing the cool application of technology. At their heart is the Apple crew of 'geniuses', on hand to help customers find out how to get the best out of the technology. Unlike other electrical retailers, no one is on a sales bonus or trying to sell anything. What matters most is making a deep personal connection built on seeing Apple as trusted experts. It is probably also worth noting that Apple Stores do not generate great returns directly for the business, but do build greater depth and a longer-term relationship with the customer. The example at Apple takes us to the next level of customer happiness.

CASE STUDY Fresh Direct – USA

This need for connection and honest relations is now being translated into real-time business connections. The desire to connect has spawned an outpouring of advice on YouTube, with everything from how to get the most out of your central heating system to how to make the perfect chocolate cake. At Fresh Direct, the online fresh food retailer in New York, they give all of their fresh fruit a rating, based on a real assessment of what the product actually tastes like. Out-of-season strawberries may be juicy, but won't be bursting with flavour; avocados can be purchased all year round, but out of season may well offer a stringy imitation of the soft lush fruit. That's exactly what Fresh Direct tells their customers. There is no hype, just complete transparency, helping to build trust in their produce, recognizing that fruit is something that people usually like to see feel and smell before purchasing. Fresh Direct has now taken the freshness idea one step further and allows shoppers to see directly into their preparation kitchens where individual cheese is being sliced and cakes are being baked overnight fresh for the next morning's delivery.

If greater depth of relationship is established by being more honest with a customer and sharing information that traditionally a company may have thought of as giving them an advantage, then the next level of happiness is about moving from passing and receiving things to making a contribution and establishing a relationship.

Level 3 happiness – 'giving': derived from contributing long-term happiness

This is the happiness that comes from giving of yourself to others and putting others first. Happiness level 3 is to a degree at odds with happiness level 2, because it is the opposite of competing with others. Level 3's major difference is that it has an external focus; it is about giving to others, not what is in it for you.

Connecting with customers here is about giving and receiving, about really helping customers beyond what we have to do. It is about leaders creating coaching environments for their people so that they can be themselves with their customers, enabling people to develop true relationships, which can and do make a difference.

CASE STUDY Trader Joe's – USA

Trader Joe's, the innovative US supermarket chain, has a clearly stated purpose – to listen and to carefully respond to the needs of those they serve. This mission has created a culture that supports loyalty and customer service through personal contact above all. The underlying message is that Trader Joe's wants to establish a personal relationship. In 2007, Mark Mallinger and Gerry Rossy from California State University looked at the impact of Trader Joe's culture on their business strategy, observing that major decisions at the company are carefully scrutinized to determine the extent to which they help maintain what Trader Joe's call 'a neighbourhood store' feel. For example, for several years Trader Joe's resisted incorporating conventional scanners at their checkout stands. The concern was that customers would consider the technology a move towards becoming a traditional supermarket and thus risk losing the homely connection between customers and staff. Continuous change in their inventory mix, however, demanded that they scan barcodes at the checkout. Eight years ago they therefore began experimenting with this shift in technology. Piloting the new technology, they found a way to ensure that the 'bleep' as items were scanned did not get in the way of cashier-customer conversation. The success of the Trader Joe's model is evidenced by the fact their revenues per square foot are triple those of a typical supermarket – an amazing performance which Trader Joe's puts down to their combination of product line and customer service culture.

A visit to my local grocery chain underlines the point. The store has the same layout as other convenience stores which are closer to home but I choose to shop there, not because I have any affinity to the chain, but because of the friendly person at the checkout who always goes the extra mile, remembers me (and most other shoppers) and makes me feel like a valued customer. Somehow I leave the store feeling a little better about life.

Starting a chain reaction

It turns out that this good feeling has real value and that good service can actually give us as much of a buzz as meeting a friend or watching a favourite sports team. In research undertaken on behalf of American Express, two in three volunteers saw their pulse rates increase, their breathing slow and their sweat glands swing into action when shown images of workers going the extra mile for customers. In other words, it was something that they enjoyed. The research was reviewed by a neuroscientist, Dr Jack Lewis (2014), who observed: 'We are so surprised when someone provides excellent service it causes a bigger response in the brain, similar to what we see when people are feeling loved.'[3]

Dr Lewis also pointed to evidence that people who have had a good experience will go on to behave kindly towards others. 'This pro-social behaviour, a good deed being passed, occurs because people have felt such a positive response to how someone has behaved towards them.' Despite the benefits of connecting with customers in this way, fewer and fewer shoppers believe that this is the kind of service that they are receiving. Customer dissatisfaction has been particularly evident in the ever-growing domain of call centres.

The challenge of running call centres that can deliver for both customers and employees is a global issue. In Singapore, a great deal of work is going on to help the nation capitalize on its advantages as a service hub for the Asia-Pacific region. By any measure, it is a highly successful economy and being great at service is a key factor in the country's continued success. However, one plank of its service-led strategy, call centres, is not working effectively at all, experiencing high levels of staff turnover due to the stress imposed by negative customer interactions. In a recent article in the *Singapore Business Review*, Gemma Calvert identified how call centres can improve both their service and the experience of their staff. Dr Calvert was Chair of Applied Neuroscience at the University of Warwick and her research on the neuroscience and psychology of consumer behaviour has been featured widely. Now CEO of Neurosense in Asia, she is dedicated to understanding how findings from neuroscience can be applied effectively in business.[4]

Calvert refers to a recent study combining online and lab-based experiments and involving over 1,600 people from four different countries. This found that the act of delivering good-quality customer service not only benefits the receiver but, intriguingly, also delivers measurable positive health benefits for the individual providing that service. The results revealed that receiving and delivering excellent customer service caused a chain reaction of positive responses in both the provider and receiver's bodies, increasing their heart rates and perspiration levels as excitement and exhilaration increased, and decreasing breathing rates as anxiety and stress levels were reduced. It turns out that a great customer service experience is beneficial not only to the bottom line but also to our health. When we receive great service, oxytocin is released in the brain, and this 'trust' hormone makes us feel good, a feeling which we then pass onto others in a positive 'ripple effect'.

However, the tests also showed that defensive behaviour in response to complainants served only to fuel negative interactions, which then had a snowball effect on people's mood and subsequent social interactions throughout the day, causing stress and ultimately depression and anger. The research found that it was far more difficult for a customer to continue to adopt an aggressive stance if the service provider on the other end of the telephone, or in-store, did not mirror their behaviour. If you want happy sales staff, Dr Calvert observes, 'brain science suggests that making people aware of the feedback loop associated with positive social interactions can be directly beneficial'. Perhaps most fascinating of all was that giving great service was found to be both physiologically and emotionally more pleasurable than receiving it. Evolution seems to have hard-wired us to be highly attuned to positive social interactions and as such, it seems we experience greater gratification being of service to others than the other way around, thus ensuring vital social cohesion. Making meaningful connections with others provides the basis for seeing your customer relationships in a completely different way.

If creating relationships is the key to making customers happy, it explains why the search for this sense of connectedness is leading companies to look to move beyond their normal frame of reference in order to create real communities.

Level 4 happiness: being–derived from experiencing meaning (enduring happiness)

We recognize in this category those experiences that are beyond what we are capable of doing purely on our own. This is about a sense of completeness through participation in something bigger than ourselves – often described when we get lost in a piece of music, hearing children sing, or sharing laughter with others. It is about finding a deeper meaning and participating in the common good.

Level 4 customer leadership is about creating a collaborative environment with customers, where barriers between the company and the customer are removed and there is full engagement of equals. It is in these contexts that the customer can experience being part of something. This kind of connected leadership helps to foster a sense of community belonging.

For example, in response to the new online competitive threat, the Walmart organization has been thinking outside the box on how it might provide a different kind of home delivery service to customers. At one Walmart store in California, the company is reviewing a radical plan to ask in-store customers to drop off packages to internet buyers on their way home. The notion that a major retailer could shift some of its activity to become more community-based, getting shoppers to deliver groceries to neighbours who are perhaps elderly and not mobile, would be a radically different way of looking at what has been a faceless online transaction up to now. But it points to the way that more community and personal solutions are being developed. The plan at pilot stage in 2013 would put the world's largest retailer squarely in the middle of a new phenomenon sometimes known as the 'sharing economy'.

The sharing economy is developing at a phenomenal rate and is redefining the boundaries between conventional business and community life. TaskRabbit is one example of an organization leading the way in establishing such new connections. TaskRabbit enables trusted people to help make money by helping their neighbours by running errands, cleaning, fixing a fence – whatever job needs doing. Founded in 2008 by Leah Busque in Boston, it is now based out of San Francisco and offers the chance of creating a level of community connectedness and genuine interaction that would seem to have been lost. Other experiments in connectedness are allowing individual car owners to loan out their cars to vetted individuals in California; 56 per cent of people in San Francisco are now considering doing this. Google are now on a similar path, having launched their 'Help-Out' community, which connects people with a desire to learn how to do something, with someone who is willing to teach that topic, at a price agreed between them. John Chambers, CEO of Cisco recently predicted that these developments will drive efficiency in all aspects of our lives. Similarly, as Yahoo CEO Marissa Mayer noted, if 1.5 million people have let 'strangers' into their homes to perform tasks for them as part of TaskRabbit, it takes trust in a radically different direction.[5]

CASE STUDY IKEA – China

Meanwhile, in China, senior citizens are finding furniture, coffee and love at IKEA. In 2011 the *Wall Street Journal* reported that retired Chinese workers were looking for love but not wanting to meet people at bars or karaoke joints. Instead they choose to go to IKEA in Shanghai's Xuhui shopping district and meet every week at the cafeteria. IKEA is helping them take a second shot at romance![6] At the weekly IKEA 'romance session' in Shanghai, the elderly arrive in swarms of 70 to 700 to get the free coffee (offered to holders of the IKEA family membership card). Zhou Hong, the official IKEA card-swiper, says she typically hands out an average of 500 coffee cups each time the group meets. At first IKEA tried to discourage the groups of seniors; now they are trying to manage this community, as the IKEA experience spreads into the mainstream. The strategy of fostering a sense of community at their stores seems to be paying off; 8 of the 10 biggest IKEAs in the world are now located in China with 40 per cent more customer traffic than other countries. IKEA is now planning to up its nine locations to 17 stores by 2015 to meet demand from the nation's growing middle class, who aspire to western lifestyles at affordable prices.

How technology is redefining relationships with customers

The reconnection with customers is fast becoming a necessity because of the way technological advance is accelerating. Barriers that we used to think of as standard between companies, products, services and customers are fast becoming obsolete because every device, every appliance, every product that we use or consume is rapidly being equipped with software that tracks where it is, how it's performing, what its usage is and whether the customer is happy with it. This 'internet of things' where every device is constantly communicating critical information only speculated on in 1999 by British technology pioneer Kevin Ashton a decade ago is fast become a reality, far beyond the confines of our smartphones and tablets. Machines and devices of every kind will have embedded sensors picking up relevant information and transmitting it back to technicians and professionals who will be able to advise us on how to get better use of the device we are using. The spectrum will range from car insurance companies, able to offer lower rates to careful drivers, to toothbrush manufacturers like Philips who have already started to embed sensor technology in toothbrushes and will in future be able to link this information with dental technicians. Running shoes and football boots are already being fitted with devices that link to applications in mobile phones and back to a 'health instructor'. Advanced wearable devices are already monitoring heart rates, blood sugar and sweat levels. This information is already being sent to private physicians in the United States, who can provide advice on health, exercise and dietary activity. It sounds expensive, but compared with the cost of medication when things go wrong, this kind of technology could save enormous sums of money. Indeed, technology has the potential to enable every product to become a service and present the opportunity to form new, different, and deeper relationships between customers and companies. But are companies ready to reconnect in this radically different way, to turn the possibilities of technology into more meaningful relationships? And surrounded by all this technology, how will customers react to the invasion of their privacy that this new level of intimacy could represent? Handled well it could help people feel like companies are helping them make life easier; handled badly it could cause customers to haul up the drawbridge and refuse to let any of these devices into their homes.

These examples indicate that retailers recognize they can become a more integrated part of people's lives. In their book *Connected*, Nicholas Christakis and James Fowler (2009) have observed how such social connections can create large patterns in the wider social networks. They propose that happiness can no longer be viewed as merely a function of an individual experience or choice, but also as the way a group of people interact. Their research into how networks operate shows that people have far greater influence, when connected through groups, than we ever thought before. People can be substantially influenced by others with whom they have no direct relationship but who are in some way part of their network, connected through friends or friends of friends. Programmes like Weight Watchers and Alcoholics Anonymous work in precisely this way, cultivating ties and group solidarity, and spreading positive attitudes. It turns out that everything from health, to anxiety, from happiness to pain, can spread through people to people networks at incredible speed in what Christakis and Fowler (2009) call an 'epidemic of attitudes'.

So if higher levels of happiness are created and can be spread by meaningful relationships between people, how can companies facilitate such social connections to foster customer engagement and create a point of difference in a world where everything is increasingly looking the same? The place where this live experiment has gone furthest is online, in the creation of new business models, which are serving to bring people together in very different ways.

Communities and clubs

As we have seen, human beings are programmed to want certain things. The top needs for most are having a sense of connection, belonging and the feeling of being understood. These needs are often met through families, clubs and communities. When companies begin to focus on building communities, it has a powerful impact that forges these deeper emotional bonds.

Starbucks, which had lost its way as a brand, decided that the best way of getting back on track was by reconnecting with its customers and working with them to improve the Starbucks offer. On the return of founding CEO Howard Schultz, it launched 'My Starbucks Idea', tapping into its loyal customers who know better than anyone else what people want from Starbucks (Ramaswarmy and Gouillart, 2010). The site is at once a crowdsourcing tool, an online community and a market-research method that brings customer priorities to light. Customers can submit, view and discuss submitted ideas along with employees from various Starbucks departments – 'Idea Partners'. The company regularly polls its customers for their favourite products and has a leaderboard to track which customers are the most active in submitting ideas, comments, and poll participation. As one participant commented, it's like a weather vane: Starbucks know which way the wind is blowing. Starbucks is a great example of a physical brand that is being social and engaging with its customers and, as a result, they are always at or near the top of nearly every major brand-ranking in social media. Developing this sense of community maintains authenticity and relevance because the company is constantly adapting to the changing needs, interests and values of the people who give them meaning.

Another example of a product company that has used this approach to really connect with its customers is US shoe brand Vans. A relatively small niche company by global standards, the team at Vans has marked out their space by going to extra lengths to really engage with their customers. Regularly running events across the United States, their latest was the Vans Community Skate Jam, which saw hundreds of committed skateboarders turn up at the Whistler Skate Park for an all-day event with prizes, free hot dogs and live music. The young user community, sporting the trademark thick, rubber-soled, canvas-topped shoes, are embracing the Vans spirit. However, it isn't simply bringing people together in this way that marks out Vans' approach; it's their continuing support for communities of skateboarders, linked through online groups across the United States, that has given the brand a sense of identity.

CASE STUDY   Wiggle – UK

This is a pattern that is also seen at the UK by online cycling specialists, Wiggle. With a calendar of events lined up for the year ahead, Wiggle is fast becoming the 'place to be', promoting the cycling sport, but also creating fun communities. The New Forest Sportive in the spring of 2014 is a case in point. Hundreds of enthusiasts turned up to take part in a community activity facilitated by the company, from people who just wanted to take part to keen cyclists who may or may not have bought any products from the company; they came along to feel part of something bigger than themselves. Mike Snell, Commercial Director, stresses that this isn't just smart marketing:

> It very much reflects the ethos of the company. Everyone who works here loves cycling and we regularly go out for long cycles at the end of the day. It brings everyone in the business together; for many people the love of cycling is the reason they work here, and hopefully that translates into the way we introduce new ideas for our customers. Everyone is a real user and expert on bikes, everyone has an opinion.[7]

People who attend these events feel part of the Wiggle community, posting their pictures of events on the Wiggle site.

CASE STUDY   Parkrun – UK and Global

Weekends across the United Kingdom are clearly changing. A nation once better-known for its cream teas and love of spectating, is now getting active with the help of other activities facilitated by corporations working to create communities around their core offer. For example, Sweatshop,

Adidas, and PruHealth are collaborating with a non-profit organization to connect with amateur runners. James Brilliant reported in the *Guardian* (London), 11 March 2013 that, 'every Saturday at 9 am tens of thousands of amateur runners are ditching the duvet in favour of lacing up their trainers and pounding their local park over 5km'. The movement began in south-west London in October 2004 and the 'parkrun' bug has now spread across the world, with events in the United States, South Africa and New Zealand. The success of parkrun can largely be attributed to its simplicity and accessibility. Unlike Sweatshop and Adidas, parkrun is not trying to promote a product (it doesn't have any) and is a not-for-profit venture, runners of any ability simply register online, turn up at their park and run. After the event each runner is e-mailed their results and provided with a permanent web page, with a history of all their runs. It is this communal sense of running for the people by the people that is central to the parkrun philosophy. 'We have an emphasis on community participation – it's about communities of like-minded people coming together, making friends and staying healthy,' said Tom Williams, UK Parkrun Manager.[8]

A 'third place' to connect

There is a tendency to think that the idea of connecting communities of people together only happened with the emergence of the internet. However, in their work using MRI data and research into the neural correlates of decision-making, neuroscientists J H Fowler and D Schreiber (2008) have demonstrated that we use very large parts of the brain, known as 'the default-state network', to monitor our social interactions. We are wired, say Fowler and Schreiber, 'with a predisposal to be social'. According to sociologist Ray Oldenburg, we are driven to create domestic, work-based and social connections. Oldenburg (1999) describes the social connections as 'Third Place', which brings an additional sense of identity and belonging. As society has become increasingly fragmented, the social institutions that used to fulfil this role have declined, but the need to connect with others in this Third Place has not. This section will explore how some organizations are starting to reconstruct these Third Places in our lives and shows how powerful they can become.

In 1995, Albert Muniz Jr and Thomas C O'Guinn (a specialist in the sociology of consumer consumption) presented a paper in which they coined the phrase 'brand communities' to capture the idea of 'a specialized community based on a structured set of social relations among admirers of a brand'. One company that has led the way in this arena is Harley-Davidson, the US motorcycle brand.

CASE STUDY Harley-Davidson

It has long been associated with the term *life-style brand*, but in many ways this definition misses the point. What marks Harley-Davidson out is the connection it has been fostering between all the people who ride Harleys; it is this social connection that makes the Harley story special, and has pulled the product along with it. Back in 1983 Harley was looking into the abyss, on the verge of collapse, facing an assault by faster, cleaner and more user-friendly Japanese bikes from the likes of Honda and Kawasaki. By contrast, the Harley was seen as big, ugly, difficult to manoeuvre, leaking oil and popular only with 'hairy bikers'. In 1983, at the height of its problems, Harley decided to establish a company-run owners group, affectionately known as HOG (Harley Owners Group). It now has in excess of 660,000 paying members from over 115 countries. This is not, however, a marketing-led initiative; it is instead strategically integrated into business-wide goals and runs throughout all of Harley's activities. Many of its most senior executives ride Harleys, demonstrating the pride they have in the company and also enabling them to better understand the experience of owning a Harley. The company prides itself on having decisions at all levels grounded in this community perspective and believes that it is this community of riders who rightfully own the brand. However, it has been the company's ability to channel the energy of its customers, helping them to shape a multifaceted community, creating real identity and belonging that is particularly noteworthy. This sense of connection has been successfully channelled by the company to help it to redefine the products and the accessories it makes. By methodically focusing on meeting these needs, the company has built substantial new businesses around motorcycle customization, riding gear, motorcycle-inspired fashion and even home decoration. It also offers services in motorcycle rentals and rider training businesses, a museum, shipping and travel. While being a US vehicle manufacturer remains a tough challenge, the organization has created a sustainable platform for the future, based around its people. Understanding why the Harley Owners Group (HOG) works is key to understanding what it takes to make connections work.

According to sociologist Ray Oldenburg, there are four characteristics of Harley's approach:

- it primarily serve the interests of community members;
- it has a persistent identity that also allows personal expression;
- it facilitates communication and interaction with other members;
- it is compelling enough to attract members to congregate around it.

However, the emotional connection to what the company stands for is equally important. 'If you want to fit in, take the bus,' shouts the HOG's Facebook page. While many businesses build products that try to please everyone, Harley are focused on striking a chord with their riders, and are not scared to polarize opinion. The view at Harley is that their customers need a cause to champion. For individuals fed up with their 'me-to' lifestyles, being different by being part of something bigger than themselves, was central to that appeal.

The HOG is a huge owner-driven community, but it is all managed by Harley. Every HOG chapter is sponsored and tied up with a Harley dealership. Harley uses this vast network to keep its ear to the ground. These communities cement the emotional bond between the company and each HOG member, by inviting their members to open days and product launches. The community is therefore treated as an exclusive club, with real benefits, which are only available to members, alongside which other loyalty style clubs can seem a pale imitation. For Harley it ensures that they have something that is highly aspirational.

The ultimate level of connection between an organization and individuals is where communities turn into fan bases, where the fans become the brand and, to a large extent, create and shape their own life with the consumer product as only a part of that experience.

Creating a fan base so 'you'll never walk alone'

At the end of 2013 David Cameron visited China. At the end of the state visit a major banquet was organized for Chinese leaders and dignitaries. The idea was that this would be an opportunity to meet and discuss important business matters which could bring the two countries closer together. However, without exception, the biggest interest of the evening was reserved for the English Premier League trophy, with dignitaries queuing up to have their photographs taken with it. British football clubs have massive support around the world. Teams like Manchester United and Liverpool are the best-supported and are both ranked by *Forbes* in the world's top six clubs, with brand values exceeding £500 million. Liverpool's motto 'You'll Never Walk Alone' captures the sense of solidarity that fans feel in being not only *attached* to a club but feeling part of a movement. It reflects the deeper connection the club has with its fan base in over 200 officially recognized branches across 30 countries in addition to a massive unofficial supporter base. What is the attraction? In his book *The Secret Life of Sports Fans*, Eric Simons (2013) highlights the importance of the interpersonal relationships and real connections which football clubs offer global supporters. According to Megan Gambino, editor of Smithsonian.com, 'the fan relationship is basically a real relationship in your brain, in which the sports team becomes a part of you in a very real sense'.[9] Being attached to the extent that you identify with a group, whether it's a sports team, a political party, a boy band or a Harley-Davidson, can affect how your body reacts and influence how you feel.

Making this kind of connection is potentially hugely powerful for organizations. Researchers have shown that people who are involved with your organization or its products as a fan are likely to spend up to 50 per cent more on your products than other regular customers. Edwina Dunn, founder of Dunnhumby, the consumer analysis business behind retail loyalty schemes at Tesco in the United Kingdom and Kroger in the United States, has spent over 25 years understanding consumer buying patterns and what drives shopper behaviour. Her new venture, Starcount, is an organization that specializes in tracking and facilitating the development of fan bases. As Dunn observes ' if you can convert just a small percentage of people from being [merely] customers into becoming true fans by building a more meaningful multi-layered relationship, then the potential business upside is significant. Putting it simply fans stay loyal and over time spend money with you.'[10] The innovative Star Count approach makes linkages between regular brands and special fan relationships to create more opportunities for deeper connections.

One organization that is embracing the development of new kinds of relationships is the UK's Guardian Media Group, which has created several different vehicles through which their readership can become far more engaged with and through their organization. For example, the *Guardian* Masterclasses cover topics from cookery to photography to writing and tap into the desire of readers to take their interests to the next level. Many of the speakers at these events demonstrate the authority of the media organization in these subject areas, but also enable the readers to form relations with other readers who physically attend these seminars and classes. There are other forums, which Guardian Media Group are creating online, through which these personal passions can be pursued, from book clubs to discussion forums. The *Guardian* is building very different connections and a far more engaged relationship with its formerly passive readership. A similar example is seen with several magazines, including *National Geographic*, which facilitates the formation of communities of interest beyond the magazine. These highly popular communities help to ensure the magazine becomes a far more integral part of readers' lives than they ever could be as a standalone purchase.

Conclusion

The degree to which organizations can connect with customers to form deeper relationships will be critical to both their success and the type of society we are able to create as the 21st century develops. Customers want to have meaningful and trusting relationships with companies, yet all around they are feeling increasingly disconnected, 'ripped off', bored and sensing they are being processed by a large machine. They often feel powerless to influence organizations that seem too big to care, distanced by a technology that risks creating as many barriers as problems it solves. Many organizations have seen this most vital of relationships as simply a series of transactions to be managed efficiently.

This chapter has explored what being truly connected to the customer can look like and how these connections can form the basis for establishing new communities of interest. Ultimately these communities need to be mobilized to turn passive customer–company links into meaningful moments that customers can identify with, want to be part of and remain loyal to as fans.

Establishing these connections with customers requires a different approach to leadership: understanding the importance of the personal connection a customer wants to have with both their products but also fellow shoppers, customers and fans. This opportunity to create lasting relationships requires leaders to grasp opportunities for redefining where the boundaries lie between the life of the organization and the lives of customers. We can see how those boundaries have become completely porous in relationships as different as the TaskRabbit schemes, which extend old ideas of 'village handymen' to the 21st century and the HOGs of Harley.

As we have seen, reconnecting thoughtfully can help customers create deeper relationships not only with the company but also with wider communities of people who share similar interests. Some of these links may at first be tangential but if companies can foster these connections they will create greater fulfillment, meaning, and happiness for individuals.

Eight steps to reconnected leadership

Step 6 – reconnecting to customers: Leadership actions

1 Active customer policies. Leaders have to start with a thorough review of all main points of customer contact so that they can consider the following:

- Are contracts with your customers clear, transparent, easy to understand and unlikely to cause misinterpretation? If not, they are likely to contribute to feelings of mistrust and you should conduct a simplification review. (One might think here of receiving a 20-page mobile phone contract that is in impenetrably small writing, relying on the sales assistant in the shop to tell you that the £40-a-month bill covers everything and then finding out that after three months you have spent several hundred pounds more than expected.)

- A reconnected leader would change those policies that may result in customer selecting options that are not right for them. They would also set out to share information and knowledge openly so that customers can make better choices. Leaders would have to ensure that their people are trained to communicate this information in the right way at the right time. However, most importantly, it requires leadership action to help colleagues to understand what is really in the best interests of the customer.

- Aim to move from a passive assumption of trust to an active approach to building trust. For example, ensure customer returns are always handled courteously handled without having to escalate and train all staff to be able to handle these customer situations.

2 Coach for service

- Develop leaders as effective coaches for all frontline colleagues to build confidence and encourage the development of connections with customers.

- Provide training and support for call centre-staff to develop confidence to better deal with negative calls, as in the examples we saw from Singapore (see page 203).

- Remove automated call-handling and increase the amount of time call-centre staff are allowed to spend answering customer queries.

3 Create customer power groups

- Create opportunities for your customers to talk to each other online about your products and services. Enable customers to make positive suggestions (and sometime negative suggestions) to other customers about best use of products etc.

- Create environments in which customer ideas are formally considered and fed back, celebrating and rewarding ideas that are taken up.

- Make the information flowing out of this site a driving force for improvement and not a sideshow owned only by someone in marketing or communications.

4 Create customer clubs as an opportunity to connect but also effectively make all your customers insiders:

- Identify with your team which products or services present the best opportunity to create an experience-based club or events that customers can attend for low/no cost. These activities should showcase your products at their best and also – crucially – help to develop relationships with the people who use your products and services.

- Help your customers to connect with other user of your products to form affiliations.

5 Connected experts

- Formally connect your internal experts with your frontline colleagues and customers so that the expertise that exists within your organization can be shared with the customer. Regard this not just as a transaction, but more importantly as an opportunity to build understanding and share learning. Viewed in this way, your internal experts become 'masters' within the organization, mentoring others in their development.

- Ideally run formal events at which your experts can meet customers to share ideas.

---

1 The rise of the customer-led economy, *Economist* Intelligence Unit Report, 2013

2 Jeremy Clarkson, *Sunday Times*, January 2013

3 Jack Lewis and Adrian Webster, What can neuroscience teach us about customer service? www.mycustomer.com, 24 March 2014

4 Predicting consumer behaviour, *IEEE Pulse* magazine, 14 February 2013; and *Singapore Business Review*, 27 September 2013, both by Gemma Calvert

5 Marissa Mayer, 2014 is the tipping point for the internet (reporting on the World Economic Forum), *Wall Street Journal*, 22 January 2014

6 Yang Jie and Laurie Burkitt, In China, IKEA is a Swede place for senior romance, *Wall Street Journal*, 1 December 2011

7 Discussion with Mike Snell, Commercial Director, Wiggle, October 2013

8 James Brilliant, Parkrun, the running revolution, *The Guardian*, 11 March 2013

9 Megan Gambino, The science of being a sports fan, Smithsonian.com, 25 March 2013

10 Interview with Edwina Dunn, Chief Operating Officer, Star Count, May 2014

Step 7: Inspiring connected innovators

09

"Organizations which are open and innovative will reap huge rewards; those which aren't will probably not exist in ten years' time. (JOHN CHAMBERS, CEO, CISCO)

Introduction

Innovation is key to maintaining competitiveness, creating jobs and improving the quality of life for everyone in society. It is particularly important today, with fresh challenges facing the planet and the wider economy. The world's most innovative companies attract a premium on their share price. Research at the INSEAD Business School has shown that keeping hold of this premium depends on the ability of leaders to encourage and connect new ideas across the organization.[1] This is where many organizations struggle, with their bias towards hierarchical decision-making, silo-working and a short-term driver mentality. Reconnected leaders need to help their organizations become far more fluid, flexible and porous if they are to maximize the likelihood of catching and deploying the best ideas.

In this chapter we will explore how leaders can create a different mindset within their organizations, one that is consciously based on a 'design by connection' mindset. We will consider how the boundaries of such organizations are far less delineated, and how leaders can enable workers to become highly collaborative. We will show how bringing together people from diverse backgrounds can create open environments where challenge is fundamental to success. Throughout we will consider case studies from organizations who have learned that such connections are critical, and we will see how trust is vital if such new development is to occur. Finally we will consider those actions that a reconnected leader can put in place to initiate innovation in their own organizations.

FIGURE 9.1   Reconnected leadership model: Inspiring connected innovators

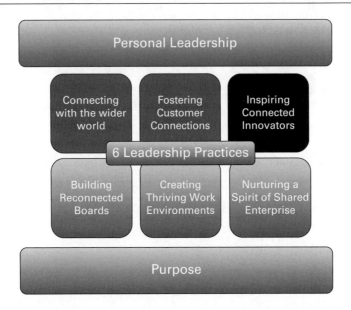

A 'design by connection' mindset

In his book, *The Living Company*, De Geus (1999) studied large and well-established 'long-lived' companies and found that they had a number of features in common:

- They were more akin to thriving eco-systems rather than rigid and heavily centralized structures, with a devolvement of decision-making to the right level. As a result, they were more tolerant of 'activities at the margins'.

- They tended to be highly active in partnerships and joint ventures.

- The boundaries of the company were less clearly delineated – local groups had more autonomy over their decisions than typical in large corporation.

- They were always listening, scanning their environments and constantly seeking opportunities. Because of their decentralized nature and strongly shared culture, it was easier for these companies to spot opportunities in a changing world and act decisively to capitalize on them.

In other words, managers were more connected in long-lived organizations than in ones that were overtaken by the innovation of others. Unfortunately many organizations still view innovation in a hierarchical way, while kick-starting 'innovation drives' through the appointment of chief innovation officers. According to a survey by the consultancy Cap Gemini (2012), in the last year alone the number of chief innovation officer roles has grown from 33 per cent to 43 per cent of major quoted companies.[2] While the appointment of a chief innovation officer can undoubtedly help focus energy and provide a short-term boost while the board figures out what it is really trying to do, it runs a deeper risk of sending a message to the wider business that innovation is covered, that they can relax, that there is someone else who is now doing the thinking and they can go back to concentrating on the day job. This hardly seems like a recipe for catalysing radical ideas.

If we want to unleash innovation, to make it once again the lifeblood of our organizations, we need a rethink, to move towards what Gray and Van der Wal (2012) calls a 'design by connection mindset'. To understand what that may look like, we will begin by looking at a group of individuals who developed the systems that underpin most of our smartphone technology, extending access to information and education across an unprecedented number of people. Surprisingly perhaps, these individuals are known as 'hackers'.

Highly collaborative workers: Hackers

Eric Von Hippel is a Professor at MIT Sloan School of Management and one of the leading thinkers on user innovation. In perhaps his most important work *Democratizing Innovation* (2005), he digs back into the early development of software and identifies how completely open it was. He recounts the story of hackers and how the unique hacker ethos first developed:

> In the early days of computer programming, commercial 'packaged' software was a rarity so that if you wanted a particular program for a particular purpose, you typically had to write the code yourself or hire someone to write it for you. As a result much of the software of the 1960s and the 1970s was developed in academic and corporate laboratories by scientists and engineers. These individuals found it a normal part of their research culture to freely give and exchange software they had written, to modify and build on one another's ideas, and to freely share their modifications. This communal behaviour became a central feature of 'hacker culture'. Indeed, in communities of open source

programmers, the term 'hacker' is still regarded as a positive term that is applied to a talented and dedicated programmer.

Similarly Stephen Levy, in his book *Hackers* (2010) highlights a positive ethic within the hacker community that has grown and spread around the world since these early days. According to Levy, there are six Hacker principles:

1 Access – anything which might teach you something about the way the world works should be unlimited and total.
2 All information should be free.
3 Promote decentralization and therefore mistrust authority.
4 Hackers should be judged by their hacking ability not their position.
5 You can create art and beauty on a computer.
6 Computers can change life for the better.

The hacker movement developed further under the impetus of Richard Stallman, a brilliant programmer in MIT's Artificial Intelligence Laboratory, who founded the Free Software Foundation and set about developing a legal mechanism that could preserve free access for all to the software developed by software hackers. The idea of free software did not immediately become mainstream as industry was especially suspicious of it. However, in 1998, Bruce Perens and Eric Raymond founded the Open Source software movement, which has continued to develop to become an important part of the software landscape.

Why has this happened? The strong ethic seen amongst software developers plays a very important part but there are also practical operational reasons. Eric Raymond, one of the early pioneers of the movement, describes Linus's law of software debugging and argues that: 'the same task can be speeded up and the cost substantially reduced when it is opened up to a great number of software users that each have a piece of the information required to fix it'. According to Raymond, in almost every situation, given a large enough number of people, the fix will be obvious to someone.

So highly collaborative working can speed up complex problem solving by a huge factor, but can it create new ideas and products? Perhaps the best-known community-led development within the Open Source World is the operating system Linux. Linux was based on software originally developed by Richard Stallman and further enhanced by Linus Torvalds in 1991. Linux powers systems such as mobile phones, tablet computers, network routers, building automation controls, televisions and video game consoles.

Indeed the Android system, in wide use on mobile devices, is built on the Linux software kernel. The Linux development community is a highly disciplined and highly skilled group of people working together towards the highest standards. Yet they achieve this without any command and control leadership. Instead, their success rests on the power of their connections through a unifying of visions, ethos, purpose and value set.

CASE STUDY Wikipedia

Wikipedia provides a final example of how this kind of collaboration by disparate groups of expert users who work together towards a common cause. The concept of holding all the world's knowledge in a single location dates back to the ancient libraries of Alexandria, but it took until 1938 for H G Wells' book of essays to glimpse the future, when he wrote of what he called the World Brain, 'It is probable that the idea of an encyclopedia's full possibilities have still to be realized.' Wikipedia was formally launched in January 2001 by Jimmy Wales and Larry Sanger. By 2014, Wikipedia had grown to include over 30.5 million freely usable articles in 287 languages, making it the world's sixth most popular website. However, initial progress on the project was incredibly slow, with only 12 articles developed in the first year. The project was on the brink of failure if it continued to be managed along traditional lines. Wales and Sanger discussed various ways to create content more rapidly. Two ideas were perhaps central to their success. The first was Richard Stallman's concept that no central organization should control editing and that it should rely on the contributions of the many and be monitored by all. The second was that it should be based on the Wiki, invented by Ward Cunningham, which enables communities to write documents collaboratively, using a simple mark-up language and a web browser (the word 'Wiki' is derived from the Hawaiian word for 'fast'). In their book *The Wiki Way*, Leuf and Cunningham (2001) described the essence of the wiki concept of fast collaboration as follows:

- A wiki invites all users to edit any page or to create new pages within the wiki website, using only a plain-vanilla web browser.
- A wiki is not a carefully crafted site for casual visitors. Instead, it seeks to involve the visitor in an continuing process of creation and collaboration that constantly changes the website landscape.
- A wiki allows non-linear, evolving, complex and networked text, argument and interaction.

- A defining characteristic of wiki technology is the ease with which pages can be created and updated.
- It differs from blogs or most other such systems in that the content is created without any defined owner or leader; it thereby allows structure to emerge according to the needs of the users.

What is noteworthy is that success was by no means a foregone conclusion. Yet this non-profit enterprise has gone on to outstrip the rate of development of major software competitors like Microsoft's *Encarta* and well-established names like *Encyclopaedia Britannica*.

But what is perhaps most startling about the development of Wikipedia is how far it differs from the way in which most conventional organizations conduct innovation. Most organizations (75 per cent) rely on internal resources for their innovation activities, while only one in four enterprises appear to be engaged in cooperation on their innovation activities. This cooperation might be with other enterprises within the group, suppliers, commercial laboratories, universities, or public research institutes.

It is worth exploring some of the other factors that have made the Wikipedia project such a success. In contrast to the turf wars that feature in so many big organizations, in Wikipedia no one owns any turf. Coordinated activity occurs through a commitment to a shared purpose, underpinned by a common ethos and a set of standards on how people should connect. Operating in this way – by connection, rather than by command and control – enables one person's work to be seamlessly linked to others'. It is a world in which the user community decides what is acceptable. This does, of course, lead to errors but it is the speed of learning and renewal that overcomes these bugs at an incredible rate. It is also apparent from Wikipedia – and indeed more generally on the web – that having clear protocols to facilitate those links to a defined standard is fundamental. Given that most organizations are still predominately designed on the basis of models that were invented in the 1890s, it is perhaps hardly surprising that companies struggle to see how they could move towards such a free-form environment. Yet it is exactly the power of organizing without organizations that will mark out the future as Clay Shirky (2008) outlined in his book *Here Comes Everybody*.

As we have seen, this new kind of environment, where users interact within their customer communities, often creates 'useful tools and infrastructure that increase the speed and effectiveness with which users can develop test and diffuse their innovations' (Von Hippel, 2005).

Creative collaborations

Together we create our future.

(Vera John-Stiener, 2005)

According to research by Professor Brian Uzzi, 'Most of us think of creativity as an innate individual talent, something that we are born with' (Lehrer, 2012). This is hardly surprising, as the image of the individual has a powerful hold over us. As cultural myths about pioneering nation-building have combined with a century of scientific argument, we have been pointed towards the notion of modern self as a largely 'self-actualizing' being. This image has been reinforced by a constant stream of business books where leaders are portrayed as individual 'superheroes', featuring the likes of Lee Iacocca, Jack Welch, Louis Gerstner, Richard Branson, Anita Roddick, Bill Gates and Steve Jobs. These books all single out one individual who has made the difference, applied creative genius or just had the guts to go further. These images have become deeply embedded and fascinate and inspire us to embark on bold adventures or difficult undertakings. This perspective was perhaps initially shaped by Jean Piaget, the renowned thinker on child and human development. His theories were developed in the early part of the 20th century, but it was not until the 1950s that his ideas truly took hold in the United States. Piaget (2001) placed the 'lone seeker of knowledge' at the heart of the cognitive development journey in the western mind. It is an idea that is now deep-rooted.

However, in her book *Creative Collaboration*, Vera John-Steiner (2005) contrasts this trajectory of thinking with the work of Lev Vygotsky, the Russian architect of a school of thinking known as 'cultural-historical psychology'. John-Steiner proposes: 'We have come to a new understanding of the life of the mind. The notion of the solitary thinker still appeals to those moulded by the western belief in individualism. However, a careful scrutiny of how knowledge is constructed and artistic forms are shaped, reveals a different reality.'

Recent scientific research supports the contentions of Vygotsky, revealing that invention and discovery are actually shaped in quite different ways to our accepted view of the world (Miller, 2013). Brian Uzzi, distinguished Professor of Leadership at The Kellogg School of Management, is one of the leading thinkers on how creative discovery actually works. He wanted to find out if individuals acting alone produced better results than collective undertakings. To test this question, he looked in detail at what worked best in science, collecting data from 21 million scientific papers published worldwide between 1945 and 2005, along with 1.9 million patent findings over a 15-year period. Using the mechanism of a citation to mark out exceptional work, Uzzi, presenting at a TEDx conference[3] shared insights from five years of study that had found that the collaborative efforts were better and more significant than the efforts of individuals. His research also showed that the level of collaboration had shifted massively. In 1950, the number of individuals with citations versus the number of collaborative efforts was about 50/50; by 2000, this number had swung completely in favour of collaborative teams, which now represented 90 per cent of all papers with citations. What was also fascinating from his research was that individual teams are roughly the same size that they were 60 years ago, but they are now far more disparate, operating across geographic and cultural boundaries. The work showed that teams that came from the most dislocated backgrounds, brought more variety of background to the table and produced the highest level of success.

What is equally staggering is that this had really started to happen in the 1970s, before the internet began to accelerate this trend. Professor Uzzi then investigated what kind of collaborators improved the chances that these collaborative undertakings would do better. He found that, when choosing collaborators, people tended to make choices on two dimensions. The first was how much experience an individual had: were they a novice with a lot of fresh ideas, or a seasoned operator? The second dimension was whether the individual selected was well known to them, with a strong track record over time ('prior relations') or whether they had no connections with this person. Professor Uzzi found that low impact teams tended to be made up of people who had worked together a lot in the past. In these situations, although the team may work together well, they tend to produce a low level of impact in terms of innovative outcome. To test these findings further, Uzzi conducted a review of Broadway musicals dating back to the late 1800s all the way up to the present day's Jukebox Musical formats. What the research found was that the sweet spot was created when a mixture of prior experience is combined with fresh perspectives, ie experience with expertise.[4] At one level this vindicates something we have long known about teams. However, what shines through most strongly from this work, is that it is the diversity of talent combined with the quality of the connections that delivers the greatest impact.

FIGURE 9.2 Impact of group composition on creativity and results

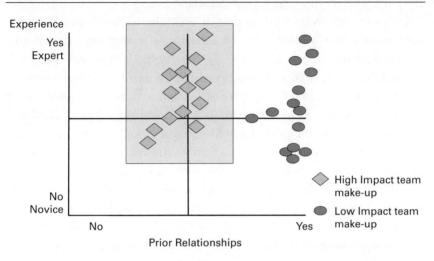

NB: Diagram based on research and presentation given by Professor Brian Uzzi–Kellogg School of Management 2013 Northwestern University, USA

Diverse Teams Win

The study by Professor Uzzi and his team at Northwestern University Kellogg School showed that teams made up only of people who had worked together before, irrespective of their expertise, had a lower impact in terms of their creativity and results, than teams made up of a diverse group of individuals. Teams with a mix of people who had never worked together, some who were inexperienced with others who were experts.

This rigorous scientific research is echoed in the reviews of eminent sociologist Randell Collins, who looked at the great works of science throughout history, and in the work of Professor Vera John-Steiner, who considered collaborations between great scientists and artists and observed that 'the construction of a new mode of thought relies on and thrives with collaboration'. Her work reinforces the view that if we are willing to look, the world is full of the benefits of individuals connecting to create innovative results. Some of these creative collaborations manage to mesh different backgrounds and forms into fresh styles; others completely transform their fields. When we look beyond our organizations we can perhaps see this most clearly in the productive partnerships of Watson and Crick, Marie and Pierre Curie, Georgia O'Keeffe and Alfred Stieglitz, or Aaron Copland and

Leonard Bernstein. This work all serves to illustrate that the mind, rather than thriving on solitude, is clearly dependent upon the reflections, renewal and trust inherent in sustained human relationships.

Unfortunately, when considering diversity in organizations, the spotlight usually moves quickly in the direction of compliance, or towards individual rights and equality of opportunity. Both approaches are just and valid, but we need to move beyond these narrow interpretations to embrace the richness that diversity of background, of experience and of thought can bring. We need to move beyond just bringing new blood into an organization and hoping that will be a good thing. What the research shows is that we need to take a radically different view on the value of diversity, which shifts it from a peripheral compliance concern of the board, to one which puts it the heart of the business's innovation and renewal. Leaders need to foster connections with different communities and different traditions, looking for people who have not all completed the same pathway through college followed by a succession of bigger jobs in the same industry. It also requires leaders to encourage people in their teams to take on different interests beyond work. This is particularly important when it comes to the development of teams. The research of Professor Uzzi clearly shows that the ability to blend and mix teams from many backgrounds creates the right conditions for innovation to thrive. It is in the edges, the boundaries between one form and another, that new realities are crafted. In the United States, for example, it is second-generation immigrants who are bringing together two cultures to demonstrate the highest levels of creativity and registering the greatest number of patent applications in the US patent office.

Lee Fleming (2010), Professor of Engineering at Stanford, explains this through the analogy of a mountain biker who specializes in jumping off high platforms and also happens to work with an orthopaedic surgeon who is interested in reducing back injury; this kind of unusual mix is the type of collaboration which results in new thinking and ultimately in the development of mountain bike suspension systems that protect the spine. In Fleming's view, innovation happens best when people use their membership of two distinct communities to combine previously disparate elements to produce a new synthesis. Professor Uzzi (2012) observes that his work has caused him to think about creativity less as the spark of individual inspiration and more as an import–export operation, where people bring ideas from one area (in which it may be common practice) to another, where it is novel, to produce highly innovative breakthroughs.

Synapses – The web of trust

In spite of rapid advances in many aspects of commerce, we have held onto our construct of organizations as machines with inputs and outputs, controlled by pulling levers. This desire to retain control over complexity has caused leaders to try to map the processes with step-by-step charts, showing how each cog connects with the next. The trouble with this mechanistic controlling model of reality is that it doesn't work well in a highly complex and fast changing environment.

So is there a better way of thinking about organization that better fosters innovation? Fritjof Capra's work on living systems certainly suggests that a different outlook is required if we want to foster innovation (Capra, 2003). Rather than viewing 21st-century organizations as machines, Capra proposes the analogy of organizations as 'living organisms' with a will of their own, which you can't control but you can cultivate to encourage growth in the right way. Such complex systems also have their own distinctive characteristics – most notably their ability to learn and adapt and to thrive on constant feedback from their environments (the world outside). From this they develop a memory of what works and what doesn't.

As we have seen, in order to drive up innovation through high levels of ideas exchange, sharing and collaboration across boundaries, organizations must become much less hierarchical and leaders must move their thinking from control to connectivity. Connectivity will become the asset that defines the culture of winning organizations. But how is it that creative connectivity seems to flow in some environments and not in others?

Sir Charles Scott Sherrington won the Nobel Prize in 1932 for his groundbreaking work on neurons. He showed how neurons signal to each other and to other cells such as those in muscles – literally sparking ideas to trigger action (Burke, 2007). Synapse comes from the term 'synaptein' which was coined by Sherrington from the Greek *syn* (together) and *haptein* (to clasp). Visible only through an electron microscope, these small gaps are filled by chemicals that allow the neurons to pass from one cell to another.

Innovation today depends on fostering rich combinations of people, both within and beyond a business. A model like this works badly where decisions have to be passed up and down hierarchies, rather than working directly with the one key person. This borderless world requires complete transparency and trust.

John Holland is part of a movement trying to change our view of organizations – from environments controlled by the directions from the top or centre, to ones that operate like a city that continues to change, thrive and grow, through what appears to be a process of constant renewal.[5] We can't control all the activities in cities, but we can provide them with critical infrastructure and a limited set of standards. According to Professor Geoffrey West from the Santa Fe Institute in the United States, in these highly complex environments, knowledge flows seamlessly and energy and creativity are unleashed in a self-managing and self-sustaining way. West found that as cities double in size they produce a further 15–20 per cent increase in productivity as measured through the rate of innovation. He believes this is driven by the number of connections that are made between people, often meeting at random and sharing ideas. But in order to work, these environments rely on strong cultures and high levels of trust.[6] In a trusting environment, observes Vera John-Steiner (2005), 'radical ideas are respectfully considered, opportunities for full participation are guaranteed and peers and co-workers are influential in creative outcomes'. To foster such environments requires a different kind of leadership.

Here again lessons can be drawn from the experiences of the technical community. Open innovation communities value technical contributions above all, eschewing titles and even democracy in favour of proven technology capability (Chesbrough and Appleyard, 2007). According to Lee Fleming, they also typically have a 'strong aversion to non-technical sources of prestige and authority'. In such technical innovation environments it is clear that trust is not based on a person's position within the organization, nor for that matter on their ability to display strong management characteristics; rather, trust comes out of respect for the capability and judgement that an individual demonstrates through the technical work that they do. Formal management is far less trusted than this hierarchy of technical respect. This respect and trust then spreads through a network of technical connections, enabling a leader to mobilize dense and cohesive networks, in part because they are embedded in such networks themselves.[7]

What the research into Open Source communities has shown is that fluidity come through webs of trust, based on individual respect, which can traverse all traditional organization boundaries, forming what Professor Von Hippel has described as 'innovation communities'. The research also indicates that, linked through common purpose and bringing rich creativity at the boundaries where they meet, these communities are led by very different kinds of people.

Robert B Cialdini, author of the 2006 best-seller *Influence: The psychology of persuasion*, proposes that companies need 'to set up systems that ensure collaborative exchanges whether or not the collaboration seems necessary to the management'. Professor Cialdini believes that innovation is all about connections; it is a 'contact sport'.

The edge of chaos: Making innovative connections

As outlined earlier, in western tradition there is still a tendency to see innovation as a distinct activity, a separate function conducted in labs. That view is changing as emerging economies and small countries demonstrate that there is a very different way to make innovation happen.

Jugaad *Innovation*

The growth of *Jugaad* in India is one such example. A very different approach to innovation, it places connections at the heart of its philosophy. *Jugaad* is a Hindu term applied to a creative or innovative idea, providing quick, alternative ways of solving a problem. It grew out of its application to situations in which improvisation was essential, often taking place in remote and poor regions that lacked resources. The *Jugaad* movement has now gathered a community of enthusiasts that sees the approach as proof of India's burgeoning creativity, in addition to offering a cost-effective way to solve the challenges of everyday life in a fast-developing economy. *Jugaad* is all about frugality and flexibility and is marked out by its inclusive approach.

CASE STUDY ChotuKool – India

One example of *Jugaad* in practice is the development of the Godrej–ChotuKool refrigerator. Traditional refrigerators can cost upwards of $350 in India, and are therefore out of reach for those struggling to emerge from poverty. Made from plastic insulation material with wires running inside, the ChotuKool model works on the basis of the Peltier effect, effectively pulling heat out of the box. It can hold a temperature of 4 degrees, which may not be good enough for making ice, but is just fine for keeping food chilled and stopping it from going off quickly. The refrigerator retails at a tenth of the price of a standard fridge unit and, at $35, is an aspirational solution to the problem of food storage for Indian people. Its stripped back simplicity encapsulates the *Jugaad* philosophy perfectly: to do the job that's required, and no more, no bells or whistles. The low cost and 'just right' solution came about as a result of what inventor Gopalan Sunderraman calls a 'full community immersion'. As he told the *WIPO* Magazine: 'Only when you jump into the fishbowl can you learn how

FIGURE 9.3 *Jugaad* innovation

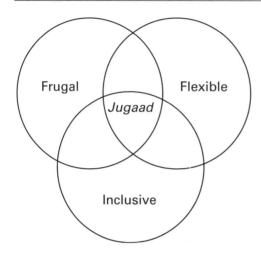

This figure shows the components which make up Jugaad design. The connections made through such an inclusive approach to new product development, is one of the reasons why Jugaad is bringing a freshness back to design. Finding out exactly what the customer does and doesn't value allows innovators to produce stripped back, simple, low-cost solutions which highly competitive.

the fish live. If you're outside the fishbowl observing, you cannot understand what the fish go through.'[8] This requirement for a new kind of connectedness is not confined to low-cost items or roadside start-ups. The conglomerate Tata have recently announced the Nano car, which is being sold in India for less than $1,300, a fraction of the price of a similar model in the West. Its design logic was again based on Jugaad principles, which have been popularized by Navi Radjou, co-author of *Jugaad Innovation* (Radjou *et al*, 2012) and a thought leader on business innovation and leadership.

CASE STUDY   The Aakash tablet – India

This type of innovation isn't just about low-tech frugality. The Aakash (meaning 'sky' in Hindi) is a tablet computer that sells for just $22 to students or $39 to other citizens. Reuters reported that the tablet could end the digital divide and give the poor in all countries access to computing and the rest of the world. The Aakash puts tablet computing into the hands of people that would never be able to afford such technology and in so doing is transformative. The tablet is the size of a paperback, features a touch screen and comes complete with video conferencing and wi-fi. It was originally supported by the Indian government, who bought 100,000 for school children in deprived areas. CEO Suneet Singh Tuli told *Guardian* Media that:

> *The development of the tablet stemmed from a realization that lack of internet adoption in many parts of the world was primarily due to lack of affordability... We're bridging the gap by offering cost-effective, high-specification devices and internet access that offers excellent value to all.'*

The Aakash has the second-largest tablet computer sales in India ahead of the Apple iPad and is just behind Samsung. The device is now going global and was launched in Africa in partnership with World Vision in the development agency's projects in African countries. However, this technology isn't just a solution for emerging economies; the *Jugaad* approach is now spreading beyond India, finding applications around the world. A commercial version of the Aakash has been launched in the United Kingdom and the United States. Called The Datawind UbiSlate tablet and now made in the UK, it was launched at the end of 2013 for only £30 and $38 in the UK and the US respectively, massively undercutting all its rivals, but focusing on people in low-income communities and schools. In a business world where complexity has overrun and corporations have become cut off from the customers they are trying to serve – a bit of collaborative *Jugaad* thinking may just be what we need.

The United States continues to be the most innovative place in the world. Silicon Valley ranks as the global number one in terms of having the right mix of people, ideas and finance to not only start up technology companies, but to also build them to full independence. There are only two places in Europe and the Middle East that rank in the global top 10: London, which is the most successful start-up location in Europe, and Tel-Aviv, which has a very different story to tell according to *Tech Magazine* White Board.

With the highest density of start-ups in the world, there are now 63 Israeli companies listed on NASDAQ – more than Europe, Japan, Korea, India and China combined. Almost 40 per cent of Israeli hi-tech employees work in the research and development (R&D) departments of multinational companies like Intel, Microsoft, Cisco or Google, all of which have subsidiaries in the country. Tel Aviv has the highest output of start-ups and a healthy mix of start-ups in all stages of development. Importantly, as part of this mix, Israel attracts a high number of immigrants to keep its start-up culture freshly topped up with new ideas and talent. This remarkable track record of innovation is seen by many as the archetypal start-up nation, with much of that activity taking place in advanced technology. In the New York Times best-seller *Start-Up Nation*, Dan Senor and Saul Singers identify the factors creating the conditions that have propelled Israel into this leadership position. They observe that 'fluidity, a key ingredient for entrepreneurialism, is produced when people cross boundaries, turn societal norms upside down and agitate… to catalyse radical ideas'. William Baumol, a Professor at Princeton, argues that this ideal environment is best described as 'the edge of chaos'. He defines the edge as 'the estuary region where rigid order and random chaos meet and generate high levels of adaptation, complexity and creativity'. With its porous and fluid boundaries, the Israeli experience provides a template for others to follow, with many traits that are similar to the *Jugaad* movement. However, Senor and Singer are at pains to point out that this is not enough. They highlight some unique cultural facets of the Israeli environment, of which two stand out in particular. First is the strong sense of identity, combined with hard work and team discipline that come out of the experience of national service, which all Israelis go through. Second is something that Israelis refer to as *rosh gadol*, which literally means 'big head'; this is not referring to arrogance, rather the ability to think for themselves rather than just following instructions. However, the meaning of *rosh gadol* goes further and emphasizes that people should use their judgement to not blindly follow, but rather to improvise to do what works and always what is right, even if that means 'challenging the chief'. It means that Israeli technology start-ups are always pushing the boundaries. The Indian and Israeli environments in many ways could not be more different, but they do share some of the same ethos whether in *Jugaad* or *rosh gadol* mindsets, emphasizing the need for fluidity, inclusion to help people to challenge conventions and improvising on a shoestring.

These are also characteristics that may tend to surface most frequently in modern urban environments. Research in the United States found that a disproportionately high number of technology patents are created in a small number of urban areas. Even in the best-known technology cluster, the centre of gravity is rapidly shifting from the leafy suburbs of Silicon Valley to the city of San Francisco. In Britain, some urban environments are becoming global centres of technological innovation in their own right, with eco-system connections between science, small start-ups, bigger enterprises, education and the arts providing fertile soil within which innovative developments can grow. These are 'incubator environments', creating talented fermentations that are well suited to growing and spreading ideas quickly. At the other extreme, a radical set of developments are emanating from China. Judge Business School Professor and author of *Dragons at Your Door* Peter Williamson describes how Chinese business is quickly connecting innovation with customers: it's 'probably the best sandpit in the world right now for quickly getting new products to market, testing them with real customers and improving them'.[9]

From research and development to connect and develop: How connecting and developing improves innovation

Some very large organizations have now recognized the central importance of creating a more porous structure, with far greater connections to a diverse set of college institutions and small creative start-ups. In doing so, they are creating their own 'disruptive environments' where ideas and experience can collide. One organization that recognized the risk it faced from becoming too large and too bureaucratic is Procter & Gamble.

CASE STUDY Procter & Gamble

Procter & Gamble (P&G) is a true behemoth of an organization. Founded in 1836, it had sales of $83.68 billion in 2012, serving 4.6 billion customers around the world. Larry Huston and Nabil Sakkib were senior figures in Procter & Gamble's corporate research and development function based in Cincinnati, and in 2006 they talked about their changing perspective on how development needs to produce breakthrough ideas. They observed that most companies were still clinging to what they called the 'invention model', which is centred on a bricks-and-mortar R&D infrastructure and the belief that innovation must principally reside within an organization's own four walls. To be sure, these companies are increasingly trying to buttress their labouring R&D departments with acquisitions and selective innovation outsourcing. However, as Huston and Sakkib explained, by 2000 it was clear to them that their invent-it-ourselves model was not capable of sustaining high levels of top-line growth. 'Our R&D productivity had levelled off, and our innovation success rate – the percentage of new products that met financial objectives – had stagnated, squeezed by nimble competitors, flattening sales, lacklustre new launches.' They recognized that the world's innovation landscape had changed yet they hadn't changed their innovation model since the late 1980s. So in 2003 they launched their 'Connect & Develop' initiative, which opened the doors of their innovation process to the outside world for the first time. In 2013 they enhanced the approach by launching their Open Innovation website, aiming to speed and simplify external innovation connections, linking innovators directly to top company needs, and P&G business leaders directly to external innovation submissions.

The approach allows P&G to review new ideas more quickly and more efficiently for strategic fit or scalability across the business. 'Our focus is on strengthening areas of our open innovation work to deliver more discontinuous, breakthrough innovations. Part of that work means making connections both easier and more effective,' said Laura Becker, General Manager of Connect & Develop.[10] P&G's approach is highly porous, actively connecting with and bringing in fresh ideas to the heart of their organization. The website lets innovators link directly to P&G's posted needs, which are organized by business area and searchable by topic. As a result of this work, there are now more than 2,000 global partnerships, which have delivered dozens of global game-changer products to consumers, accelerated innovation development and increased productivity, both for P&G and its partners. The website has served as P&G's 'open front door to the world', allowing any innovator anywhere to share their innovations with the Company.

One recent example of how P&G's Connect & Develop initiative works is the Academia Partnership established between them and the University of Leeds in the UK. A distinctive feature of the partnership is its innovative approach to getting collaborations working on the ground. Within P&G, a dedicated 'Connect & Develop' Board identifies the potential academics partners for key projects, while university researchers are also encouraged to approach P&G with ideas. With intellectual property and confidentiality issues already covered by the strategic partnership agreement, work can get under way very quickly. P&G's joint projects with Leeds include more than a dozen PhD and post-doctoral projects, but the partnership also gives the company broader access to expertise across the university.

Equally important to P&G's academic connections are its strategic partnerships with other organizations. For example, through a 'Connect & Develop' relationship with MonoSol of Indiana on the development of its Tide washing brand, P&G created 'Tide Pods', which is on track to becoming a $500 million-brand in its first year. To fully enable the project to flourish, the MonoSol and P&G teams had to function as one. P&G brought a deep history of cleaning, while MonoSol brought the world's leading experience in water-soluble film delivery systems. The chemistry behind Tide Pods grew out of the close collaboration between the two companies, with the film and detergent chemically designed to work together. Developing the sophisticated chemistry to enable this product took years of work and resulted in patents pending for both MonoSol and P&G.

P&G has achieved a staggering 60 per cent uplift in innovation since initiating its Connect & Develop programme. This demonstrates the extent of potential growth in innovation for organizations that can better connect with external partners and find ways to make effective collaboration work.

By doing so, they are effectively acting as an innovation hub for technology development – fostering the development of expertise and enabling what can often be very small start-ups to achieve scale. The P&G approach demonstrates that this kind of partnership does not need to involve acquisition, although it does involve investment of time, money and expertise. It is unsurprising that a number of organizations have sought to create these relationships with smaller companies through venture funds, as outlined in the example of Google and also in operation with the likes of BT and IKEA. What is exciting about the P&G approach is that it retains the element of openness, providing the freedom for creativity and continuous learning on all sides. These are as such both commercial and intellectual relationships, and mirror some of the learning we explored earlier about Open Source development. Innovating in this way fully articulates the benefits of connection.

CASE STUDY Unilever, a Foundry for ideas

Like rivals Procter & Gamble, Unilever has been keen to collaborate, recognizing the growing imperative to connect with audiences in more meaningful ways beyond ad campaigns. Unilever has been prominent amongst the brands in devoting time and resources to cultivating these collaborations with tech companies and has thrown open the doors to start-ups everywhere through the creation of The Unilever Foundry, a new platform that unites the company's efforts to work with start-ups. The Foundry will serve as Unilever's flagship, global tech collaboration and investment programme. Keith Weed, Unilever Chief Marketing and Communications Officer, says the Foundry initiative is unique for its 'pitch to pilot' approach. As part of the three-pronged programme, start-ups can submit ideas to the Foundry site which will host a series of projects on different themes. Successful applicants will get $50,000 and a chance to create a pilot programme with a major Unilever brand. The Foundry is linked to Unilever's existing venture capital arm. It is about shifting corporate mindset, to emulate the processes and mentality of start-ups, making the shift from the over-baked, over-tested campaign mentality to a more nimble approach. 'We spend a lot of time doing planning and perfecting,' says Weed. 'What start-ups do is launch and learn. It's good for us.' Unilever see this as an opportunity to shape the future.[11]

Conclusion

Throughout this chapter we have explored how innovation is built on trusting relationships allowing information and insight to flow across fluid boundaries. We saw the first examples of the power of this kind of communal behaviour set out in the 'Hacker' principles developed at MIT in the late 1960s and early 1970s where highly decentralized and non-hierarchical structures helped to facilitate open access to information and spurred an environment of constant learning. We showed how these ideas were taken further in the creation of Wikipedia and how the rules of 'fast collaboration' enabled content to be created without designated owners or leaders.

The research of Professor Brian Uzzi and his team demonstrated just how powerful such collaborative working can be, showing how collaborative teams outperform lone individuals in their creative output, by a factor a three to one. Professor Uzzi's research also noted that the more diverse the teams were, the more creative they were.

We then considered how these components of successful innovation were being activated in radical ways by being immersed in local communities to produce different and cheaper solutions in the *Jugaad* revolution that is sweeping India. The fluid exchange of information, insights and ideas present in India were also evident in the start-up nation that is modern Israel, which once again emphasized the need for completely porous boundaries and open and collaborative environments. The Israeli innovation experience also highlighted a need to create environments in which individuals feel confident enough to be able to challenge their leaders and the status quo, to take their own path. Once again this ties back to the ideas discussed in Step 4 – where leaders nurture a spirit of shared enterprise, when they enable people to gain real mastery in their own areas and allow individuals the autonomy they need to express themselves fully.

For those who might believe that such radical thinking is all well and good, but only works in start-up environments, we considered how two behemoths of the consumer goods industry, Procter & Gamble and Unilever, have used these ideas to reignite their product development pipelines by consciously creating highly collaborative 'connect and develop' environments, in which their own employees and those of partners, start-ups and academic institutions can work seamlessly together.

However, the success of all these new connections relies also on the ways leaders enable webs of trust to be woven around what Frijtof Capra called 'living organisms'. To pull these threads together the role of a leader must be transformed from a locus that is still centred on control in many organizations, to one centred on connectivity.

A reconnected leader therefore has a pivotal role to play in creating the conditions in which such environments can flourish. Their focus is on creating a sense of solidarity, where people are working together towards a common purpose, where there are high levels of subsidiarity with decisions consciously made in a decentralized way and where diversity of views are welcomed in an open spirit of reciprocity. Such highly connected approaches are outstripping more conventional innovation rates around the globe.

We can already see that leaders who can inspire such communities for innovation will find themselves acting as hubs where truly borderless communities of highly committed individuals come together to produce their best work, motivated not by the money but rather by the opportunity of working with respected peer groups on highly meaningful activities.

The power of connection in innovation is captured in what the Chinese call 'Red Thread Thinking'. In her book about the ancient Chinese legend, Debra Kaye recounts how the myth can help us to rethink the practical benefits of connection.

According to the myth, Chinese gods tie an invisible red thread around the ankles of those that are to meet or help each other in a certain way: 'The thread may stretch or tangle, but never break.' Just as people are destined to meet and connect, so too will the best innovations result from unexpected affinities and relationships, provided that the conditions are created in which those connections can happen. These red threads of innovation are the connecting strands of relationships woven of knowledge, memories and insights that leaders weave together to create a multi-textured fabric of seamless interconnectivity. It is a powerful and useful image, one that is worth remembering when leaders are exploring how to best move their innovation agenda forward.

Eight steps to reconnected leadership

Step 7 – Reconnecting through innovation: Leadership actions

1 Develop structures and process to support innovation. Organization structures in many businesses rely on formal organization lines drawn on charts. If such ideas of organization ever did work in practice then they do not work today. The ability therefore of leaders to design porous, fluid and agile organizations that facilitate the

movement of people and ideas is key to becoming a connected innovator (see Chapter 4 on connected work environments).

2 Develop innovation skills. Hal Gregersen, Professor of Leadership at INSEAD and co-author of *The Innovator's DNA* (2011) believes that five key skills can be taught to aid 'disruptive innovation':

- Questioning allows innovators to challenge the status quo and consider new possibilities. Any innovation always starts with a question.

- Observing helps innovators detect small details – in the activities of customers, suppliers and other companies – that suggest new ways of doing things.

- Networking permits innovators to gain radically different perspectives from individuals with diverse backgrounds.

- Experimenting prompts innovators to relentlessly try out new experiences, take things apart and test new ideas.

- Associational thinking – drawing connections amongst questions, problems or ideas from unrelated fields – is triggered by questioning, observing, networking and experimenting and is the catalyst for creative ideas.

3 Crowdsource plus – Crowdsourcing is defined as 'the practice of obtaining needed services, ideas, or content by soliciting contributions from a large group of people and especially from the online community rather than from traditional employees or suppliers'. Opening up a problem to a pool of diverse talent can lead to huge gains. However, it can have major disadvantages, most notably that many of the solutions developed can be weak and shallow solutions from people who don't invest the time or fail to understand the nature of the challenge. The volume of ideas can also make it costly and counterproductive for a company to evaluate each and every one. The difficulties are not with the idea of opening up innovation, but with an unwieldy execution. To ensure that the ideas that you do tap into are worth having, there are some key initial steps to follow:

- Identify who you want to be members of your virtual think tank – your experts of choice. With technology these people could be anywhere in the world. Nurture a link with these people, or get your team to each pick one and get them interested in work you are doing.

- Identify a specific topic that you need to develop some fresh ideas around.

- Create a forum (online or real-time face-to-face) where you can facilitate a really in-depth discussion about the topic.

- Conduct these CrowdSource Plus sessions with a mix of core and new members on a regular basis. It is a less expensive way of creating the Connect & Develop model outlined in P&G's approach and can be a first step towards deeper collaborations. The plurality of perspectives on a certain idea can really open up new directions of thinking.

4 Mini innovation labs (MILs) – MILs can quickly and inexpensively pull people from across an organization to look at ideas and make recommendations. Given small budgets, such teams can deliver big breakthroughs quickly, without necessarily distracting others from the day job. MIL's have the added benefit of accelerating talent development and exposing the best and brightest to the top of the organization on tangible initiatives rather than plodding through more conventional management development processes. Linked with some of our top research facilities, these mini-labs can become real innovation incubators, fostering a different outlook across the whole enterprise. To achieve the most effective implementation of MIL's, the following approaches should be considered:

- Start with small initiatives that, even if they fail, will not dent your performance or the confidence of the team. Use these experiences to then scale up and spread ideas. By using real world environments to field test ideas (using the ideas of *Jugaad*), you will get immediate feedback on whether they work. Also, because they are in real-world settings, you will find that other business unit managers in your operation will be keener to take them on, without having to go through the normal presentation and pushing process that takes up so much time.

- Identify a key issue facing the organization/business unit.

- Identify a group of people who will be involved in developing an innovative solution. Build a blend of experienced and new talent and where appropriate a mix of internal and external talent. Also ensure the group includes frontline people from the unit that has been targeted to act as the MIL and give them a development objective while the MIL is under way.

- Allow the group to work in real-time, within a real part of the business, to test out their ideas in practice – to see what works and what doesn't. Remove the normal financial reporting constraints from the unit while the MIL is under way; otherwise this will kill the initiative.

- Have the people leading the MIL report back to the senior management team on the progress they are making and the recommendations they would make.

5 Shared purpose and identity:

- To foster an innovative environment, it is essential that the business or unit develops some common principles for operating.

- Emphasize the behaviours identified in Chapter 2 on purpose and principle – solidarity, reciprocity and plurality – to consider new ideas while being clear about your own.

- Also see Step 1 on purpose.

6 Viral spread:

- Where possible, avoid formal low-interaction presentations as a means of spreading ideas in your business or unit – people like to feel that they are masters of their own destiny, particularly when it comes to new ways of doing things.

- Remembering that it is peer-to-peer recognition that is a strong motivator, set up regular peer-to-peer reviews between parts of your business, where people have to go and see, learn and feed back what they have seen and what they are going to do differently.

7 Create a hinterland of connections:

- Leaders need to create links with multiple organizations that act as an amplifier of the creative process that is going on within an organization. A reconnected leader will be at the forefront of forging such links, actively looking for where new ideas are coming from and making it their business to ensure that the organization is as actively hooked up to the widest possible network.

- As a first step to establishing a link with a university, invite them to come in and look at your organization through people spending time with you in the form of internships or PhD projects.

- Also encourage links with small start-ups in your area, perhaps as business mentor, or indeed just through some form of ideas forum.

8 Encourage others to start small:

- Let people know that you are interested in their fresh ideas about the business and make it your business to spend time talking to people about the work that THEY are doing.

- Find out about their 'red thread' connections beyond the immediate workspace; encourage them to bring some of this thinking to work.

- Fostering these kinds of dialogues will start to build trust. The more you watch and listen, the more people will gain in confidence that they can try out new ideas.

- Watch, listen and adapt.

9 *Rosh gadol* sessions:

- To foster innovation you have to encourage more people to develop a *rosh gadol* attitude, which we explored in our review of start-ups in Tel-Aviv. *Rosh gadol* is all about 'challenging the chief'. Above all it's about trying to get everyone thinking about moving the agenda forward.

- However, just challenging the chief without the individual innovation to demonstrate that there is a better way, is just obstructionism. To avoid misunderstandings, encourage people to think of a 'better way' and persuade others in the team that their ideas are sensible – then, going with the energy of the group can create a powerful force for change.

- Once you are confident in setting this tone for your working style one to one – consider running a *rosh gadol* talk-back session with the wider team – workforce. These sessions are always difficult to encourage real challenge, so the groundwork you do one-to-one is going to be key.

---

1 Hal Gregersen, Senior Affiliate Professor of Leadership at INSEAD, The world's most innovative companies 2013, @INSEADknowledge, 2013

2 Based on a study by Cap Gemini Consulting and IESE Business School, *Baseline* Magazine, April 2012

3 Brian Uzzi, TEDx Northwestern University, 2012

4 *ibid.*

5 John Holland, Building blocks and innovation, TEDx University of Michigan, October 2010

6 Geoffrey West, A physicist solves the city, *New York Times*, 17 December 2010

7 Tatiana Bouzdine and Marina Bourakova-Lorgnier, Learning and capabilities: The role of social capital within business networks, European Conference on Organisational Knowledge, April 2004

8 Gopalan Sunderraman, *WIPO* Magazine, India, December 2013

9 Peter Williamson, Cambridge Judge Business School, YouTube, December 2012

10 Connect and Develop launches new website, P&G.com, February 2013

11 Teressa Iezzi, Unilever looks to forge new partnerships with startups, www.fastcocreate.com, May 2014

Step 8: Personal leadership

Introduction

To change the way we lead, we first need to change the way we think about our own personal leadership qualities. In this chapter we will examine how we can create a new model for personal leadership that underpins connectedness and integration and considers the actions leaders can take to bring this new leadership approach to life. As we have seen, poor leadership judgement becomes more likely when leaders are insufficiently connected to the new realities in increasingly volatile and uncertain global markets. Indeed, according to research conducted by Boston Consulting Group (BCG), 50 per cent of all organizations recognize that they have not developed sufficient leadership capability to meet the new challenges facing their organizations. Rosalind Torres, a Partner at BCG, believes that most companies and business schools are not equipping their leaders effectively and goes so far as to observe that much leadership development is paradoxically stunting their leaders' development.[1] Leaders must consider whether what they are thinking and doing continues to be relevant, and learn to work in a way that lets them anticipate changes in the world, in their business and in their lives. To do so effectively they must become far more connected to employees, the wider organization and the world around them. Throughout this chapter, we will explore how leaders can bring this extra dimension to their leadership.

We have so far considered how two of the three pillars of reconnected leadership function. Step 1 focused on the need for leaders to reconnect their organizations with a guiding sense of *purpose*. We then looked at how purpose could be operationalized through a series of six leadership practices, each bringing a different dimension of connectivity into play. We will now turn our attention to our last and critical chapter: Step 8 and the dimension of *personal leadership*. Personal leadership is critical in reconnecting because it both activates and integrates all the other steps we have discussed so far, while also ensuring that connection is something that occurs at a personal level. Without the personal leadership of Step 8, a new statement of purpose will remain as only words on a page. Without personal leadership, introducing new leadership practices risks becoming a series of isolated projects rather than a radically different way of operating the business.

As we discussed in the introduction to the book, we are at a turning point in our history and new forces are being unleashed. We have captured how these forces relate to our businesses under the theme of *connection*. We have seen how to build connections that run across porous boundaries to inspire innovation and foster connections that transform interactions with customers into relationships with meaning. We have seen how to build connections with the wider world that reflect our responsibilities as integrated members of communities. We have also observed how to create connections between people that nurture a spirit of sharing and enterprise, and which bring people together in ways that enable them to thrive and tie them to a purpose, providing everyone with a greater sense of meaning and direction. The power of reconnecting in this way can be deeply transformative, requiring everyone in an organization to re-imagine their relationships to create

FIGURE 10.1 Reconnected leadership model: Personal leadership

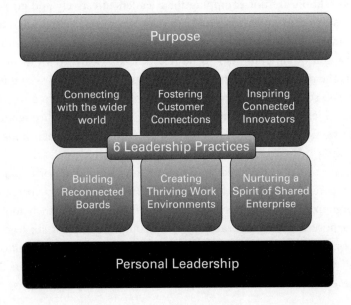

greater collaboration, transparency, sharing and empowerment in all aspects of their work. This chapter will consider a new approach to personal leadership, which will enable and underpin these other pillars of the reconnected leadership model.

Creating a pivotal leadership axis

The focus of this approach to personal leadership is not about deepening theoretical understanding or defining leadership competencies (of which there are already far too many definitions). Rather, it is about striving to create a better foundation from which we can lead in an increasingly volatile world. In Confucianism, the dilemma of creating a point of stability in a dynamic environment is encapsulated in the concept of a 'constant pivot', which makes it possible to maintain a sense of dynamism while retaining stability, honesty and sincerity in volatile situations. A simple pivot is often shaped like a triangle, with a strong base rising to an apex, which facilitates flexibility and movement. Providing stability and flexibility, strength and fluidity at one and the same time, a pivot enables us to remain constant and connected simultaneously to what may appear to be conflicting demands. It provides an unwavering centre in a changing world. It allows us to move past 'either/or' thinking and beyond weak compromise to create a point from which the greatest leverage can be

FIGURE 10.2 Personal leadership model 1

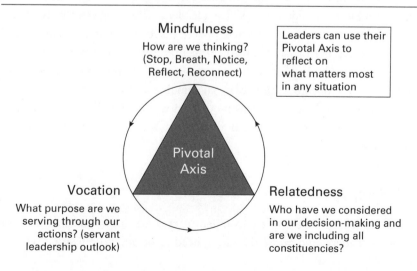

Mindfulness
How are we thinking?
(Stop, Breath, Notice,
Reflect, Reconnect)

Leaders can use their
Pivotal Axis to
reflect on
what matters most
in any situation

Pivotal
Axis

Vocation
What purpose are we
serving through our
actions? (servant
leadership outlook)

Relatedness
Who have we considered
in our decision-making and
are we including all
constituencies?

achieved. Used wisely, a pivot can create an axis of energy between apparent extremes.

We can extend this thinking to our leadership model. Without the strength, balance and flexibility that comes from having a pivotal axis at the heart of our leadership approach, no amount of leadership skills development will enable us to succeed. Creating our own leadership 'pivot' can help us to connect with all the issues around us, without losing our sense of what is important.

The three key elements in the pivot are mindfulness, vocation and relatedness:

- *Mindfulness* is about developing clarity of thought and action.
- *Vocation* is about connecting with a sense of self: being clear on what we stand for (our motivations and broader aims beyond the specifics of the immediate task and job) and being true to these.
- *Relatedness* is about connecting with the lives and outlooks of others in our organizations and our wider society.

Together these three elements can bring a greater degree of personal effectiveness, resilience, connection and satisfaction in leadership roles and beyond. The *pivotal axis* works by helping us to stop and reflect on what is right in any situation. It provides a mechanism to reconnect with our own sense of vocation and the company's true purpose while ensuring that in reaching any decision, we are connected to the people and situations we are impacting. It helps each leader to develop a framework that supports reflection and dialogue about decision-making processes, so that when they are under real pressure and have to make the toughest calls, they have a tool that they can rely on and have confidence in. When a leader is operating effectively within the *pivotal leadership axis*, they will be well placed to combine audacity and patience; drive performance and health; bring ethics together with entrepreneurialism; unite profit with a sense of purpose; integrate business and society to serve one goal, and create sustainable and shared value.

To understand better how this model can work, we will now consider in more detail each of the three pivotal elements of mindfulness, vocation and relatedness.

Mindfulness

Our volatile and uncertain environment is creating enormous pressures for leaders – leaders who, more than ever, need to be able to reflect on what is most important amid conflicting demands and busy schedules. For many leaders, the source of major pressure can be the real dilemmas they face in their work. They are increasingly confronted with apparently paradoxical challenges: improving customer satisfaction while reducing costs; increasing innovation while driving profitability; making redundancies while also improving engagement; and now improving growth while also benefiting society. If we continue to see such factors as competing forces, leaders will inevitably focus on making cost-benefit and risk analyses and arriving at trade-offs. The ability to think clearly, stay balanced and maintain perspective plays a huge role in defining what we become as leaders. amid the myriad competing challenges it is especially important for leaders with great responsibility to be able to gain focus and develop the resilience necessary to cope with these pressures. This not only makes the difference between good and bad decisions, or between a connected and a disconnected life, but also the impacts the sense that others have of us as persons of integrity.

The idea of mindfulness stems from an ancient Sanskrit word, *sati*, which literally means 'to be aware'. It is about being able to train the mind to apply its attention to the matters in hand without getting sidetracked by internal and external distractions. Mindfulness gives us space to recollect what we are supposed to be doing and to see things as they truly are, by being aware of what is going on beyond and around us, being aware of how our bodies are reacting, how our feelings are affected and how our mental processes are operating.

Bill George, the former CEO of Medtronic, writing in the *Harvard Business Review* (10 March 2014) identified four qualities that mindfulness is particularly helpful in fostering:

- clarity;
- creativity;
- compassion;
- courage in the service of others.

Mindfulness is about bringing these qualities to the forefront of our minds at the point when we are under greatest pressure and it is perhaps easiest to lose or forget them.

Once the mind is aware of what is happening it is then better placed to direct its attention. As part of this pivotal model, a leader – while maintaining attention on the needs of the current situation – would be better able to also focus on their own personal vocation, of what matters most, while also considering how their action will impact on the lives of others. These 'others' may be people whom the person may know directly or they may be distant but nonetheless affected by the actions decided upon. The ability to be aware of each of these considerations in a thoughtful and balanced way is why mindfulness is so important.

Mindfulness then, is simply a method of mental training to better focus attention on the emotions, thoughts and sensations occurring in the present moment. This awareness or attentiveness can be trained by meditational practice which allows the brain to relax and let go of anxious tensions and confusion, enabling individuals to reflect on their work and life more broadly.

In the last 30 years, the beneficial effects of using mindfulness techniques in relieving physical pain and mental distress have been subjected to significant scientific scrutiny. Mindfulness-based cognitive therapy (MBCT) has been taken to a new level by Oxford University's Mindfulness Centre, where the research is based on Jon Kabat-Zinn's pioneering work on mindfulness-based stress reduction. They have shown that MBCT prevents depression in the most vulnerable people, reducing the risk of the recurrence of severe depression by up to 50 per cent over 12 months, proving as effective as anti-depressants (Segal *et al*, 2002). As a result, relatively conservative organizations, ranging from the Bank of England to the UK National Health Service and the international professional services firm Grant Thornton, have demonstrated its uses to alleviate workplace stress levels and improve work relations. But can it improve our decision-making?

Journalist Caitlin Kelly has noted that the application of mindfulness techniques has now gone much further and is now being used extensively in high-tech organizations.[2] Google is one such organization, pushing the boundaries of its use in an initiative called 'Search Inside Yourself' (Tan, 2012). As part of the programme, Jon Kabat-Zinn (2007) observed, many large organizations were behaving as if they had ADHD, so frenetic and crazy was the level of activity, irrespective of whether there had been any reflection on whether the course of action was right or not. For Google the use of mindfulness techniques has worked because it ensures that they are getting the very best from their people in terms of creativity and collaboration. Application of the approach has resulted in a set of guidelines that leaders and staff are being asked to follow:

- Stop what you are doing.
- Breathe deeply.
- Notice how you are experiencing the emotion in your body.

- Reflect on where the emotion is coming from in your mind (personal history, insecurity, etc). Reconnect with what's important; before
- Responding in the most compassionate way.[3]

So far more than 1,000 Google employees have taken the class. People who have attended the programme report that they are no longer fazed by demanding pressures, or indeed senior executives, and they feel much more resilient.

Mindfulness clearly has benefits to offer on its own. However, its impact can be amplified when linked with the other personal leadership elements of vocation and relatedness, to which we shall now turn.

Vocation: Connecting your leadership to a personal sense of vocation

Vocation is about connecting with a sense of self, about being clear on what we stand for beyond the specifics of the immediate task and job and being true to this. However, the pressure to achieve and the constant focus on a narrow set of financial outcomes can seem to squeeze the good out of leadership endeavours, taking leaders away from the way they would prefer to behave, causing them to lead an increasingly divided life and to create different 'selves': one for work and one for home. According to Michael Naughton, from the University of St Thomas in the US: 'Dividing the demands of one's beliefs from one's work in business is a fundamental error of our age, contributing to much of the damage done by business in our world today.'[4] As we saw in Chapter 1, leaders who focus entirely on career can be working to the detriment of their family and their own physical and spiritual well-being. Furthermore, such a narrow focus can risk leaders coming to value position, status or financial wealth over lasting accomplishment and can in the process risk losing a sense of balanced judgement in the process. So, how do such divisions occur in practice?

Geoff Moore (2012) of Durham University proposes: 'When multiple pressures crowd in on us, it is virtue that gets crowded out'. Much of this pressure arises from the context and people a leader is working with, as Dan Airely demonstrates in his best-seller *Predictably Irrational* (2008). Airley, a professor of psychology and behavioural economics at Duke University in Durham, North Carolina, has spent years exploring aspects of decision-making in his 'social labs', showing how people's decisions can be swayed hugely by what he calls 'social and contextual factors', particularly how peer pressure can shape leadership behaviours in our biggest corporations. Airley found that people find it particularly easy to 'fall in' with others' actions if they come from the same social background, even where that course of action is not appropriate. His research showed that when leaders find peers in their sector making deals in a particularly lucrative area, copying questionable practices becomes not only accepted but is seen as an essential and normal way of keeping up. The herd instinct kicks in far faster than we might like to think. This was particularly true where the rewards were high and the perceived likelihood of being caught was low. Airley's research shows that this group 'instinct' applies even when it comes to activities considered to be 'cheating the system'. It is apparent that people with only financial measures to navigate by, find it relatively easy to get involved in activities such as rate-fixing when many of their peer group are also involved, because the financial return is there. The excuses we hear from our children 'that everyone else was doing it', apparently remain a dormant phenomenon in all of us. The experiments also showed that such actions become more palatable the more detached people are from the consequences of their behaviour. This is a worrying observation given the bankers dealing in credit default swaps from the 20th floor of a New York skyscraper were about as detached as they could get from the circumstances someone in Detroit trying to secure a first mortgage for their family. Airley's research illustrates just how easy it is for perfectly 'good' people to step beyond the scope of what we would all consider 'good' behaviour if the conditions are conducive to doing so.

What is perhaps most fascinating about Airley's work is how such 'cheating behaviours' could be curtailed. Airley found one of the most startling impacts on behaviour occurred when he asked people to recite the Ten Commandments, before being put into one of his social lab 'cheating tests'. Many individuals were not religious and most could not recite the commandments. Yet strikingly, he found that most people would not cheat in any of the subsequent 'cheating' tests that he had devised. Airley re-checked his findings by asking others to read and sign a university 'honour code' before completing the next set of tests; once again the students did not cheat. Airley concluded that the process of bringing front of mind a sense of 'what being good was about', no matter how unrelated to the task in hand or someone's religious beliefs, clearly had a profound impact on people's subsequent behaviours.

Developing a sense of vocation

> You need to find a way to live your life that doesn't make a mockery of your values.

> (Bill Ayers)

Any leader – and indeed, any worker – is faced with the question: What am I working for? There are typically three ways leaders can answer this question. The first answer is seeing work as just a job and all about the money, the next bonus or paying for the next holiday or new car. This view of work comes wrapped up with the notion of acquiring things. The second answer for many leaders is that it's all about the career, about achieving things, about doing more. The issue with these answers is they fail to address a wider question: What am I living for? As we saw in earlier chapters, when people work just for the money, work satisfaction goes down while giving over everything in life to a career is too small to hold the human spirit. Significantly both of these outlooks are orientated towards what we can get out of work. If, on the other hand, we can find a wider sense of what work is about and connect it with what we are living for, our emphasis shifts to what we can give through our work. This third answer lies at the heart of what developing a sense of leadership vocation is about. Vocation in the broadest sense requires a shift of perspective from the narrowest sense of a job (a series of tasks) and career (a progression and development of responsibility and earnings) to a more holistic sense: a cause worth pursuing for the benefit of many, bringing a stronger connection with all.

The sense of developing a vocation is a way of combatting the divided life, resisting the insularity that provokes careerism, competition, distrust and disloyalty, and instead seeking a vision for a life of greater unity and integrity. By doing so our work can take on a different dimension and contribute to a sense of meaning in our lives. Developing a sense of personal vocation in our work can also provide the counterweight to the competitive pressures which can, as we have seen, so easily squeeze out the way we would prefer to behave as leaders, compromising our sense of who we are and what we believe. Developing a sense of vocation can help us retain the sense of personal identity that forms the basis for being authentic and behaving with integrity as a leader.

Dan Airley's social lab tests earlier showed us just how easy it can be to become compromised as leaders as we strive to deliver. Earlier commercial eras knew that such personal compromises often led to larger problems. In Venice, the Bridge of Sighs takes its name from the sighs of regret heard from prisoners who were marched across the bridge to the courts. The prisoners were allowed to take one last look back before they disappeared into their cells. What they would have seen around the palace walls were beautiful carvings intended to bring to mind the things that mattered most to business leaders of the Venetian era: temperance (balance between self- and public interest, self-control and prudence), humility (spirit of self-examination and selflessness), charity (respect for others), patience (moderation and peaceful conflict-resolution), kindness (compassion and trust), chastity (humanity and honesty with oneself and others) and diligence (integrity, work ethic and steadfastness). While the images on the top of the Doge's Palace provide a salutary reminder of what a good life *should* be, it is also quite evident that business people then as now were unsure how to bring these ideals into play at the heart of their activities.

Most recognize that the idea of developing our own sense of vocation can be deeply challenging. When we think about leading through a deep sense of vocation we may end up thinking of figures like Mother Teresa, who dedicated her life to helping the poor and excluded of the Calcutta slums. In doing so, we run the risk of elevating her and others to a sphere we too easily persuade ourselves we cannot reach. In fact, Mother Teresa's work was marked out by its practicality. She ran a large organization covering over 90 countries, which brought its own pressures and demands. She was a hands-on operator working on the ground in difficult conditions with as much to show us about fortitude and focus as about compassion and charity.

As we have seen in Chapter 1, simply trying to insert a code of ethics into our businesses may look good on a corporate website but does little to actually help leaders to re-imagine and reframe the way they work. Alternatively, we can recognize that developing our own sense of vocation is a long-term undertaking, which we need to grow and nurture. This is quite different from most outlooks on leadership development, which tend to see skills as things to be acquired and a new style as something which can be grafted on. Instead, developing a sense of leadership vocation can only come through commitment, practice and reflection.

To this end, we need to consider a series of questions, which over time will help us to frame our own sense of vocation and start the process of bringing 'what matters most' front of mind, no matter what the pressures of the job. The overarching question is whether we see ourselves as being here to serve others or to serve our own ends. Frighteningly, we see an increasing number of leaders who seem at least on the outside to be consumed by this self-seeking outlook. For such individuals, their sense of self-worth can become a function of their performance at work or the opinion of others. Inevitably, if we put our sense of self up for grabs every day our lives are going to be full of significant ups and downs. Instead we need to move ourselves to a place where we can ask a series of questions which are not contingent on events but remain constant over time. We will return to these questions in more detail later on in this chapter. For now, we will turn to consider the third element of the pivotal axis – *relatedness.*

Relatedness: Connecting your leadership approach to the world around you

Relatedness is about the degree to which an individual leader is connected with the world beyond their immediate relationships. It extends far beyond the notion that we are all connected via ubiquitous technology.

To explore this idea further, it may be helpful to step outside the narrow confines of our normal western business constructs and examine this concept by reference to three very different cultural examples of what relatedness can mean from across the globe.

First, let us consider an example from Africa. Originating amongst the Zulu, Ndebele and Bantu people of South Africa, the concept of *Ubuntu* means 'the belief in a universal bond of sharing that connects all humanity'. This idea of connectivity was a guiding principle for Nelson Mandela in the 1990s as he steered the transition from apartheid to majority rule in South Africa; it allowed Mandela to be bigger than the group he was expected to represent and to reflect the greater needs of all South Africans. *Ubuntu* asserts that it is society that gives human beings their humanity and is a quality that we owe to each other. It is a quality that cannot be removed or changed because of circumstances. Desmond Tutu said: '*Ubuntu* speaks of the very essence of being human. . . My humanity is inextricably bound up in yours. . . A person is a person through other persons. . . what dehumanizes you inexorably dehumanizes me.'

Ubuntu suggests that an individual's success can only be long-lasting if it has considered the success of all. As such it encompasses ideas of solidarity, in which leaders seek opportunities to bring people together by serving the broadest community. It also reflects ideas of plurality in which a leader knows what they stand for, yet manages to combine this with an openness to enrichment from others.

CASE STUDY Cashbuild – South Africa

In an interview with Otto Schramer, Peter Senge asked: 'How do you begin to help people collectively, in an organization setting, to tap into the real reserves for organizational learning, for profound change?'[5]
One answer lies through the collective and spiritual process that is *Ubuntu*.
One company that has stretched its boundaries to include everyone is 'Cashbuild', based in South Africa and founded by Albert Koopman, an Afrikaans business

visionary, who designed a variety of structures that ensured meaningful participation of thousands of employees at every level. In their book *Sawubona Africa: The great indaba* (Lessem and Nussbaum, 1996) Elton Bondi explained how the Cashbuild process worked: 'Hundreds of opinions, complaints and problems raised by worker representatives were categorized into five areas of customer, employee, competitor, the company and suppliers.' The Cashbuild philosophy was born out of these central issues and was aimed at fulfilling two fundamental goals:

- to provide people with a holistic organizational structure;
- to integrate the entire company into one participatory team.

This reflected key wider principles at Cashbuild: 'that it is the responsibility of every individual to play a part in finding solutions to problems'. This commitment to community participation and communal learning culminated in a two-day *indaba,* or gathering, with over 300 elected representatives, and while it involved considerable up-front costs, it meant that long-term relations were far superior. Such large-scale collaborative exercises reflect the spirit of *Ubuntu* and foster mutual respect as Verna Allee, visiting lecturer at Oxford University and Hanken Swedish School of Business and an expert in innovation in complex environments put it: 'By working from a philosophy that no one group of people can understand a real system, the goal is to find a way to have the whole system reflect on its behaviour and change itself' (Nussbaum, 2003). We are now starting to see radical, lighter-weight, versions of this idea re-emerge in business, enabled by technology, such as the 'JAM' sessions, which are now regularly facilitated by IT systems business IBM, by bringing diverse communities together from across the globe in all kinds of organizations. One such JAM event occurred at global professional services firm, Grant Thornton, who with over 35,000 people in 80 countries, used a giant multi-day JAM session in 2014 to bring everyone in the firm together into a giant collective discussion involving tens of thousands of people, to review what really mattered most to people. The data engine helps to identify what are the major global and local themes and these are then worked on as priorities for development. Reaching out in this way to mass groups of people is also happening in the way start-ups raise funds through Crowdsourcing, to the way Starbucks is using mass engagement with customers to drive real engagement with its brand. Despite the intervention of technology, there is something deeply humanizing in the experience of listening to mass groups of other people, hearing their voices and their realities, before you can understand your own. This lies at the heart of relatedness and the *Ubuntu* outlook on life. It seems that technology is making it possible for all of us to rediscover the value and power of the collective mind and spirit.

A second example of relatedness can be found in Chinese thinking. This is about a deep obligation to maintain relationships and meet commitments. The idea stems from the Confucian principle of *Guanxi*, a belief that isolation is bad for the human spirit and therefore leaders should encourage everyone to become integrated into multiple social relationships. At the heart of this philosophy lies the belief in reciprocity, such that if a person helps someone, the person who has been helped should in turn help the other. This reciprocity explains how historic ties have been augmented over the years as people have used their *Guanxi* relationships to assure each other of their trustworthiness, ensuring that at all times honour is maintained throughout all of their trading and other relationships. In an Anglo-Saxon sense, this relates to a time when 'my word is my bond'. Clearly, like any set of connections it can be abused and insular, but in its truest sense *Guanxi* can provide a basis for stability in society because the connections across all groups can provide a self-regulating environment in which honour and ties prevent people from being exploited. A leader fostering *Guanxi* is therefore setting out to deepen trust and understanding between all those they have connections with. The webs of *Guanxi* tie Chinese business leaders into a cohesive economy and capture and extend what is meant in the West by the phrase 'social capital'.

Our third example comes from Scandinavia, where social capital as an economic and social model has taken a different course from much of Anglo-American capitalism. One of the factors behind this is the principle of *Hygge* (pronounced 'heu-gah'), originally a Norwegian word but subsequently absorbed into Danish culture. *Hygge* is a pervasive element of national culture and is about a sense of togetherness, well-being and the basis for forming trusting relationships beyond family to the wider community along with a stronger connection to the environment. It is about stewarding and sustaining people and resources for both this and future generations. It captures an uncomplicated, practical notion that we should weave greater connectivity into daily life.

It is interesting to note how much these three separate ideals, from the radically different cultures of Africa, China and Scandinavia, share in common. They remind us that relatedness is about far more than a technical, functional or process connection. It is about the formation of relationships of meaning and value, through which we develop real understanding and trust and see the humanity and dignity within each other. Together they offer up a radically alternative way of thinking about aspects of personal leadership. Rather than acting as isolated soloists or even individual members of a team, they offer a different outlook on life. In seeing ourselves as part of this greater whole, we open up the possibility of contributing towards, and deriving for ourselves, a greater sense of meaning and value.

To understand where they are on the dimension of relatedness, a leader can begin by looking at their diaries or appointment calendars: Who are leaders spending time with and on what topics? Where are they travelling? And what are they reading? If the answer is the same people as last month and last quarter, then the world – or more precisely their perspective on it – is narrowing. If this is the case, then how well are they personally positioned as a leader to distill fresh insights and understand potential discontinuities? However, developing relatedness as a leader is not about becoming a tourist, simply passing through different environments and maintaining pre-existing 'external' view of things. It is about getting to the margins of their business environment and sharing different experiences.

A person with this sense of relatedness and connection has the potential to significantly change the way individuals and groups interact with one another: they are open and available to others, affirming of others and do not feel threatened by others. Seeing ourselves and our organizations as part of a connected whole in this way can fundamentally change the dynamic of business and society and open up significant new opportunities.

FIGURE 10.3 Personal leadership model 2

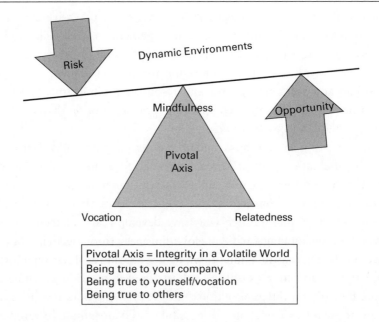

Conclusion

The three areas of mindfulness, vocation and relatedness come together to form a Pivotal Axis for a leader, enabling them to bring to life a very different approach to leadership. As we have discussed, the pivotal axis creates stability and dynamism by enabling leaders to be more reflective, and more grounded by connecting to their own vocation while relating more of their decisions to others beyond the immediate organization. The Pivotal Axis can provide individual leaders with greater resilience and the basis for developing their own strength of character while also opening themselves up to other external perspectives. It can therefore support leaders with their own dynamic process for dealing with the conflicting demands that are ever present in volatile times, while maintaining a greater sense of personal balance.

Throughout this book we have discussed how our three pillars of purpose, leadership practices and personal leadership, together form a framework for reconnection. However, there are three important considerations that any leader will need to address before starting out on the journey to reconnect:

- First, that each leadership pillar – if implemented alone – is likely to have little impact. For example, the creation of a *purpose* statement alone, which is not also reflected in changes in leadership practice or behaviours, can lead to the kind of cynicism we saw in Part 1.

- Equally, changes in leadership *practice* without similar clarification of an organization's purpose can lead to confusion. Such approaches frequently result in 'disconnects' occurring between what people believe is important and what is happening in different divisions of the same business.

- Finally, changes in personal leadership *behaviour* that are not part of a more coordinated approach can lead to stress and tension at the frontline as employees and customers find themselves confused and often torn between new expectations in one area and old ways in another.

This final point is important for any company looking to manage the transition from a controlling model of doing business to one which relies on connection. Liberating individuals, who have previously been working in the old ways, to become connected requires judgement and courage. Here it is important to acknowledge the difference between leaders and visionaries.

Reconnected leaders must not only see the future but must also respect the past and embrace the people who need to participate in the changes we have discussed, so that their fears of losing control, face, money or power do not sabotage their bold intentions.

A leader must integrate the changes they want to see across purpose, leadership practices and personal leadership and carefully iterate and evolve a way forward while addressing the following dilemmas:

- How do we foster solidarity through sharing a sense of purpose while also creating an environment where diversity of view is welcomed?

- How do we create a sense of identity while having porous borders through which new ideas and people flow freely?

- How do we connect with the wider world while also remaining focused on our own business priorities?

- How do we develop a shared sense of ownership across an enterprise while also increasing an individual sense of accountability?

- How do we ensure leaders take on greater accountability while also ensuring authority is decentralized as far as possible?

- How do we combine all of these efforts to produce a fair return for society and shareholders, at the same time?

- How do we share power with others, while ensuring that the difficult challenges reconnection will raise are anticipated and the courage to deal with them is not dissipated?

Personal leadership is therefore critical because it is the place where conflicting demands from the volatile environment discussed in Part One meet the new ways of working discussed in Part Two.

Figure 10.4 provides an outline of how leaders can navigate the journey to reconnection. This, then, is the eighth step to becoming a reconnected leader.

Eight steps to reconnected leadership

Step 8 – Reconnecting through personal leadership: Leadership actions

Moving from good principles to good practice is where the real challenges and difference lies. Set out below are a number of actions that you can put in place to develop your own Pivotal Leadership Axis.

FIGURE 10.4 The eighth step to reconnected leadership:
Purposeful organization and leadership development

Top-down development

B Consider how your company's purpose needs to change to ensure that it reflects views captured in **A**

C Refine your company's purpose and define which leadership practices will need to change

Powerful purpose

D Implement new leadership practices effectively across your company

Practice of leadership

A Start by considering what you personally value or worry about in society and then at work

Personal leadership

E Reflect on your personal leadership, checking for alignment. Where are there gaps or tensions?

Bottom-up development

These questions are initially intended to be used on a personal level to help us think about how we see our work but can subsequently be used to enter into a dialogue with people both inside and outside of our business about the way we are operating as a leader in practice. Used wisely, they can help us develop as more contemplative leaders:

1 First we need to look at how we treat people in our daily work lives and challenge ourselves as to think about whether our actions demonstrate that people really matter. We can ask ourselves, are we really connecting with other people or are we purely making decisions in a self-interested, self-determined, closed way? If other people really do matter to us, are we acting in solidarity with them and avoiding actions which cause inequality?

2 The second question to ask ourselves is how we are running our organization. Are we giving people freedom and responsibility that

their role demands? Are we allowing people to develop and to contribute to the decision-making process, at all levels? Are we allowing each person to take the responsibilities they are capable of taking? Or are we creating dependency by reserving decisions unnecessarily? This all requires careful weighing, to ensure responsibility for the right decisions is being taken at the right level.

3   The third question for someone working to become a reconnected leader is: are we creating reciprocal relationships and are we building trust? The foundations of trust we discussed earlier start with basic honesty and integrity, ensuring everyone receives what they are entitled to or can reasonably expect. This is the first stage of building trust. However, as a reconnected leader we need to ask ourselves: can we go beyond this minimum, using all the knowledge and capabilities we have at our disposal to provide benefits that people would like and value but could not strictly expect or demand?

4   The fourth question is about knowing who we are, while valuing diversity of thinking and cultures. Are we favouring curiosity and inclusion over suspicion and exclusion of those who think differently?

5   The fifth question for a reconnected leader is the degree to which we see our role as a steward, using our knowledge, influence and experience to connect and collaborate with others for the benefit of all. As a reconnected leader, do we accept responsibility for the impacts we and our organization are having and are we taking steps to develop people, nurture values, preserve and restore existing resources?

These are complex and challenging questions. They do not produce easy, simple or fast answers. They are designed to cause us to reflect in our hectic schedules. However, using these questions on a regular basis can help every leader to develop their own sense of personal vocation, examining how they are acting and by doing so develop a deeper sense of what they are about, what they stand for and what they believe in. The aim of the questions is to make conscious and regular a process that people often go through unconsciously, sporadically and irregularly.

If we want to become a reconnected leader with a stronger sense of vocation, then the more we work at this kind of reflective process on our own or with a coach or with our teams, the stronger our sense of vocation will become.

To ensure that we return to these questions discussed in understanding our own vocational journey, we need to build them into the rhythm of the way we lead and run our organizations. To help us do this we can keep a 'vocational journal', which captures our reflections and answers on the

TABLE 10.1 Personal leadership: A framework to guide decision-making

DEFINING PURPOSE	
Each person is a someone, not a something (DIGNITY & VALUE OF PEOPLE)	Show respect for the dignity of each person and for the whole person; never use people merely as a means to achieving business objectives. Respecting the whole person includes thinking of people in all their various roles in relation to the business: as employees, customers, suppliers, investors and citizens. Demonstrating respect means setting a purpose and seeking outcomes that enable each person to reach his or her full potential, not least being able to contribute fully to building relationships and communities both within the workplace and beyond. Such purposes and such outcomes engender trust between people and between business and society.
Delivering value by serving society (THE COMMON GOOD)	Genuinely aim to promote the good of society as a whole through the provision of goods and services that benefit society; never use stakeholders, and society as a whole, as a mere means to business success. This gives meaning to the purpose of the business within society and demands innovation to achieve that purpose alongside a financial return. Society and communities of people determine the licence, and freedoms, of business to operate and grow; these will be broader if business actively aims to reduce harm and produces goods that are truly good and services that truly serve.

(Continued)

Behaviours needed to build character and achieve purpose

Other people matter (SOLIDARITY)	Freedom with responsibility (SUBSIDIARITY)	Building trust and trusted relationships (RECIPROCITY)	Valuing diversity and building bridges (PLURALITY)	Stewardship of people, values and resources (SUSTAINABILITY)
Judge decisions as good, or not, in the context of the best values, expectations and needs of those with whom we should seek to build relationships. Do not make decisions in a self-interested, self-determined, closed world that does not weigh sufficiently the impact on others.	Allow people to develop by being able to contribute to making decisions at all levels. Do not create dependency through reserving decisions unnecessarily to higher levels in the hierarchy, or lose accountability through inappropriate delegation. Give people the freedom, and support where	Start with basic honesty and integrity so that each and all receive what they are entitled to or can reasonably expect. This is the first stage of building trust. Then go beyond this minimum, using knowledge and capabilities to provide benefits that people desire and value but cannot expect or	Be clear as to who you are and what you stand for, combining this with an openness to enrichment from others, valuing diversity of thinking and cultures. Favour curiosity and inclusion over suspicion and exclusion of those who think differently. Maintain consistency of purpose and	Acknowledge and seek to measure the impact the business has on people, values, resources, and the environment. Accept responsibility for those impacts. Then take steps to develop people, nurture values, preserve and restore existing resources and create new ones where possible so that others

Make a fair contribution to society and avoid actions that cause inequality. Opportunities shoud be sought to serve the broadest community, including the underserved, the underprivileged and the excluded; not to emphasize the divide but rather to bring people together, through new job opportunities, innovative goods and services, and new markets.

necessary, to take on the risk of decision-making and to have a voice in their work, thus fostering innovation, creativity and a sense of shared responsibility.

demand, in particular in situations of information asymmetry or power imbalance. Fair and efficient markets depend on trust and trusting relationships.

values while embracing diversity, encouraging closeness to people, markets, innovation and growth.

may enjoy their benefits. Use your knowledge, influence and experience in collaboration with others for the benefit of all.

questions outlined above, and in particular to see how we are applying our reflections to the real-life situations within our business lives. Such a journal would be purely for ourselves and, unless we chose to do so, not for sharing with others in our organization. It should capture some of the dilemmas and difficult choices that arise through the course of the year. The journal can then be returned to later reflect further on choices we have made and the rationale we use at different times for the decisions we make. The journal is designed to prompt a greater level and depth of reflection than that which we are accustomed to in modern business life. It could be completed monthly or quarterly and in so doing can act as a counterbalance to typical business processes such as quarterly financial reviews and quarterly sales forecasts, which tend by their very nature to be more tactical. Reflection is not the same as holding ourselves to account – it is not intended to be a judgemental exercise. However, over the course of time, it will help us to start to evolve the leadership options we consider and will help us approach things gradually in a different way.

While this kind of reflection will come naturally to some, others may find every reason possible to avoid undertaking the work. For this reason it may be helpful to work with a vocational coach, a person who you can work with to help you work through the questions outlined above to find your own unique vocational path. Your initial answers can then be used to provide the basis for reflection against the subsequent actions you take in your business life. Choose a coach who can act as a reflective partner to help you consider whether the way in which you address business dilemmas is in line with your vocational path.

A third way of bringing this sense of vocational journey to life is to find a group of people with whom you can share your work experiences and dilemmas and who can share their own with you. Such a group would best be served by finding people from other situations and environments, so that the discussions do not end up with the normal excavations of corporate life. Such a group would usually have a moderator who will help to keep returning to the simple questions which were outlined earlier.

These three kinds of work on your vocational journey can be complementary – covering individual reflection, one to one work and collective activity.

To practice mindfulness (*sati*) we need to pause to reflect on what we are doing, to check first how our actions and thoughts in the moment relate to our personal sense of purpose or vocation and the degree to which our actions may be augmenting or harming our degree of relatedness to others both around us and beyond our immediate circles.

A greater sense of relatedness can be developed by spending time and interacting with groups who do not share your perspective on the world. Actions could include:

- Inviting in hostile NGOs to aspects of your environmental strategy and policy planning meetings, to act as specialists who may well bring a different perspective to that which is held within your organization.

- Spending time eating with staff in your canteens, not on a separate table with your own group of managers or worse yet in your office.

- Become a volunteer working in frontline service delivery with excluded groups in your community, or by sending your future leaders to work with NGOs on projects that your organization can directly assist with.

- Relatedness also comes by changing the constituent members of your board to have more people with a greater level of diversity, or in establishing advisory board groups, which are designed to offer alternative and innovative view points.

Exercise

To check on your progress to making better decisions as a reconnected leader try an exercise which will help you to take stock of how connected you are. To do this one approach is to use a model developed by Stewart D Freidman (2014) called *Four Circles*.

Here you start by drawing four circles representing four domains: work, home, community and self. The circles should be varied in size to reflect first how much you really value each area, and then complete a second cut, by examining how much time you spend in each circle. Do the circles shrink or get bigger? Do they stand close together or far apart? Then think about the values, purpose, and actions you pursue in each domain – are they compatible or in opposition? Imagine what life would be like if your aspirations in all four circles – and the means by which you achieved them – lined up perfectly, like the concentric rings of a tree trunk? Most people would see that as an unattainable ideal but what if there was a greater degree of alignment?

Exercise

In another exercise outlined by Friedman (2014) – which he calls conversation starter, but which I would term connection starter – individuals are asked to bring an item that is important to them such as a photograph and explain why it matters to them, the values it represents and how it fits in to what that person is trying to achieve at work. Then a colleague repeats the exercise sharing their own item and why it matters to them. This forms the basis of starting to discover what matters most and starts to break down some of the compartmentalization that normally gets in the way of people being their true selves at work.

Exercise in mindfulness

A mindful minute

Create space in any part of a day – but especially before and after meetings – to stop for one minute and before entering the meeting, sit or stand somewhere quietly and pause. After taking a few long breaths in and out, simply reflect on what you want to personally get out of the meeting. When that surfaces, write it down and then ask yourself in a similar way – pick one other person who will be at the meeting – and keep them in mind while repeating the exercise with the question: What do they want and need from this meeting? Entering the meeting with this sense of calm and clarity is a tool that – in the situation – helps improve decision-making and in the longer term, helps to bring greater integration of all decisions around your own sense of purpose.

Jamming

Creating a live and meaningful dialogue with wider and more diverse communities requires greater planning. However, that shouldn't mean that it is too difficult. As we discussed in earlier chapters, organizations like IBM and the Guardian Media Group will help to facilitate and moderate curated discussions which maximize the input from multiple groups in real time, driven by the things which matter most to them. As a leader, the challenge is to be an active participant in these groups, yet allowing others to comment in ways that ensure that they contribute fully in their own way (even if you strongly object to what they may be saying). There are many platforms that are making such online jam sessions a new feature of organizational life; however, to be transformative, leaders must engage actively and not wait to have results complied by their marketing or HR teams.

1   Rosalinde Torres, TEDx, Boston Consulting Group, October 2013
2   Caitlin Kelly, OK Google, take a deep breath, *New York Times*, April 2012
3   Search Inside Yourself programme, in-house Google video featuring
    J Kabat-Zinn, YouTube, 2007
4   Michael Naughton, Business as a calling, Business Ethics Conference,
    University of St Thomas (video)
5   Closing the feedback loop between matter and mind, May 1966

Conclusion

11

If you want to go fast you go alone. If you want to go far you go together. (AFRICAN PROVERB)

When eras change, history teaches us to expect great winners and losers along with great upheaval and uncertainty. The purpose of this book has been to highlight the changes we are witnessing, to consider their implications and to set out a course of action.

Our central theme has been *connection*. As we have seen, connection is at the very heart of what this new era is about. Furthermore, 'the old ways' are themselves proving to be a source of disconnection. Our central focus has been leadership, because the biggest risk faced by business and society today is not the shift to a more interconnected and interdependent world, but that our leaders continue to behave in ways that are no longer appropriate or effective. It seems that disconnected leadership is getting in the way of the decisions we need to take to shape a better future.

It would be easy for leaders to acknowledge the need for greater connection at a superficial level, given that we are all now technologically more connected than ever before. However, the multitude of media channels disguises the fact that – at a deeper level – our connections are breaking down. The word *company* originally has Latin roots, *com* (together) + *panis* (bread). So a place where we break bread together was the origin of the idea of company. *Companion* also comes from the same Latin root, someone you break bread with. Today the stark reality is we rarely see each other as companions. We no longer sit down to eat our meals together with colleagues, preferring instead the isolation of a sandwich at our desks. This sense of increasing isolation doesn't stop in the office. We no longer know the people down the street, because we never see them and, it seems, have little in common; we can no longer understand the person from a disadvantaged part of town because we do not hear their voice; and we cannot comprehend the needs of someone from a developing country because we have never sat in their home or experienced what it is like not to have access to our every want and need.

Throughout this book we have therefore attempted to draw out and explore what connecting could mean in terms of the practices that business leaders engage in every day – how leaders run or participate in board decisions; how leaders do or do not inform those meetings with views from a landscape beyond the doors of the boardroom; how leaders can create or mend the bonds that bind people together inside an organization so that they can not only commit but also rediscover much of the spirit that has been leaking away. These are difficult questions but if a leaders want to inspire others they will need to ask themselves difficult questions about how they can give everyone a sense that they share in the decisions, struggles and rewards of the enterprise. Leaders need to rekindle this torch within themselves so that they can pass it on to others within their companies, serving the greater need rather than just their own. These are fundamental changes but can bring a transformative energy to life in the hearts and minds of people within an organization and in their relations with the world beyond.

Looking at those practices which connect companies with the wider world, we have asked how leaders could help their business to become more embedded in community – seeing the needs of those around the business not as separate or distinct but as essential in guiding the organization in the way it carries out its activities. We also discussed how this change in the need for greater connection is affecting customers, while they also start to recognize that the path to happiness may well not lie in ever more consumption. We can see all around us that customers are searching out more authentic connections, that they are increasingly sceptical of the promises from corporations and trust far more the insights they receive from friends and other customers. This search for authenticity is part of a deeper quest for meaning and relationships. We also saw how the desire for trusting relationships is an essential ingredient in helping organizations to find better and more innovative ways to develop new products and services, seeing how removing barriers and building trust can open up new avenues and opportunities.

The other unwritten practice of reconnected leaders will be how they make the connections between all of these activities – understanding how it is almost impossible to create a true sense of shared enterprise if nonexecutive directors don't have first-hand exposure to what is happening on the frontline; understanding how becoming embedded in communities is a prerequisite for meaningful and lasting relationships with customers; how building a long-term value requires a connection right through the supply chain to understand the degree to which their activities are sustainable.

The analysis we have conducted indicates that our leadership practices can no longer be misaligned with the purpose we develop for our organization. Expecting customers to be treated honestly and with care requires that *all* people are respected and treated with dignity. Striving to achieve high levels of trust means that people both inside and beyond the company need to be able to air a critical voice and recognizing this truth is crucial if people are to gain and maintain the courage to 'speak truth to power'. We have also seen why people highly incentivized to behave as individual contributors struggle to put the interests of the common good above and beyond their own.

These then are the real challenges of connection, and they will place very different challenges at the doors of leaders. They will need to draw on different resources that will not be found in competency manuals. Instead, personal leadership will in future examine how well an individual has created their own connections and how well this is helping to build resilience, a balanced outlook and a sense of relatedness to the world beyond.

This final point brings us back to the start of our journey, because connection cannot be an intellectual exercise conducted and clarified at strategic 'away days' or management events. Modern leaders need to be much more part of this world so that they can not only understand it but also respond to it personally. Leaders therefore need to create time, to connect with the world and come to know it better. This book has set out the first eight steps on the journey to become a reconnected leader and open the door to fully engaging in our increasingly interconnected world. Only by stepping through that doorway can reconnected leaders feel the excitement of the new age we are entering and hope to influence it to be the kind of place we all want to live in.

REFERENCES

Acemoglu, D and Robinson, JA (2012) *Why Nations Fail*, Crown Publishing, Random House

Agar, H (1942) *A Time for Greatness*, Little, Brown & Company

Airely, D (2008) *Predictably Irrational*, HarperCollins

Akerlof, GA and Kranton, RE (2010) *Identity Economics: How identities shape our work, wages and well-being*, Princeton University Press

Bains, G (2007) *Meaning Inc*, Profile Books

Baker, J (2007) *The Report of the BP US Refineries, Independent Safety Review Panel* (The Baker Report), January

Balibar, E (2013) *John Locke: Identity and difference*, Verso Books

Barton, D and Wiseman, M (2014) Focusing capital on the long term, *Harvard Business Review*, January

Bass, BM and Steidlmeier, P (1998) *Ethics, Character and Authentic Transformational Leadership*

Bastone, D (2010) *Not for Sale: The return of the global slave trade*, HarperCollins

Bennis, WG, Goleman, D, O'Toole, J with Ward Biederman, P (2008) *Transparency: How leaders create a culture of candor*, Josey-Bass

Birkinshaw, J, Foss, NJ and Lindenberg, S (2014) Combining purpose with profits, *MIT Sloan Management Review*, Spring

Bishop, B with Cushing, RG (2008) *The Big Sort*, Houghton, Mifflin, Harcourt

Blasi, JR, Kruse, DL and Freeman, RB (2013) *The Citizens Share*, Yale University Press

Bondebjerg, I (2013) *Heritage Film and Cultural Policy*, Leeds University Publications, March

Brin, D (1998) *The Transparent Society*, Perseus Books

Buiter, W (2008) Lessons from the North Atlantic financial crisis, NewYorkFed. org [Online] http://newyorkfed.org/research/conference/2008/rmm/buiter.pdf [accessed 16 September 2014]

Burke, RE (2007) Sir Charles Sherrington's *The integrative action of the nervous system* : S centenary of appreciation, *Brain – A Journal of Neurology*, Oxford Journals, **130**, Issue 4, Oxford University Press

Capra, F (2003) *The Hidden Connections: A science for sustainable living*, Flamingo

Capra, F (2004) *The Hidden Connections: A science for sustainable living*, Anchor Books

Catmull, E (2008) How Pixar fosters collective creativity, *Harvard Business Review*, September

Caulkin, S (2013) Masters in Management Magazine, *Financial Times*, May

Chesbrough, HW and Appleyard, MM (2007) Open innovation and strategy, *California Management Review*, University of California, Berkley, 50, No1, Fall

Christakis, NA and Fowler, JH (2009) *Connected: The surprising power of our social networks and how they shape our lives,* Little, Brown

Christensen, C (1997) *The Innovator's Dilemma: When new technologies cause great firms to fail,* Harvard Business Press Books

Christensen, C (2013) Clarendon Lecture, Oxford Said Business School, 19 June

Cialdini, RB (2006) *Influence : The psychology of persusasion*, Harper Business

Clarke, N and MacLeod, D (2009) *Engaging for Success*, Engage for Success

Cole, J (2012) US Deputy Attorney General James M Cole, speaking at GSK Press Conference, Washington DC, 2 July

Deci, EL and Ryan, RM (1985) *Intrinsic Motivation and Self-Determinaton in Human Behaviour*, Plenum, New York

Deci, EL and Ryan, RM (2000) *Intrinsic and Extrinsic Motivations: Classic definitions and new directions*, Contemporary Educational Psychology, University of Rochester, www.Ideallibrary.com

Deci, EL and Ryan, RM (2002) *Handbook of Self-Determination Research,* University of Rochester Press

Deci, EL and Ryan, RM (2004) Intrinsic Need Satisfaction: A motivational basis of performance and well-being in two work settings, *Journal of Applied Social Psychology*, V H Winston & Sons

De Geus, A (1999) *The Living Company*, Harvard Business Review Press

Deloitte (2010) The Shift Index, Deloitte Consulting

Deming, WE (2000) *Out of Crisis*, MIT Press

Denning, S (2010) *The Leader's Guide to Radical Management*, Jossey-Bass

Department of Health (2013) *Hard Truths*: The Government response to the Mid Staffordshire NHS Foundation Trust Public Enquiry consultation paper, *Strengthening corporate accountability in Health and Social Care* 2013

Desai, M (2012) The incentive bubble, *Harvard Business Review*, March

Dikolli, S, Mayew, W and Nanda, D (2011) CEO *Tenure and The Performance-Turnover Relation.* Springer Science+Business Media

Drucker, PF (1964) *The Practice of Management*, Harper and Row

Drucker, PF (1993) *The New Society*: *The anatomy of industrial order*, Transaction Publishers

Duckworth, AL (2013) A conversation with Angela Lee Duckworth, *Educational Leadership*, 71, Number 1, Resilience and Learning Pages, September

Durand, R and Vergne, J-P (2012) *The Pirate Organisation : Lessons from the fringes of capitalism*, Harvard Business Review Press

Dweck, C (2012) *Mindset: How you can fulfil your potential*, Constable & Robinson

Dyer, J, Gregersen, H and Christensen, C (2011) *The Innovator's DNA: Mastering the five skills of disruptive innovators*, Harvard Business Press

ERC (2005) US National Business Ethics Survey, 21 December

Ernst and Young (2013) Annual Fraud Survey

Festinger, L (1962) *A Theory of Cognitive Dissonance*, Stanford University Press

Fleming, L and Singh, J (2010) Lone inventors as sources of technological breakthroughs: Myth or reality? *Management Sciences*, 56, Issue 1, January

Fleming, P and Jones, MT (2013) *The End Of Corporate Social Responsibility*, Sage Publications

Foucault, M (1977) *Discipline and Punish*, Pantheon Books

Freedland, C (2012) *Rolling Stone* Magazine interview, 23 October

Freeland, C (2012) *Plutocrats*, Penguin

Friedman, SD (2014) Work + Home + Community + Self, *Harvard Business Review* [Online] http://hbr.org/2014/09/work-home-community-self/ar/1 [Accessed 17 September 2014]

Goshal, G (2005) *Bad management theories are destroying good management practices*, Advanced Institute of Management Practices and London Business School

Gratton, L (2013) Restoring faith in leadership, *Forbes* [Online] www.forbes.com/sites/lyndagratton/2013/05/02/restoring-faith-in-leadership/ [accessed 16 September 2014]

Gratton, L (2014) *HR* magazine, 15 May

Gray, D and Van der Wal, T (2012) *The Connected Company*, O'Reilly Media

Green, K, Morton, B and New, S (1998) Green purchasing and supply policies: Do they improve companies' environmental performance?, *Supply Chain Management: An International Journal*, 3, Issue 2, pp.89–95

Grouzet, FM, Sheldon, KM, Kasser, T, Ahuvia, A, Dols, JMF, Kim, Y, Lau, S, Ryan, RM, Saunders, S and Schmuck, P (2005) The structure of goals across 15 cultures, *Journal of Personality and Social Psychology*

Hamel, G (2011) First, let's fire all the managers, *Harvard Business Review*, December 2011

Hammer, M and Champy, J (2003) *Re-engineering the Corporation*, HarperCollins, New York

Hammond, R (2013) Conversation with Professor Rebecca Hammond, Blueprint for Better Business discussion

Hankin, S (1997) The war for talent, *McKinsey Quarterly*

Harding, D and Rovit, S (2004) *Mastering the Merger*, Bain and Company, Harvard Business School Press, Boston, Mass.

Heffernan, M (2011), *Wilful Blindness*, Simon & Schuster

Hopkin, P (2013) 7 factors of supply chain failure, *Supply Chain Management* Magazine, www.supplychainmanagement.com, 26 June

Huston, L and Sakkib, N (2006) Connect and develop: Inside Procter and Gamble's new model for innovation, *Harvard Business Review*, March

James O'Toole (2007) *Speaking Truth to Power*: A white paper, Markkula Centre for Applied Ethics, Santa Clara University

Jaques, E (1956) *Measurement Of Responsibility: A study of work, payment, and individual capacity*, Tavistock

Jaques, E (1964) *Time-Span Handbook: The use of time-span of discretion to measure the level of work in employment roles and to arrange an equitable payment structure*, Heineman

John-Steiner, V (2005) *Creative Collaboration*, Oxford University Press

Kabat-Zinn, J (2007) *Coming to Our Senses*, Hyperion,2006

Kahneman, D (2011) *Thinking Fast and Slow*, Penguin Books

Kakabadse, A and Van den Berghe, L (2013) *How to Make Boards Work*, Palgrave Macmillan

Kaku, R (1997) The path of Kyosei, *Harvard Business Review*, July

Kant, I (1790) *Critique of Judgement*

Kaplan, S and Minton, B (2008) *How Has CEO Turnover Changed?* [Online] http://faculty.chicagobooth.edu/steven.kaplan/research/km.pdf, Chicago Booth University, August

Keller, S and Price, C (2011) *Beyond Performance,* John Wiley

Kilner, J (2014) *The Curated Ego*, lecture at the National Portrait Gallery, London, sponsored by StudioStrike (a not-for-profit organization), March

Kofman, F (2006) *Conscious Business: How to build value through values,* Sounds True

Kondratieff, N (1984) *Long Wave Cycle*, translated by G Daniels, Richardson and Snyder

Lally, P, van Jaarsveld, C, Potts, H and Wardle, J (2009) *European Journal of Social Psychology*, 40, July

Lau Tzu, *Tao Te Ching*,Vintage Books, 1989

Lehrer, J (2012) *Imagine: How creativity works*, Houghton Mifflin Harcourt

Leonard, A (2012) *The hourglass economy,* www.salon.com, September

Lessem, R and Nussbaum, B (1996) *Sawubona Africa: The great indaba*, Cape Town, Zebra Press

Leuf, B and Cunningham, W (2001) *The Wiki Way,* Addison-Wesley

Levy, S (2010) *Hackers* O'Reilly Media

Llopis, G (2013) 7 reasons employees don't trust their leaders, *Forbes* [Online] www.forbes.com/sites/glennllopis/2013/12/09/7-reasons-employees-dont-trust-their-leaders/ [accessed 16 September 2014]

Lys, T, Naughton, J and Wang, C (2013) *Pinpointing the Value in CSR*, The Kellogg Institute, Northwest University, March

MacLeod, D and Clark, N (2009) *The MacLeod Report*, Engage for Success

Malcolm, J (2011) *Iphigenia in Forest Hills: Anatomy of a murder trial*, Yale University Press

Mayer, C (2013) *Firm Commitment*, Oxford University Press

McIntyre, A (1984) *After Virtue: A study in moral theory*, University of Notre Dame Press, 1984

McIntyre, A (2000) *A culture of choices and compartmentalisation*, Notre Dame Centre for Ethics and Culture

Mich, MLK (1998) *Catholic Social Teaching and Movements*, Twenty-Third Publications

Milgram, S (1974) *Obedience to Authority: An experimental view*, HarperCollins,

Miller, P (2010) *The Smart Swarm*, Penguin Group

Miller, R (2013) *Vygotsky in Perspective*, Cambridge University Press

Moore, G (2012) Virtue of governance: The governance of virtue, *Business Ethics Quarterly*, **22**(2)

Muniz Jr, A and O'Guinn, TC (2001) Brand community, *Journal of Consumer Research*, University of Chicago Press, **27**, No. 4

Naughton, MJ (1996) *The Integration of Liberal and Professional Education*

Nayar, V (2010) *Employees First, Customers Second*, Harvard Business Press

Nin, A (1961) *Seduction of the Minotaur*, Swallow Press

Norman, J (2013) *Edmund Burke: Philosopher, politician, prophet*, William Collins, HarperCollins

O'Brien, G (2011) The week in ethics: Columns on ethics, leadership and life, http://theweekinethics.wordpress.com/ 5 April

ONS (2013) Ownership of UK quoted shares, Statistical Bulletin, Office for National Statistics, September 2013

Parliamentary Select Committee for Science and Technology (2013) Improving the Commercialisation of Research [Online] www.publications.parliament.uk/pa/cm201314/cmselect/cmsctech/559/559.pdf [accessed 12 June 2014]

Paul, P (2014) Business, society and the future of capitalism, *McKinsey Quarterly*, May

Pepper, D and Rogers, M (2012) *Extreme Trust*, Portfolio/Penguin

Peterson, C and Seligman, MEP (2004) *Character Strengths and Virtues: A handbook and classification*, Oxford University Press

Piaget, J (2001) *The Psychology of Intelligence*, Routledge

Pinckaers, S (1995) *The Sources of Christian Ethics*, T&T Clarke, Edinburgh,

Pink, DH (2002) *Free Agent Nation: The future of working for yourself*, Business Plus, Warner Business Books

Pinto, D (2014) *Capital Wars*, Bloomsbury Publishing

Polyani, K (2001) *The Great Transformation*, Beacon Press (USA)

Porter, ME and Kramer, RR (2011) *Creating shared value: How to reinvent capitalism – and unleash a wave of innovation and growth*, Harvard Business Review, January

Priestland, D (2012) *Merchant Soldier Sage: A new history of power*, Allen Lane

Ramaswarmy, V and Gouillart, FJ (2010) *The Power of Co-creation: Build it with them to boost growth, productivity and profits,* Free Press, Simon and Schuster

Rand, A (1961) *The Virtue of Selfishness*, Signet Penguin Books

Reichheld, F and Markey, R (2011) *The Ultimate Question 2.0*, Harvard Business Review Press

Rock, D, Davis, J and Jones, E (2013a) *People and Strategy*, **36**, Issue 2

Rock, D, Davis, J and Jones, E (2013b) One simple idea that can transform performance management, *People and Strategy*, **36**, Issue 2

Rolheiser, R (1999) *The Holy Longing: The search for Christian spirituality,* Doubleday Books, Random House

Rowson, J (2011) Social Brain Project, Royal Society of Arts

Salz, A (2013) *Salz Review: An independent review of Barclays' business practices*, 3 April

Sandel, M (2012) *What Money Can't Buy: The moral limits of markets*, Penguin

Sandel, MJ (2012) What isn't for sale? *The Atlantic*, April [Online] www.theatlantic.com/magazine/archive/2012/04/what-isnt-for-sale/308902/ [accessed 12 June 2014]

Schor, JB (1992) *The Overworked American*, Basic Books

Scoble, R and Israel, S (2006) *Naked Conversations: How blogs are changing the way business talks*, John Wiley

Segal, ZV, Williams, MG and Teasdale, JD (2002) *Mindfulness-based Cognitive Therapy for Depression*, Guildford Press

Seligman, M (2011) *Flourish: A new understanding of happiness and wellbeing,* Free Press, Simon and Schuster

Semple, J (1993) *Bentham's Prison*, Clarendon Press, Oxford University Press

Sen, A (1999) *Development as Freedom*, Oxford University Press

Sennet, R (2012) *Together: The rituals, pleasures and politics of cooperation,* Allen Lane

Sergiovanni, TJ and Starratt, RJ (2002) *Sources of Authority*

Seth, JN, Sisodia, RS and Wolfe, DB (2007) *Firms of Endearment,* Wharton School Publishing

Shih, WC and Thurston, T (2010) Intel NBI: Intel Corporation's New Business Initiatives, Harvard Business School Case 609–043, Faculty and Research (revised)

Shirky, C (2008) *Here Comes Everybody:The power of organising without organisations,* Penguin Press

Simons, E (2013) *The Secret Life of Sports Fans,* Overlook

Smihula, D (2011) Long waves of technological innovations, academic paper, 12 July

Sonnenfeld, J (2002) What makes great boards great, *Harvard Business Review*, September

Stark, M (2002) *The State of the US Consumer 2002*, Saatchi & Saatchi

Tajfel, H (1982) *Social Identity and Intergroup Relations*, Cambridge University Press

Tan, C-M (2012) *Search Inside Yourself,* HarperOne, HarperCollins

Tata, R, Hart, S, Sharma, A and Sarkar, C (2013) Why making profits is not enough, *MIT Sloan Management* Magazine, Summer

The Tata Way (n.d.) Group Publications, Tata Sons Ltd [Online] www.trf.co.in/media-corner-mainmenu-33/journals-mainmenu-71/doc_download/257-the-tata-way-foreword-by-cyrus-p-mistry.html [accessed 22 September 2014]

Timpson, J (2010) *Upside Down Management*, John Wiley

Turner, JC (1982) *Towards a Cognitive Redefinition of the Social Group*, Cambridge University Press

Tutu, D (2000) *No Future without Forgiveness*, Random House

Von Hippel, E (2005) *Democratising Innovation*, MIT Press

Webley, S and Dryden, P (2005) *Ethics at Work Survey*, Institute of Business Ethics

Wells, HG (1938) *World Brain*, Methuen

Wenger, E (1998) *Communities of Practice: Learning meaning and identity*, Cambridge University Press

Whalen, J, Barrett, D and Loftus, P (2012) Glaxo in $3billion settlement, *Wall Street Journal*, 3 July

Wilson, EO (2012) *The Social Conquest of Earth*, Liveright, W W Norton

Yalnzyan, A (2012) The Economy Lab, *Globe and Mail*, Toronto, Canada, 3 May

Zuboff, S (1988) *The Age of the Smart Machine: The future of work and power*, Basic Books (USA)

INDEX

NB: eight steps to reconnected leadership are indexed as 'steps to reconnected leadership'
NB: page numbers in italic indicate figures or tables
NB: references are indexed as 'chapter references'

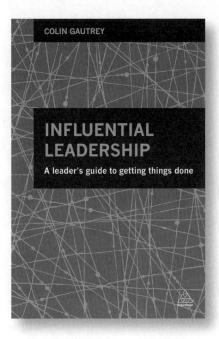

Also available from **Kogan Page**

CREATING AUTHENTIC ORGANIZATIONS

Bringing meaning and engagement back to work

Robin Ryde and Lisa Sofianos

KoganPage